SHAW'S 2023
SOUTH CAROLINA GUN LAW

Contributors:
Roy G. Harmon, III, Esq.
James Patrick Kelley, Esq.
Robert K. Merting, Esq.
Sgt. G. Curtis Moore, Jr.
Major Michael M. Nunn, Esq.
Henry R. Schlein, Esq.

Important Information on Updates

The author, contributors, and Legislative Consultant always try to keep up with the most current developments in firearms law. But statutes can be amended and new case law created. While the law generally moves slowly, changes do happen and they can happen abruptly. The author also recommends that you visit and "like" his Facebook page (https://www.facebook.com/scgunlaw) to frequently to keep abreast of current topics regarding South Carolina gun legislation and court activity. Similarly, the author, contributors, and Legislative Consultant make no express or implied warranty as to the accuracy or completeness of that information.

FOR MORE INFORMATION AND **UPDATES** VISIT:
https://www.facebook.com/scgunlaw

SHAW PUBLISHING, LLC
27 South Main Street, Suite L
Travelers Rest, SC 29690

ISBN: 978-0-9817469-9-9

Warnings & Disclaimer:

The authors have thoroughly and extensively researched the materials in this book to ensure accuracy. However, the authors, publisher, distributors, references, links, and retailers specifically disclaim and assume no liability or responsibility whatsoever for its use, reliance on its contents, reliance on any subsequent nor do they assume any liability or responsibility for errors, inaccuracies, omissions, misrepresentations or any inconsistency contained herein. Further, the authors, publisher, distributors, references, links, and retailers specifically disclaim, any and all possible liability premised upon reliance of this book, or any subsequent updates, including, but not limited to, liability for negligence or gross negligence. This book, along with any subsequent updates, is not rendered as legal advice, is the opinion of the authors, and should not be relied upon as legal advice. For legal advice, an attorney should always be consulted regarding specific questions and how your specific questions relate to specific facts, instances, and circumstances. This is especially true because the law changes and some legal advice can only be given when an attorney knows the subtleties of your question. Moreover, legal opinions sometimes vary and the opinion of one attorney might differ from another attorney's opinion. All warranties, express or implied, including those for implied warranty of fitness for a purpose and implied warranty of merchantability are disclaimed expressly herein.

ISBN: 978 - 0 - 9817469 - 9 - 9 $24.95

Dedication

This book is dedicated to Robert D. Butler, J.D., D.C., formerly of Lexington County. He is the founder of GrassRoots Gun Rights, SC. He's a preeminent South Carolina firearms legal leader, and the strongest Second Amendment defender I have ever known. His help with this book, and his early advocacy for South Carolina gun owners and possessors cannot be overstated.

Forward

Sharing a love of the law and protecting the individual right to bear arms is a freedom that Steve and I deem worthy. We support our Attorney General, Alan Wilson's relentless efforts to uphold and defend the Second Amendment on behalf of South Carolinians by teaching attorneys and judges across our state at Steve's annual gun law continuing education seminar.

When Steve discovered that I was the progenitor and initial sponsor of the Concealed Weapons Permit (CWP) law in South Carolina, he contacted me about writing this foreword.

In 1995, I was a newly elected State Representative in the General Assembly full of idealism and energy. After only six weeks of service, I began to contemplate why South Carolina, a state, steeped in a history of identification with firearms wasn't on the forefront of self-protection gun laws like Georgia, Texas and Florida.

Quickly, I filed a bill that created the legal skeleton for our CWP law. Within days, I had 105 co-sponsors for the bill in the House of Representatives. However, the news media was ruthless with their fear mongering reporting trying to thrust sordid imagery of the "Wild West," and describing me as a lone rebel with "blood on my hands."

With the help of two, special friends and Second Amendment advocates, Ralph Baker and Rick Daniel (deceased), researched the guns laws of other states and provided vital information that enabled the bill to gain momentum.

After minimal debate in the House of Representatives, the bill crossed over to The Senate. It was discussed, debated, and filibustered for a year in The Senate chambers.

My friend, Congressman Joe Wilson (then Senator Joe Wilson) navigated the call for cloture, and the bill crossed the finish line in the Senate. Governor David Beasley signed the bill into law in 1996.

This gun law has proven its necessity, popularity and functionality over the past 25 years. It has helped ratify the notion that individuals have the right to defend themselves if that dreadful need arises. Furthermore, the Second Amendment means what it means – the right to bear arms shall not be infringed.

However, possessing a firearm is not sufficient. Gun law education is paramount; the law-abiding citizen has a duty to know the law of carrying and self defense. Steve's book is a must read. It is a comprehensible reference of South Carolina's gun laws in laymen's terms. He has broken down the legal jargon; simplified sections of the federal and state laws and then woven it into an intelligent guide for you.

As citizens, we have a duty to know the law, and Steve's book provides a pathway of knowledge. Enjoy the book!

W. Jeffrey "Jeff" Young, Esquire
Former State Representative

Contents

Chapter 1
The Right to Keep and Bear Arms

You are Responsible for your Own Protection

A common myth is that the police are under a duty to protect you. A police officer, deputy, or law enforcement officer is not under a duty to protect you. (See the chapter on self-defense). You are responsible to protect yourself from threats of death or serious bodily harm. Further, threats generally occur so quickly that it is impossible for police to respond in time. When seconds count, police are, at best, minutes away. This legal reality is discussed further in the chapter on self defense but the practical and legal reality is that you are responsible to protect yourself from deadly threats.

The Natural Right to Personal Defense

Natural rights are those rights existing outside of any government, constitution document or any other institution. The United States Constitution does not create natural rights. Instead, it protects natural rights. The right of an individual to defend against a threat is a natural right and arms are an excellent means to defend against threats of deadly force. The U.S. Constitution specifically protects an individual's natural right to keep and bear arms.

American Character

The ownership and possession of firearms by law-abiding citizens is central to the American experience. Since the Pilgrims, Boston Tea Party, and creation of the Constitution, Americans have had firearms. The Stamp Act angered us, the Declaration of Independence defined us, but a British attempt to confiscate our firearms at Lexington and Concord started the war for independence and freedom. Guns are an inseparable part of the American character.

Articles of Confederation

The Articles of Confederation predated the United States Constitution. These articles loosely held together the states, but they also allowed the states to be autonomous and sovereign.

Those Articles provided the states would maintain well regulated militia as well as sufficient guns and equipment for that militia. Generally, the states provided a private right of gun ownership and nowhere did the Articles contradict the states in that regard. Where a state did not specify the right, it was presumed and not challenged.

United States Constitution

In 1791, the Bill of Rights became the law of the land. The Second Amendment guarantees and protects the pre-existing right to keep and bear arms, it does not establish the right. The exact wording is as follows: "A well regulated militia, being necessary to the security of a free state, the right of the people to keep and bear arms, shall not be infringed."

Anti-Individual Gun Rights Obfuscation

Anti-individual gun rights activists sometimes get away with obfuscating the plain meaning of the Second Amendment. They say that it only guarantees the right to a well regulated militia and not an individual right to have guns. However, this exact issue was discussed during the Articles of Confederation. During those debates, the liberal obfuscation was explicitly rejected. The anti-individual gun rights obfuscation is a twisted argument positing that the Second Amendment only protects a State's right to an armed militia, but that individuals do not have a right to keep or bear arms.

Historical Context of the Second Amendment

The Second Amendment does not specifically say that we have a right to be provided with a well regulated militia. It does, on the other hand, presume that a militia is a requirement of any free state. By implication, this means that the framers of the Constitution intended for us to have a well regulated militia. When the Constitution was written, militias were made up of all citizens who had a gun and knew how to use it. The overall number of members in the combined colonial militias was much greater than that of the professional military. During the early part of the Revolutionary War, the only troops existing were groups of ordinary armed citizens who organized militias. The colonists had no regular professional military as we know it today.

The key concept to the militias was the lack of government control. The militias were regulated, but that regulation was done internally. Members voted for the leaders of their individual militias. Everyone was a volunteer and could leave at any time and there was no funding from any level of government. The result is that the government did not control the militia.

The aim is a nation run by the people where the people to have the power and not the government. It is critical to keep the populace armed as a fighting force to discourage and repel a tyrannical home front government as well as foreign invaders.

Anti-individual gun rights activists claim that there is no need for armed citizens because we now have the military branches and National Guard. Notice however that the militia is entirely different from the military branches and National Guard. The National Guard is funded by the government. The government makes the rules and chooses the leaders. The members of the National Guard are not free to leave until dismissed. The fact that the National Guard is funded and controlled by government makes it ineffective at dispensing with a tyrannical government. Therefore, we still need an armed populace to do this job, should it become necessary.

Finally, America is about freedom and the pursuit of happiness. Millions of Americans enjoy owning, collecting, shooting, cleaning, trading, admiring, bragging about, and cursing their guns.

Additional Support of the Constitutional Protection

A full discussion of the Second Amendment is beyond the scope of this book. Numerous resources are available for individual study of the subject. Simple searches on the internet or at your local library should provide you with a good start. The authors encourage you to always be ready to defend this vital right. A recommended scholar is NRA Counsel Dr. Stephen Halbrook, Esquire. His legal research and writing is included in the *McDonald* and *Heller* briefs discussed next.[1]

Recent Activity of the United States Supreme Court

The United States Supreme Court has recently taken-up the two most important Second Amendment right to bear arms case in its history: *Heller v. District of Columbia* and *McDonald v. Chicago*. In the 2008 *Heller* case, the Court decided whether the right to keep and bear arms is an individual right, unconnected to service in the militia, or a collective right that applies only to state-regulated militias. By a five to four margin, the Court held that the Second Amendment protects an individual right to possess firearms for lawful use, such as self-defense in the home.

The *McDonald* case involved a challenge to a Chicago ordinance that basically banned private handgun ownership in the city. In another

---

[1] www.stephenhalbrook.com

five-four split decision, the Court held that an individual's right to keep and bear arms is incorporated and applicable to the states through the Fourteenth Amendment's Due Process Clause. The Court found that the Fourteenth Amendment makes the Second Amendment right to keep and bear arms fully applicable to the States.

It is important to note that the Court reiterated in both decisions that the Second Amendment only protects a right to possess a firearm in the home for lawful uses such as self-defense. The Court stressed that some firearm regulation is constitutionally permissible and the Second Amendment right to possess firearms is limited. The opinions ruled that it does not guarantee a right to possess any firearm, anywhere, and for any purpose.

On the heels of these two landmark cases, the US Supreme Court has taken on the question of whether the Second Amendment prohibits a government from criminalizing a person from carrying a firearm outside of the home. On June 23, 2022, the Supreme Court published its opinion for *New York State Rifle & Pistol Association v. Bruen*. Here the Court ruled that the ability to carry a pistol in public was a constitutional right under the Second Amendment.

The South Carolina Constitution

In addition to the guarantees provided for in the United States Constitution, the Constitution of the State of South Carolina also guarantees the right to bear arms. The exact wording of Article I Section 20 provides, "A well regulated militia being necessary to the security of a free state, the right of the people to keep and bear arms shall not be infringed." The astute reader will notice that, excepting two omitted commas, the South Carolina Constitution uses the exact same words as the United State Constitution. The same analysis is applicable to it as is applicable to the Second Amendment to the United States' Constitution.

The "Policy" Power of the States

Much of the gun and weapons law that you will need to know comes from the South Carolina Code of Laws. The state derives authority to regulate firearms through its implicit *police power*. The term police power is basically legal slang and not very illustrative of the real nature of the power. Often, the term makes people think of police officers. A more correct terminology would be *policy* power. A state can make policies that provide for the health, safety, and welfare of its residents. State policy is codified in the statutes (South Carolina Code of Laws) and regulations (Code of Regulations) that implement the statutes.

The policy power of states is generally the strongest power that a state has. Courts historically give great deference to state attempts to provide for the health, safety, and welfare of its residents. A court will find a statute or regulation Constitutional if the state can show virtually any rational basis for enacting the law. For instance, if the legislature and governor determines that wearing dress shoes causes excessive wear to sidewalks, the state can pass a law that prohibits the sale of dress shoes in the state.

Where the state runs into limitations on its policy power is when a statute or regulation infringes upon fundamental rights. Fundamental rights are rights that are so important that they deserve special protection. Examples of fundamental rights are voting, worship, political speech, and bearing arms. If a statute or regulation infringes upon a fundamental right, courts will require the state to have a compelling reason for the law and to prove that there is no less restrictive way to accomplish the goal of the legislation. This has historically been a very high hurdle for states to overcome. Therefore, laws that infringe upon fundamental rights are generally struck down by the courts as unconstitutional.

The South Carolina Code of Laws

Using its policy power, South Carolina regulates guns, weapons, ammunition, and explosives through the Code of Laws. Executive agencies such as SLED and the South Carolina Department of Natural Resources implement the Code of Laws with regulations. Finally, executive departments such as the Highway Patrol and various police and sheriff's offices execute and enforce the Code of Laws and regulations.

County and Municipal Home Rule Power

South Carolina is a home rule state. This means that local governments like counties, cities, and special districts are free to make their own local legislation and regulations for their own health, safety, and welfare. However, where the state regulates a subject area or specifically prohibits a local government from regulating a subject area, the local government must subordinate itself to state law.

State Law Trumps Local Ordinances

Since the South Carolina legislature has chosen to regulate the subject area of guns, weapons, and ammunition, local governments are not free to make laws that contradict or otherwise impair the state statutes and regulations. Section 23-31-510 of the South Carolina Code of Laws provides that,

> No governing body of any county, municipality, or other political subdivision in this State may enact or promulgate any regulation or ordinance which regulates or attempts to regulate the transfer, ownership, possession, carrying, or transportation of firearms, ammunition, components of firearms, or any combination of these things.

What this means is that your local government cannot make any laws or regulations that affect virtually anything related to guns. Therefore, if your local government makes a law or policy that contradicts the state statutes, you can bring that law before a court and it will likely be found in violation of state statutes. Further, the statutes prohibit a local government from confiscating firearms or ammunition unless the confiscation comes incident to an arrest.

Be aware, however, that the state statutes do allow local governments to pass laws that deal with the discharge of firearms, public brandishing of firearms, and brandishing of firearms during major disruptions of order such as riots, insurrections, and during natural disasters (see Chapter 6 for the definition of *brandishing*). In the case of *State v. Johnson*, decided in 1907, the South Carolina Supreme Court rejected a constitutionality challenge to a Charleston ordinance prohibiting the discharge of firearms within the city limits. The court reasoned that the ordinance did not prohibit an individual from possessing a firearm on his or her premises, but merely prohibited him or her from discharging the gun within the city limits. Therefore, the ordinance was a reasonable exercise of the city's police power.

Also, the 2021 Open Carry with Training Act permits local governments to restrict ***open*** carrying on public property during public protests, rallies, fairs, parades, festivals, or other organized events for which a permit is issued. See South Carolina Code of Laws Section 23-31-520. The prohibition can only be temporary for the event, limited to the area of the event, with proper notice, and firearms cannot be confiscated except for incident to a lawful arrest.

State and Local Police and Sheriffs Enforcing Federal Law

Can state and local law enforcement officers enforce federal gun law? This question is the subject of a January 28, 2013 South Carolina

Attorney General Opinion. In short: No. Under the South Carolina Code of Laws Section 17-13-30, state and local law enforcement officers (police, sheriffs, highway patrol, etc.) are only authorized to arrest and enforce under the "criminal laws of this state." Conversely, federal law enforcement officers are specifically authorized to enforce South Carolina laws under Section 23-1-212 of the South Carolina Code. Last, the Supremacy Clause of the U.S. Constitution, as supported by the foundational case *McCulloch v. Maryland*, serves to prevent state law officials, or state law, (or anyone) from interfering with or otherwise impeding federal officers as they perform their lawful duties. See *Tennessee v. Davis*. While this and any other Attorney General opinion is not law, the Attorney General supported his opinion with federal and state cases and statues. Therefore, you should consider it to have considerable legal weight unless you convince yourself by your own study and consultation with legal counsel that the interpretation is not correct, supported, and/or valid.

Second Amendment Sanctuary State

South Carolina is a Second Amendment sanctuary state. As part of the 2021 Open Carry with Training Act, our General Assembly added Section 23-31-250 which provides that our State and local governments cannot be compelled by the feds to take any action related to an individual's right to keep and bear arms. Our attorney general has the authority to evaluate any federal mandate for constitutionality. If he deems it unconstitutional, our state and local governments cannot assist the feds. Our attorney general Alan Wilson might be the strongest and most effective Second Amendment supporter in the nation and we are very fortunate to have him and his assistants.

Chapter 2
Buying and Possessing Guns and Ammunition

Merchants that have been in business for any length of time will tell you that the first qualification to buy anything is you must have enough money. Modern merchants will tell you that there is an exception to this if you have enough credit on your credit card. Anyway, now that the obvious qualifications are out of the way, let's get to the legal requirements for buying a gun.

Registration of Firearms

There is no South Carolina Code that provides that firearms must be registered. South Carolina does not maintain a firearms registry. Likewise, except for NFA regulated firearms, there is no United States Code that provides that firearms must be registered. The United States government does not maintain a firearms registry.

Federal Concealed Weapons Permit

Neither the ATF nor any other federal agency issues a concealed weapons permit or the like. Concealed weapons permits are the province of the states.

Licensed Gun Sellers (FFL)

You will read the term Federal Firearms License or "FFL." This term means a person or business that has a federally issued license to sell or transfer guns. In general, we are talking about retail gun shops and sporting goods stores but there are many FFL holders who can legally sell guns outside of stores and shops. Some even sell out of their homes. We will discuss the details of dealers and FFL holders in a subsequent chapter. If you are not buying from a gun shop or retail sporting goods store, you should be extra careful to read both this chapter and the

Dealers and FFL Chapter to make sure that the seller is following the law.

Age for Purchasing a Handgun from a Federally Licensed Dealer

You must be at least 21 years of age to purchase a **handgun** from an FFL. *See* 18 USC 922 (b)(1). An FFL is a federally licensed firearms dealer. Both FFL and underage purchaser are subject to penalties of 18 USC 924(a)(1)(D), up to 5 years in prison and a fine.

Age for Purchasing a Long Gun from a Federally Licensed Dealer

To legally purchase a legal **rifle** or **shotgun** from a person or business with an FFL, you must be at least 18 years of age (18 U.S.C. 922(b)(1)). You must be 18 years of age to purchase the gun from a federally licensed dealer. This is federal law. *See also* Code of Federal Regulations 27 CFR 478.47.

Age Requirement to Purchase Handgun from Private Individual

Section 16-23-30(3) S.C. Code of Laws, **does not** prohibit 18 year-olds, and up, from buying a handgun from a private (non-licensed) individual. What does it mean to purchase from an individual? An individual can be a neighbor or someone selling at a gun show. It can also mean someone who is selling a gun in the classified. Be very wary though of purchasing a firearm from the "individual collection" of an FFL to get around the age requirements of FFL sales. If the seller is an FFL but wants to sell his or her private collection outside of his or her status as an FFL, both the seller and buyer should take great care to understand federal and South Carolina dealer law.

The South Carolina penalty for the seller or buyer violating the above Code, including a dealer, is a felony and, upon conviction, must be fined not more than two thousand dollars or imprisoned not more than five years, or both (S.C. Code of Law Section 16-23-50).

Federal law stacks on an additional charge and potential penalties. Generally, a handgun transaction involving a minor puts you at jeopardy of up to 5 years in prison and a fine. See 18 USC 924(a)(1)(D).

Age Requirement to Sell to or Give a Person a Handgun

Section 16-23-30(3) provides that it is illegal to knowingly sell, offer to sell, ***deliver***, lease, rent, barter, exchange, or transport for sale into this S.C. a handgun to someone under 18. You cannot provide anyone under the age of 18 with a handgun. The S.C. Code has some narrow exceptions to this prohibition for minors who are members of the Armed Forces of the United States, active or reserve, National Guard, State Militia, or R. O. T. C., ***when on duty or training*** or the temporary loan of handguns for instructions ***under the immediate supervision*** of a parent or adult instructor. Immediate supervision means the parent is right there with the minor while the minor has the handgun.

If an adult wants to gift a handgun to a minor, the adult must keep possession of the handgun and keep it away from the minor until the minor has reached 18 years of age. Same goes for inheritance. If a minor inherits a handgun, the personal representative of the estate or the minor's guardian/conservator or trustee should take and keep possession until the minor reaches 18 years of age. *See* 18 USC 922(x)(3)(A)(iv)(C).

The penalty for individuals is up to 1 year imprisonment - unless transferor had reason to believe juvenile would commit crime of violence with gun or ammunition - then it's up to 10 years. *See* 18 USC 922(x)(1).

Age Requirement to Possess a Handgun

Section 16-23-30(B), South Carolina Statutes, prohibits anyone under 18 years old from possessing a handgun. There are some narrow exceptions to this prohibition for minors who are members of the Armed Forces of the United States, active or reserve, National Guard, State Militia, or R. O. T. C., ***when on duty or training*** or the temporary loan of handguns for instructions ***under the immediate supervision*** of a parent or adult instructor. It appears the intent of this section is that the parent or adult instructor is right there with the youth as the parent or adult supervisor instructs the youth on handling or operating the handgun. The parent or instructor should not loan the handgun to a youth unless the parent or adult instructor is certain that the youth will have immediate supervision the entire time that the handgun is in possession of the youth.

Federal law, 18 USC 922(x)(2)(a)&(b), also prohibits a *juvenile* from possessing a handgun (or ammunition that is suitable for use only in a handgun). Subsection 922(x)(5) of the same title defines "juvenile" as a person under the age of 18.

Federal law gives more exemptions than S.C. law but you can only rely upon the SC exceptions above. This is because of the complicated jurisprudence of *conflict of laws* between federal and state. Simplified, the South Carolina Code provides for additional restrictions beyond federal law - therefore, South Carolina's further restrictions are the law to follow. If you want to fully understand why, study *conflict of laws* and the ins-and-outs of *federal preemption doctrine.*

Age Requirement for Purchase of a Rifle or Shotgun from an FFL.

A dealer cannot sell rifle or shot gun to someone believed to be under 18 years of age. 18 U.S.C. § 922(b)(1), (c)(1).

Age Requirement for Sale of a Rifle or Shotgun to a Private Individual

No age restrictions against private seller selling rifle or shotgun to a private buyer.

Age Requirement for Purchase of a Rifle or Shotgun - Private Parties

No known federal or state law that creates an age restriction against private buyer buying rifle or shotgun from a private seller. All other rules apply (i.e. residency, etc.).

Age Requirement for Sale of a Rifle or Shotgun - Private Parties

No known federal or state law that creates an age restriction against private person giving, loaning, providing, or selling a private person a rifle or shotgun. All other rules apply (i.e. residency, etc.).

Age Requirement to Purchase Ammunition

Again, federally licensed firearms dealers cannot sell handgun ammunition to anyone under the age of twenty-one (21) years. As to non-FFL ammunition sellers, there is no apparent controlling legal authority. Certain types of ammunition are used in both handguns and rifles. *Example*: an under 21-year-old should not tell FFL he is buying .22 caliber for a rifle when, in fact, he is buying it for a .22 caliber handgun.

What is Residency?

A person is a resident of a State in which he or she is present with the intention of making a home in that State. Read on for more details.

Military Residency

A member of the Armed Forces on active duty is a resident of the State in which his or her or her permanent duty station is located. If a member of the Armed Forces maintains a home in one State and the member's permanent duty station is in a nearby State to which he or she or she commutes each day, then the member has two States of residence and may purchase a firearm in either the State where the duty station is located or the State where the home is maintained. 18 U.S.C. 921(b), 922(a)(3), and 922(b)(3); 27 CFR 478.11.

Dual State Residency

If a person maintains a home in 2 States and resides in both States for certain periods of the year, he or she may, during the time the person physically resides in a State, purchase a firearm in that State. However, simply owning property in another State does not alone qualify the person to purchase a firearm in that State. 27 CFR 478.11.

Moving Residences

A person who lawfully possesses a firearm may transport or ship the firearm interstate when changing his or her State of residence. If using a moving company, the person must notify the mover that firearms are being transported. He or she should also check State and local laws where relocating to ensure that movement of firearms into the new State does not violate any State law or local ordinance. 18 U.S.C. 922(a)(4) and 922(e); 27 CFR 478.28 and 478.31.

Residency for Firearms Sales or Purchases

A person may transfer a firearm to an unlicensed resident of his or her State, provided the transferor does not know or have reason to believe the transferee is prohibited from receiving or possessing firearms.

Federal law prohibits the sale of a firearm, by someone without an FFL, to any person who is not a resident of the state where the transfer takes place. Therefore, if you want to sell your personal firearm, and you live in South Carolina, you must make sure that the physical transaction of the firearm for consideration (money or other thing of value) occurs within the boundaries of South Carolina and that you are selling it to a South Carolina resident that you reasonably believe is not prohibited from possessing a firearm. Likewise, if you are a South Carolina resident, you cannot travel to another state to purchase or sell a firearm in that other state. This is because you are not a resident of the state in which you are purchasing or selling the firearm. Both you and the other person would violate 18 U.S.C. 922(a)(3) and (5), 922(a)(5) and 922(d); and 27 CFR 478.30, 478.32.

There are three exceptions:

- Temporary transfers. This means that you can loan or rent a gun to a non-resident. The temporary transfer must be for a lawful sporting purpose like hunting or target shooting and you must have no reasonable cause to believe the person is prohibited from receiving or possessing firearms under Federal law.

- Inheritance. A non-resident can receive a gun through bequest or devise upon the death of the owner. This means that you can travel to another state to pick up a firearm that you are entitled to from an estate. Likewise, you can hand-over an estate firearm to a non-resident who is entitled to the firearm as a beneficiary. As in the first exception, you must not know or have reasonable cause to believe the person is prohibited from receiving or possessing firearms under Federal law

- Face-to-Face Transaction. Under federal law, a resident of one state can travel to another state and purchase a **shotgun or rifle** if the purchase is from an **FFL** in that other state. To qualify, the gun being sold is a shotgun or rifle, the purchase is from a federal licensee and the transaction is done face-to-face. This means no mail order, no internet, and no ordering by calling over the phone. You must show up in person to purchase in the other state under this exception.

South Carolina Code of Laws 23-31-10 and 23-31-20 address non-resident purchases, sales, transfers and transporting of shotguns and rifles. These South Carolina provisions do not add any additional prohibitions over the federal law, neither do they negate any prohibitions of federal law. That's because, under the current interpretation of the *Dormant Commerce Clause*, a state law cannot negate a federal law once Congress has decided to regulate that subject area. The practical effect is this: as long as you follow federal law with respect to residency requirements for purchases, you will be following South Carolina law.

Purchasing from Out-of-State Dealer

You can buy a handgun, shotgun or a rifle from an FFL dealer in another state. However, all four of the following must be in place:

- The dealer must transfer the gun to a federally licensed dealer in your state.
- The dealer must send a copy of his license to the dealer in your state.
- Gun dealer, gun sale and gun purchase laws of both states must be completely followed.
- Form 4473 is fully filled out when you pick up the gun.

You must also be careful about transporting the gun back to your home state after you purchase it. Even if you can receive the gun legally as a non-resident, you must still make sure that it is legal to transport it and own it in every state that you carry it through on your way back to your home state. For interstate travel, see Chapter 5 on *Possessing and Transporting.*

Legal Aliens Purchasing Firearms

An alien legally in the U.S. is not prohibited from purchasing firearms unless the alien is admitted into the U.S. under nonimmigrant visa and does not meet one of the exceptions as provided in 18 U.S.C. 922(y)(2), such as possession of a valid hunting license or permit. 18 U.S.C. 922 (d)(5), (g)(5) and (y)(2); 27 CFR 478.11 and 478.32(a)(5).

Purchasing a Firearm or Ammunition as a Gift for a Juvenile

A parent or guardian may purchase firearms or ammunition as a gift for a juvenile (less than 18 years of age). However, persons less than 18 years of age may only receive and possess ***handguns*** with the written permission of a parent or guardian for limited purposes discussed earlier in the chapter. 18 U.S.C. 922(x).

Inheritance

Weapons can be transferred through a will. Individuals, including minors, can take title to firearms though inheritance. Even machine guns, suppressors and other NFA firearms can be inherited. If you are interested in transferring a firearm through a will or if you are concerned about the legality of an inherited firearm, see an estate planning attorney familiar with firearms inheritance.

National Criminal Background Check System (NICS)

The NICS is only applicable to transfers by a federal firearms licensee (FFL) and not to private sales. The NICS works by an FFL obtaining identification information from the prospective purchaser. The FFL then calls a number and connects with an NICS operator. That operator inputs the identification information into the system and the system automatically searches the vast data bases located in computers at the FBI Criminal Justice Information Center located in Clarksville, West Virginia. The main databases that get searched are the Interstate Identification Index (III) and the National Crime Information Center (NCIC). Combined, these databases have records ranging from felonies to dishonorable discharges and firearms disqualifiers in-between.

The operator runs the applicant's name and looks to see if any "hits" appear. A hit is a match or close-match in name. If a hit is found, the operator investigates further. The operator then quickly reports back to the FFL with an approval, denial, or delay pending more investigation. There is an appeal procedure for denials or delays. The Federal government does not charge for the NICS check but states may charge a small fee. South Carolina CWP holders are exempt from the NICS requirement for purchases from South Carolina FFLs.

Adjudication of Mentally Defective in South Carolina Courts

The Act contains quite a few definitions and procedures. Because of the nuances of the definitions and the likelihood of detailed hearings in commitment and guardianship and conservatorship cases (Probate Court), it would be a very good idea to retain an attorney for assistance with a case under this Act. If you are found mentally defective and reported on NICS as such, it is a process to get that adjudication removed.

A South Carolina Court can determine a person mentally defective for obvious reasons like dementia or serious mental illness, but can also adjudicate a person mentally defective for a substance addiction or even an extreme physical disability.

In a May 9, 2007 Open Letter, the BATFE explained its position regarding *mentally defective*. BATFE's position is that mentally defective is generally defined by state law and determined by state courts. Again, however, veterans have been running into trouble with NICS reporting because of examinations by VA related health care providers. Further, HHS regulations under the new Affordable Care Act are raising serious concerns about NICS reporting. Mostly though, determinations of mentally defective are made in the state mental health courts. In South Carolina, jurisdiction lies typically with the Probate Court, Mental Health Division. The typical cases are commitments, guardianships, and conservatorships.

Briefly, taking a step back at federal law, Section 922(g)(4) of 18 U.S.C. makes it unlawful for any person who has been adjudicated as a mental defective or who has been committed to a mental institution to possess firearms or ammunition. This prohibition covers two classes of persons–those who have either been (1) adjudicated as a mental defective; or (2) committed to a mental institution. These terms is defined by Federal regulation at 27 C.F.R. Section 478.11 as follows:

a. A determination by a court, board, commission, or other lawful authority that a person, because of marked subnormal intelligence, or mental illness, incompetency, condition, or disease:

    1. is a danger to himself or to others; or

    2. lacks the mental capacity to contract or manage his own affairs.

This means a formal commitment to a mental institution by a court, board, commission, or other lawful authority. It includes a commitment to a mental institution involuntarily (against your will) for mental defectiveness or mental illness or other reasons such as for drug use. It does not include a person in a mental institution for observation or any voluntary admission to a mental institution.

BATFE has historically made two distinct prohibitions and that each prohibition represents a separate disqualification. For example, a ***commitment*** means a formal commitment, not a voluntary stay. Excluded are stays for observation only. Nor does the term include a stay in a mental institution that never involved any form of adjudication by a lawful authority. Therefore, if a court did not commit you to the mental health center, you are not supposed to be reported to NICS. However, a stay that began as a voluntary stay may be subsequently transformed into a disqualifying stay if a court, board, or other lawful authority determines that a person is a danger to self or others. Moreover, a voluntary stay that is, by itself, not disabling could be later converted into a formal commitment and therefore be disabling.

b. A determination by a court, board, commission, or other lawful authority that a person, because of marked subnormal intelligence, or mental illness, incompetency, condition, or disease:

    1. is a danger to himself or to others; or

    2. lacks the mental capacity to contract or manage his own affairs.

This means a formal commitment to a mental institution by a court, board, commission, or other lawful authority. It includes a commitment to a mental institution involuntarily (against your will) for mental defectiveness or mental illness or other reasons such as for drug use. It does not include a person in a mental institution for observation or any voluntary admission to a mental institution.

BATFE has historically made two distinct prohibitions and that each prohibition represents a separate disqualification. For example, a ***commitment*** means a formal commitment, not a voluntary stay. Excluded are stays for observation only. Nor does the term include a stay in a mental institution that never involved any form of adjudication by a lawful authority. Therefore, if a court did not commit you to the mental health center, you are not supposed to be reported to NICS. However, a stay that began as a voluntary stay may be subsequently transformed into a disqualifying stay if a court, board, or other lawful authority determines that a person is a danger to self or others. Moreover, a voluntary stay that is, by itself, not disabling could be later converted into a formal commitment and therefore be disabling.

For purposes of a federal firearms disability, ATF interprets ***adjudicated mental defective*** to include anyone adjudicated to be a danger to him or herself, a danger to others, or lacking the mental capacity to contract or manage his or her own affairs. For purposes of federal law, danger means any danger, not simply imminent or substantial danger as is often required to sustain an involuntary commitment under state law. So, adjudication that a person is mentally ill and a danger to himself or others will result in federal firearms disability, whether the court-ordered treatment was on an inpatient or outpatient basis. This is because the adjudication itself (a finding of danger due to mental illness) is sufficient to trigger the disability.

The South Carolina Code of Laws provide for two procedures for arriving at adjudication of mentally defective. These procedures are *commitment* and *guardianship/conservatorship*. A commitment procedure is either emergency or non-emergency (also called judicial). In an emergency under Section 44-17-410, et seq., a first-responder such as EMS or the police or a family member typically arrive at a scene and determine that the subject is in danger to himself or others and needs an immediate evaluation by a mental health professional. The police will take custody of the subject and bring the person to a mental health center. The subject is not under arrest but is not allowed to leave. An evaluation must be made within twenty-four hours or the subject is released.

Within forty-eight hours of the involuntary admission, the examiner must send an affidavit and certification to the Probate Court. Within forty-eight hours of receiving these documents, the court must see if there is probable cause to continue the emergency involuntary hospitalization. (Saturdays, Sundays, and holidays do not count toward the forty-eight hours). Probable cause means there are still good reasons for an emergency commitment. If no probable cause, the person is released. If there is probable cause, a full hearing will be conducted at Court. The alleged mentally defective will have an attorney and the opportunity to provide the Court with his own medical exams and witnesses.

For the purposes of reporting to SLED and then NICS, there is no reporting unless, and until, final adjudication is made at the full hearing. If the commitment was for the observation and did not result in a final adjudication after full hearing, any of the judicial actions are considered temporary. Temporary court actions are not reportable to SLED and NICS short of the Court finding an extraordinary exception.

Non-emergency involuntary commitment procedures are codified in South Carolina Code of Laws Section 44-17-510, et seq. The procedure is similar to the emergency procedure but the time frames are less immediate. Further, the matter is generally begun with a court proceeding before observation or temporary commitment. Like emergency cases, no report of mentally defective is sent to SLED (and thereafter NICS) unless, and until, a final adjudication is made. Again, a person must be appointed counsel and given notice as well as opportunity to present his own experts and any other evidence.

The emergency and non-emergency commitment procedures are for forcing a person to enter a mental health hospital. Just like physical diseases that don't require hospitalization though, a person might be mentally defective but not require hospitalization. For mental defective cases that don't necessarily require hospitalization, the judicial process is a *protective proceeding* under South Carolina Code of Laws Section 62-5-101, et seq., A protective proceeding provides for judicial review and the establishment of a guardianship and/or conservatorship for a *protected person.* The court must ensure due process including notice, an attorney, and opportunity for a full hearing.

The purpose of the procedure is to determine if a person is an *incapacitated person* under Section 62-5-101(1). An incapacitated person means:

> any person who is impaired by reason of mental illness, mental deficiency, physical illness or disability, advanced age, chronic use of drugs, chronic intoxication, or other cause (except minority) to the extent that he lacks sufficient understanding or capacity to make or communicate responsible decisions concerning his person or property;

In a protected proceeding, a person adjudicated incapacitated will be appointed a guardian and/or conservator. As in commitment proceedings, only final adjudications are reported to SLED (which then reports to NICS). Temporary adjudications are not final and not reportable to SLED unless there is some extraordinary reason to do so.
Avoid a Final Adjudication of Incapacity or Mental Defective

If the adjudication is final, a report will be sent to SLED and the person will appear as a hit on a NICS check. Therefore, it is critical to take a protective proceeding or commitment proceeding as serious as you would a criminal charge. If you have legitimate defenses, you need to hire a good attorney to defend you. The legal danger is that the adjudication is not easy to undo. There are two statutes that you have to deal with. Under South Carolina Sections 44-17-620 and 62-5-306, there is relief available that will restore most rights. However, that is not enough with respect to NICS. Under the NICS, the state procedure for relief must meet with ATF's interpretation of the NICS Improvements Amendments Act of 2007. Meeting that standard has proven difficult. In fact, according to the probate judge consulted, as of January, 2014, it appears that no more than twenty people have been granted that relief nationwide.

Alcohol and Drug Patients Prohibited from Possessing Firearms

Section 44-52-165(3) prohibits patients receiving alcohol and drug addiction services prohibited from possessing firearms. The crime is a felony with the potential penalty of a fine of not less than $1,000 nor more than $10,000 or imprisoned for not less than one (1) year nor more than ten (10) years, or both. A person supplying a patient with a firearm is subject to the same potential penalty.

Dealers Must Provide You with a Handgun Safety or Storage Device

If you purchase a *handgun* from a licensed dealer (FFL), the dealer is required by federal law to also provide you with a secure gun storage or safety device. 18 U.S.C. § 922(z)(1). Most of the time, a qualified safety device will be ether a locking mechanism built into the handgun by the manufacturer or a cable lock that makes the handgun inoperable. This is **not** the same as the firearm safety. A qualified storage device is basically a lock box or locking safe. 18 U.S.C. §921(a)(34)(A)(B)and(C). There is no requirement that you use the device.

Using a Handgun Safety or Storage Device Provides Some Immunity

Even though there is no requirement that you use a handgun safety or storage device, using it for storage provides some level of immunity from civil liability. Federal law immunizes any person who is in lawful possession and control of a handgun and who uses a secure gun storage or safety device with the handgun, from a *qualified civil liability action.* Qualified civil liability action is defined as a civil action for damages resulting from the criminal or unlawful misuse of a handgun by a third party if: 1) the handgun was accessed by another person who did not have the authorization of the lawful possessor; and 2) at the time the handgun was accessed it had been made inoperable by a secure gun storage or safety device. 18 U.S.C. § 922(z)(3)(A) and § 922(z)(3)(C).

Conclusion

Make sure that you understand the law before obtaining a gun so that you do not end up with a criminal record or jail time. Do not rely solely on the gun seller, especially if the seller is not a reputable local gun shop. Always know the law for yourself.

Chapter 3
Preventing and Removing Your Legal Disability

Contributor Henry R. Schlein, Esq. (Summerville)

What is a Legal Disability?

A legal disability is a personal condition that prevents you from lawfully purchasing or possessing a gun. Legal disabilities can arise from a criminal record, mental condition, or certain other misconduct that the government deems problematic. If you have a legal disability, it is a crime for you to sell, transfer, possess, or receive a firearm.

What is the Lifetime Federal Firearms Disability?

Those with federal or state felony conviction or adjudication, or those with a federal misdemeanor conviction with a *potential* jail term of more than one (1) year, or those with a state misdemeanor conviction that carries the *potential* jail term of greater than two (2) years, virtually always have a legal disability. Notice that the word potential is italicized. That is because the law does care what the actual sentence applied is, the federal firearms disability arises or not based upon the potential penalty of a given offense as opposed to the actual sentence handed down by a judge or negotiated with the prosecutor. For a more detailed discussion of the lifetime federal firearms disability and removal of a legal disability, see *Appendix I*.

So, expanding upon the general rule above, you have a legal disability if one of the following applies to you:

- you were convicted or adjudicated for a federal or South Carolina felony; or you were convicted or adjudicated of a federal misdemeanor with a *potential* jail term of greater than 1 year or a South Carolina misdemeanor with a *potential* jail term of greater than two (2) years;

- you were convicted of a felony or a state misdemeanor with a *potential* jail term of greater than two (2) years;

- you are under indictment or information for a federal or state felony, a federal misdemeanor crime with a *potential* jail term more than one (1) year, or a state misdemeanor with a *potential* jail term of more than two (2) years. However, this might not rule-out possession of a firearm until a sentence is imposed; or

- you are fleeing another state to avoid prosecution for a crime or avoid testifying in a criminal proceeding.

Second, certain mental conditions can impute a legal disability. Therefore, you have a legal disability if one of the following applies to you:

- you are addicted to or using illegal drugs (this is true even if you are only occasionally using marijuana or other "recreational" drugs);

- you have been adjudicated mentally defective, or are committed to a mental institution, or have been committed to a mental institution sometime in the past.

> *Commitment to a mental institution* means the involuntary placement in a mental facility after some legitimate board, agency or court of mental illness determines that you have a mental defect that requires involuntary treatment. Involuntary commitment for drug or alcohol use is included in this definition.

Note though, if you had been placed in a mental facility, against your will, for observation of your suspected condition, such commitment would not count against you. Only after you have been determined to have a mental defect that requires involuntary admission to a mental facility would a legal disability arise. Voluntary admission to a mental facility is not included. So, if you think that you have some mental condition, worry about seeing a doctor first and worry about how it will affect your gun rights later (see also the National Instant Criminal Background Check (NICS) section in the *Buying and Possessing a Gun or Ammunition* chapter for more details); or

- you have been found not guilty by reason of insanity in a criminal case.

Finally, miscellaneous misconduct or other circumstances can impute you with a legal disability. Therefore, you have a legal disability if one of the following applies to you:

- you were dishonorably discharged from military service;

- you renounce your U.S. citizenship;

- you are subject to a domestic restraining order where the court found you a credible threat to the physical safety of another. Alternatively, that the court order expressly prohibits the use, threatened or attempted use of physical force; or

- you were convicted of a misdemeanor crime of domestic violence as defined in 18 USC 922(g)(9). Generally this means an offense that involves the attempted use of physical force, or the threatened use of a deadly weapon, committed by a current or former spouse, parent, or guardian of the victim, by a person with whom the victim shares a child in common, by a person who is cohabiting with or has cohabited with the victim as a spouse, parent, or guardian, or by a person similarly situated to a spouse, parent, or guardian of the victim. It doesn't apply to casual relationships unless you were living together. Under current federal law it likely includes cases where a "guilty" plea was entered vs. "no contest" plea, or where there was a trial with a "guilty" verdict, even if adjudication was later "withheld." It will always include an "adjudication" of guilt.

VA Health Care Visits and Mental Health Diagnoses

Unfortunately, some Vietnam Era and other veterans are being denied their right to keep and bear arms under some language in the NICS Improvements Amendments Act of 2007. This controversial and hastily passed federal law has the effect of allowing some diagnoses of post-traumatic stress disorder to satisfy the *adjudicated mentally defective* standard discussed above. What generally happens is a veteran will go to buy a firearm from an FFL and find that they are denied during the NICS check.

A full discussion of this Act is beyond the scope of this book but affected veterans should **consult with an attorney** to assist in removing a legal disability caused by the Act. There are procedures to gain relief found in Title 27, Code of Federal Regulations Section 478.11.

Be aware also that the federal agency HHS is currently attempting to promulgate regulations that would affect the HIPAA privacy laws for private (non-VA) visits with, and diagnoses by, mental health providers. If not stopped, this would mean that HIPAA privacy law would be repealed to allow mental health providers to turn their patients into the FBI's NICS list because of personal information, communicated in private. This would greatly expand the ability of the federal government to interfere with gun possession on otherwise law-abiding folks. In the balancing act between public safety and the natural rights of individuals to firearms, this proposed change will give more power to the government. It might also cause many people to not seek help from mental health professionals for fear of losing the freedom to possess firearms.

The Legal Danger of Domestic Violence

Under 18 U.S.C. §922(g)(9), a person charged with criminal domestic violence faces a permanent firearms disability if convicted of this offense. In addition, while the charge is pending in court, and even before any trial or conviction, the defendant may also face a temporary prohibition against owning or possessing firearms as a term or condition of bond. For example, the magistrate or bond hearing judge may impose such a restriction against the defendant as a condition of being released from jail on bond.

In the past, it was routine for a criminal domestic violence charge to be reduced to simple assault, as the result of a plea bargain, which at that time, eliminated the prospect of the firearms prohibition. However, in 2009, the United States Supreme Court effectively closed this door with their decision in *United States v. Hayes*. Therefore, if a defendant pleads "guilty" or "no contest" to, or is convicted of, the lesser included offense of simple assault, or assault and battery third degree, the defendant will still be subject to the same firearms prohibition and disability as for a criminal domestic violence conviction, if the underlying offense involved substantially the same elements.

By way of further explanation, 18 U.S.C. §921(a)(33)(A) provides that the term "misdemeanor crime of domestic violence" means an offense that:

1. is a misdemeanor under Federal, State, or Tribal law; and

2. has, as an element, the use or attempted use of physical force, or the threatened use of a deadly weapon, committed by a current or former spouse, parent, or guardian of the victim, by a person with whom the victim shares a child in common, by a person who is cohabiting with or has cohabited with the victim as a spouse, parent, or guardian, or by a person similarly situated to a spouse, parent, or guardian of the victim.

Thus, if the underlying offense involved an assault against someone with whom the defendant had a specified domestic relationship, the federal firearms prohibition would apply, upon conviction, regardless of how the charge was characterized.

Likewise, under S.C. Code § 16-25-20, it is unlawful to:

1. cause physical harm or injury to a person's own household member; or

2. offer or attempt to cause physical harm or injury to a person's own household member with apparent present ability under circumstances reasonably creating fear of imminent peril.

On the other hand, a person shall not be considered to have been convicted of such an offense for purposes of this chapter, unless:

1. the person was represented by counsel in the case, or knowingly and intelligently waived the right to counsel in the case; and

2. in the case of a prosecution for an offense described in this paragraph for which a person was entitled to a jury trial in the jurisdiction in which the case was tried, either

(a) the case was tried by a jury, or

(b) the person knowingly and intelligently waived the right to have the case tried by a jury, by guilty plea or otherwise.

In general, when someone is arrested for the charge of criminal domestic violence, the defendant is typically brought before a magistrate judge for a bond hearing. At the bond hearing, a person is told of the right to have an attorney and the right to have one appointed if the defendant cannot afford to hire an attorney. The defendant is also informed of the trial or court hearing date. The defendant's subsequent failure to appear at the scheduled court hearing could be construed as a waiver of the foregoing rights and the court would likely convict the defendant in his absence.

However, if the defendant was able to post bond without having to appear before a judge to be informed of the right to counsel, and subsequently decided not to appear in court, but to forfeit the bond previously posted, such a defendant might be able to pursue a claim that the right to counsel was not knowingly and intelligently waived, but it would be an uphill battle and the defendant making the claim would bear the burden of proof. Also, the court might not automatically decide merely to order the defendant's bail forfeited. Instead, it could issue a bench warrant for the defendant's arrest for failure to appear and have the defendant brought to court for trial.

For anyone who is subject to this firearms disability, the good news is that first offense criminal domestic violence is a misdemeanor under S.C. Code Section 22-5-910(A)(3) and may be expunged after five (5) years from the date of conviction provided:

(a) it was a first offense of any kind for the defendant, other than minor traffic tickets; and

(b) there have been no subsequent criminal offenses for the five (5) year period following the conviction, other than minor traffic tickets.

If the conviction was for simple assault or assault and battery third degree, under S.C. Code Section 22-5-910(A) it can be expunged under the same conditions, except that the waiting period is shortened to 3 years from the date of conviction.

In some cases, depending on the circumstances, the defendant may be allowed to enter the solicitor's Pretrial Intervention Program, known as PTI. Anyone participating in this program is required to pay for all costs associated with it. The defendant will typically be required to successfully complete a domestic violence counseling program, which usually lasts twenty-six weeks. Failure to attend classes and successfully complete counseling, failure to pay all fees, or getting rearrested for anything will usually result in the defendant's being terminated from the PTI program and the case being returned to the court's docket for trial. Upon successful completion of PTI, the charge will be dismissed and the defendant can have it expunged.

It may be possible for the prosecuting attorney or officer to simply defer the prosecution of the case for a certain period, such as six (6) months, during which, the defendant would be obliged to stay out of trouble and not be rearrested. At the end of the deferral period, the case would be dismissed and could be expunged by the court. It used to be common for the deferred prosecution of a case to be used in lieu of PTI, with conditions being imposed that the defendant would have to complete, such as anger management counseling or domestic violence counseling. However, our state Supreme Court has ruled that only the solicitor can operate a pretrial intervention program, so any such deferred prosecution cases must now be straight deferrals, without those kinds of conditions. However, nothing would prevent the defendant from voluntarily participating in, and successfully completing, a program of anger management or domestic violence counseling and furnishing a certificate of completion to counsel, for future reference.

Some other factors that may generally affect the prosecution of criminal domestic violence cases include reluctance or lack of desire by the complainant to press charges, which sometimes makes prosecution difficult. However, the state can still compel the appearance in court and the testimony of complainant and witnesses, but the state bears the burden of proof ***beyond a reasonable doubt*** at all times. The defendant is innocent until proven guilty and never needs to prove his or her innocence, although as a practical matter, it is usually very helpful to have a good defense attorney.

Sometimes a prosecutor or police officer may adamantly pursue the conviction to impose a firearms disability for a defendant. On several occasions, a prosecuting attorney or officer has stated to me in pretrial discussions that he or she specifically wanted a defendant to be prohibited from ever being able to own or possess any firearms. A federal agent who was making a presentation to a group of attorneys referred to a case anecdotally (although not domestic violence related, but the same point) in which he and his team specifically wanted the defendants to be deprived of their ability to ever own or possess firearms, and he was disappointed when federal prosecutor allowed those defendants to enter the PTI program, over his objection.[2] Criminal domestic violence tends to be a "hot button" topic and many police officers and prosecutors are reluctant not to fully prosecute these cases for the simple reason that the threat of further violence resulting in serious injury or death is very real. Of course, each case has its own facts and when the allegations of violence are severe, prosecution tends to get ramped up. This just serves to illustrate some of the issues concerning criminal domestic violence cases and the associated legal firearms disabilities.

---

[2] 3rd Annual South Carolina Gun Law Seminar, Summerville, S.C., February 10, 2012. Although the facts of that particular case would have justified the legal firearms disability, it was a matter about which reasonable minds could differ, whether or not to allow the defendant's to enter the PTI Program. In any event, this incident is related for illustrative purposes only and the author offers no opinion regarding any decision in this case.

Pardon

If a defendant pleads "guilty" or "no contest" to, or is convicted of, a criminal domestic violence related offense, a pardon may be possible at some point in the future. Pursuant to S.C. Code Section 24-21-940(A), "Pardon" means that an individual is fully pardoned from all the legal consequences of his crime and of his conviction, direct and collateral, including the punishment, whether of imprisonment, pecuniary penalty or whatever else the law has provided. For purposes of Title 18 U. S. C. §922(g)(1), the ATF Form 4473, and the federal Firearms Transaction Record, you are no longer prohibited from owning or possessing firearms or ammunition because of the prior criminal offense, if you have received a pardon for that offense.

For those applicants to be granted a pardon, a certificate of pardon shall be issued by the Board stating that the individual is absolved from all legal consequences of his crime and conviction, and that all of his civil rights are restored (S.C. Code Section 24-21-1000). A pardon shall fully restore all civil rights lost as a result of a conviction, which shall include the right to: (1) register to vote; (2) vote; (3) serve on a jury; (4) hold public office, except as provided in Section 16-13-210; (5) testify without having the fact of his conviction introduced for impeachment purposes to the extent provided by Rule 609(c) of the South Carolina Rules of Evidence; (6) not have his testimony excluded in a legal proceeding if convicted of perjury; and (7) be licensed for any occupation requiring a license. Although the right to own and possess firearms is not specifically enumerated in §24-21-940, the list does not purport to be all inclusive.

Restraining Orders Under the PDAA

A person subject to a restraining order under S.C. Code Section 20-4-10 (the Protection from Domestic Abuse Act) will be subject to a firearms disability for the duration of the order. See also 18 U. S. C.

§922(g)(8). To fall within this statute, this court order must meet three criteria. First, it must have been issued after a hearing of which the person restrained received actual notice, and at which such person had an opportunity to participate. Second, it must restrain this person from harassing, stalking, or threatening an intimate partner of such person or child of such intimate partner or person, or from engaging in other conduct that would place an intimate partner in reasonable fear of bodily injury to the partner or child. Third, it must either (a) include a finding that the person restrained represents a credible threat to the physical safety of the intimate partner or child; or (b) by its terms the order must explicitly prohibit the use, attempted use, or threatened use of physical force against the intimate partner or child that would reasonably be expected to cause bodily injury.

The restraining order issued under the Protection from Domestic Abuse Act is called an Order of Protection. It usually comes about when one person of a married couple, or couple who are living together, or who have a child in common, alleges that he or she was threatened or assaulted by the other. The person seeking this order is referred to as the "petitioner." Under Section 20-4-50, the hearing must be held:

(a) Within 24 hours of service upon respondent (the person against whom the restraining order is being sought), if an emergency hearing request is made and granted by the court; or

(b) otherwise, within 15 days, so long as the respondent is properly served at least 5 days prior to the hearing.

The respondent may request a continuance until this requirement has been complied with. Under Section § 20-4-30, the hearing will be held in the family court except that, during non-business hours or at other times when the court is not in session, the petition may be filed with a magistrate. The family court has the authority to order additional relief, such as custody, support, and attorney's fees, while the magistrate's court can issue the restraining order only. This process may be collateral to a criminal prosecution for domestic violence.

Arguably, there is significant potential for abuse of legal process in this type of action. On the one hand, it enables someone with limited financial resources to have prompt access the family court to swiftly obtain a protective order restraining his or her spouse or intimate partner from perpetuating further abuse, under the threat of the contempt powers of the court, as well our criminal statutes which prohibit the violation of an order of protection. On the other hand, under Section 20-4-60, it is also a fast track side door entrance to the family court to potentially obtain substantially similar relief as could be obtained in a regular domestic action, such as custody, child support, alimony, exclusive possession of the home, the car, and division of certain debts. A regular domestic action usually requires an attorney, a $150.00 filing fee, and takes several weeks before the court schedules a hearing. For a petition for an Order of Protection, there is no filing fee under Section 20-4-40(f) and 20-4-65, the forms are made available by the court, and the police victim's advocate assists the petitioner with the entire process, including going to court.

This type of legal action is civil in nature, so the petitioner, as the person making the claim, bears the burden of proof, but by the lesser civil standard of the preponderance of the evidence. In other words, by the greater weight of the evidence, meaning that the case will be determined based upon whether it is more likely than not that the claim is, or is not, valid. Contrast this with a criminal prosecution for domestic violence in which the standard of proof for conviction is proof beyond a reasonable doubt. The respondent defending against the action has different legal rights than what one would have, as a defendant in a criminal case. For example, since this is a civil case, the defendant can be called to testify as a witness against himself. If the defendant takes "the Fifth" (i.e. refuses to answer a question on the grounds that the answer may tend to incriminate himself), it can result in an adverse inference and can be used as evidence in support of the petitioner's claim. The respondent also does not necessarily have a right to request a continuance to obtain a lawyer, although the petitioner may do so.

A case in point is Moore v. Moore, in which the respondent was served at approximately 8:00 p.m. the evening before an emergency hearing scheduled for the following morning. At the hearing the next morning, the judge asked the petitioner if she was prepared to go forward without an attorney. When the petitioner said that she was, the respondent asked for a continuance to get an attorney but the court denied this request. After the petitioner gave her testimony, the court asked the respondent if wanted to give any testimony. The respondent again requested a continuance to obtain an attorney. The court again denied this request, citing Section 20-4-50. The court ultimately found against the respondent and issued the Order of Protection. Respondent subsequently hired an attorney and appealed the court's decision. The South Carolina Supreme Court affirmed, in part, and reversed in part, ruling:

> [W]e believe the Legislature intended for the findings, which result from an emergency hearing pursuant to section 20-4-50 (a), to be temporary and confined to the Order of Protection. Implicit in this conclusion is that these findings cannot be used in future litigation unless they are confirmed in a subsequent hearing on the merits.... Inferentially, a hearing conducted pursuant to section 20-4-50 (b), which provides a respondent an extended period in which to retain counsel and prepare his or her case, should be viewed as an adjudicative hearing on the merits of the action.

The essence of the ruling is that, if the respondent is served with an emergency hearing notice to be held within 72 hours, the hearing can still proceed, with or without a defense attorney for the respondent, but no finding made by the court can be used against the respondent in any subsequent proceeding (i.e., a finding that respondent threatened or assaulted his or her spouse). But if the hearing was the non-emergency, 15 day one (or perhaps if respondent were to have been granted a continuance to retain an attorney), any findings made by the court can be carried over to subsequent proceedings. In either case, if a restraining order is issued under this act, it will still carry the same firearms prohibitions for the duration of the order.

Once an order of protection is issued, how long does it remain in effect? South Carolina Code of Laws Section 20-4-70(A) specifies that the duration of an order of protection must be for a fixed time not less than six months nor more than one year unless the parties have reconciled as evidenced by an order of dismissal. It may be extended or terminated by order of the court upon motion by either party showing good cause with notice to the other party.

If the parties reconcile, the issuing court may grant an order of dismissal without a hearing if the petitioner receiving the order of protection to be dismissed appears personally at the offices of the issuing court, shows proper identification, and signs a written request to dismiss based on the reconciliation. Under Section 20-4-70(B), The order basically continues in effect unless, prior to the expiration, the family court has scheduled a hearing for temporary relief in a regular domestic action, in which case, it continues in effect until an order granting temporary relief is issued. Under 20-4-70(D) alternatively, an order of protection issued by a magistrate expires as provided under the terms of the order or upon the issuance of a subsequent order by the family court, whichever occurs first.

Sometimes these cases can be difficult to prove, where the evidence consists only of the petitioner's word against the respondent's and there is no other corroborating or supporting evidence. The court may choose, however, to err on the side of caution and issue the restraining order. Courts sometimes disfavor these types of cases if perceived to be embellished and sought only to bypass the regular domestic relations action process, which takes more time and expense for a case to be heard. One cannot help but try to appreciate the unenviable position of our family court judges, who must weigh the evidence, and who are called upon to make decisions in these cases with the wisdom of King Solomon.

These cases can sometimes be settled by agreement between the parties to mutual restraining orders without any finding of domestic abuse. A well-drafted mutual civil restraining order, which does not prohibit either party from owning or possessing firearms or ammunition would be preferred. However, a purely civil restraining order may have more lasting consequences, depending on what other terms or conditions are included, what duration, if any, is specified, and how it is drafted. Anyone facing such an action would be well advised to seek the services of a competent and experienced attorney.

Restraining Orders in Regular Domestic Relations Cases

In regular domestic relations cases, such as actions for divorce, child custody, or separation (formally called an action for separate support and maintenance), attorneys usually plead for an entire laundry list of restraining orders. Section 20-3-110 specifically allows the family court to grant an order restraining either party to the cause from in any manner interposing any restraint upon the personal liberty of, or from harming, interfering with or molesting, the other party to the cause during the pendency of the suit or after final judgment. In the experience of Attorney Henry Schlein, the language most commonly used in drafting this provision usually restrains a spouse or party "from threatening, harming, harassing, or interfering with the peaceful enjoyment of life by the other." The family court routinely grants such requests, even without cause, as Section 20-3-110 provides. The courts will often make this a mutual restraining order upon the request of either party or attorney. Sometimes the court, on its own motion, will ask the parties whether any such restraining order is desired, although neither party requested it.

The issue for concern here is that the wording of this type of restraining order looks very similar the type referred to in Title 18 U. S. C. §922(g)(8), above, and could therefore appear to implicate the federal firearms prohibition of that statute. For example, under Title 18 U. S. C. §922(g)(8), a person will be prohibited from owning or possessing firearms and ammunition if he or she is subject to a restraining order that:

1. Has been issued after a hearing of which the person restrained received actual notice, and at which such person had an opportunity to participate;

2. Restrains this person from harassing, stalking, or threatening an intimate partner of such person or child of such intimate partner or person, or from engaging in other conduct that would place an intimate partner in reasonable fear of bodily injury to the partner or child;

It either

(a) includes a finding that the person restrained represents a credible threat to the physical safety of the intimate partner or child; or,

(b) by its terms the order explicitly prohibits the use, attempted use, or threatened use of physical force against the intimate partner or child that would reasonably be expected to cause bodily injury (18 U. S. C. §922(g)(8)). Compare this with our State Code § 20-3-110:

The parties to a domestic action must be served with notice of the hearing and have an opportunity to appear and be heard. The order can restrain either party from interposing any restraint upon the personal liberty of, or from harming, interfering with or molesting, the other party (who is usually a spouse or intimate partner and/or they have a child in common.)

Although there may not be any finding that the person restrained represents a credible threat to the physical safety of the intimate partner or child, it will, by its terms, explicitly prohibit the use, attempted use, or threatened use of physical force against the intimate partner or child that would reasonably be expected to cause bodily injury.

By this comparison, it is easy to see how some overzealous prosecutor or law enforcement official might be able to construe a federal firearms violation out of something that was never meant to form the basis of such a case. This is, perhaps, a good example of the law of unintended consequences. The policy reason for the law allowing these restraining orders is obviously to protect the parties against continued and unwanted communications or contact between each other, after the breakup of their marriage or other intimate domestic relationship, which could lead to potentially lead to domestic violence. No one supposes it was ever intended to prevent the parties from owning or possessing firearms or ammunition.

This concern may be resolved, without implicating the aforementioned federal firearms prohibition, by a well-drafted mutual civil restraining order with wording that specifically protects the parties' second amendment firearms rights. A final order or decree from a family court has no expiration date and continues in full force and effect indefinitely, unless modified in the future by a subsequent family court order, based upon proper legal grounds. Anyone pursuing or facing any family court action should seek the services of a competent and experienced attorney. Below is an example of a language that the domestic practitioner can use to craft a mutual civil that will satisfy the requirements of South Carolina Code Section 20-3-110 without implicating the firearms disability associated with Title 18 U. S. C. §922(g)(8).

Domestic Mutual Civil Restraining Order

Following is sample language for a Domestic Mutual Civil Restraining Order:

> The parties agree to be mutually enjoined from molesting, bothering, annoying, or interfering with the peaceful enjoyment of life by the other party, from contacting or coming about each other's place of residence, employment, or education, and from making disparaging remarks about the other party to that party's employer, family, or acquaintances. The Court makes no finding of any domestic abuse and the parties agree, and the Court hereby requires, that this be a mutual civil ***injunction*** (as opposed to *restraining order*) only, and not one issued under any protection from domestic abuse act, stalking or harassment statute, or for purposes of any State or federal firearms laws, including but not limited to, Title 18 U. S. C. §922(g), the Brady Act, the federal Firearms Transaction Record, AFT Form 4473, or its/their successors, or any state law counter-parts, nor for any military, police, or law enforcement purposes.

In this sample language, "enjoined" is used instead of "restrained;" "molesting, bothering, annoying" instead of "threatening, harming and harassing;" and "injunction" instead of "restraining order." Here, your court order specifically says that it is not making prejudicial findings of abuse and that this order excludes any implication of any laws that give rise to firearms disabilities. Although in the example, some of the substituted terms, “molesting, bothering, [and] annoying,” could be read as being more restrictive than “threatening, harming and harassing,” the likelihood that this would pose any problems to the parties is extremely remote, provided the parties understand that the relationship they previously had between them has ended, and that they each need to move on with their own, respective lives.

Normally, there is no problem getting the parties and the courts to agree to this or similar language. However, during a divorce that recently came to court, Attorney Schlein had a different result. The case involved custody and visitation, and the parties had settled their case. They had, amongst other things, agreed to a mutual civil restraining order with language specifically exempting it from the meaning and scope of Title 18 U.S.C section 922(g)(8). But in that case, one spouse had a history of making threats of violence and harm against the other spouse, had attempted suicide, had mental health issues, and this was part of the court records.

At the final hearing, the judge declined to approve the parties' agreement with any such language that would exempt the restraining order from implicating section 922(g)(8). Moreover, the judge specifically found that the restraining order did implicate the federal firearms prohibitions for the affected spouse. Knowing all this, the parties, including the one particularly affected, nonetheless decided to proceed with their agreement and resolve their case. However, the judge left the door open for the affected spouse to present evidence in the future that the mental disability no longer obtained, in which case, the restraining order could be modified to not implicate section 922(g)(8).

Presumably because of Sandy Hook and other recent unfortunate incidents, judges may now tend to give greater scrutiny to grant or deny parties access to firearms. If you face a similar situation, you must ensure that your lawyer is specifically prepared to support his or her legal position in such cases, particularly in the present environment of heightened firearms awareness by the public.

Restraining Orders Under the Stalking or Harassment Statutes

South Carolina Code Section 16-3-1750 provides for the issuance of restraining orders between citizens who are not necessarily involved in domestic relationships with each other. The statute is collectively called the Stalking or Harassment Statute. A person subject to a restraining order under the Stalking or Harassment statute may likewise be subject to a firearms disability for the duration of the order under Title 18 U. S. C. §922(g)(8). This is because the alleged actions involve the statutory definition of an "intimate partner" or "child" thereof. The hearing for this type of case is held in the magistrate's court. The plaintiff bears the burden of proof, by the civil standard of the preponderance of the evidence. In other words, whichever party has the greater weight of the evidence.

The same types of problems with proof are present in these cases, as with other cases for restraining orders discussed above. Judges may likewise tend to err on side of caution and issue a restraining order or mutual restraining orders; or try to encourage the parties to agree to mutual restraining orders without any finding. Unlike in a criminal trial, the defendant can be called to testify as a witness against him-or-herself.

According to a March 19, 2008 South Carolina Attorney General Opinion, there is ostensibly no right to request a jury trial. The Attorney General's opinion cited case law holding that protective orders are equitable remedies so they are not triable by jury.

However, this raises more questions than it answers. First, the magistrate's court is a statutory creation of the South Carolina General Assembly. As such, it has only those powers granted to it by statute.

The magistrate's court does not have equitable powers. Second, the Stalking and Harassment statutes are just that: statutes. The restraining orders that the magistrate's court may issue in such cases are specifically provided for in those statutes. Therefore, the underlying reasoning for the opinion that there is no right to a jury trial in this type of action is arguably based upon a fallacious premise. But until our Supreme Court or Court of Appeals rules on this issue, it will remain an open question of law.

In any event, these cases can often be resolved by agreement. A well-drafted mutual civil restraining order can narrow the scope of the impact on the parties' lives in general. If a hearing is held and a restraining order is issued, it will usually be on a form order prepared by the magistrate's court, unless counsel drafts the order with leave of the court. If the court uses its form order, it is important to make sure the blocks are not checked at the bottom, prohibiting firearms possession, if the statutory criteria under Title 18 U. S. C. §922(g)(8), as discussed above, are not met.

The Bottom Line on Domestic Violence

Federal law prohibits persons who have been convicted of criminal domestic violence, or who are subject to certain related restraining orders, from owning or possessing firearms or ammunition. This can often be a lifetime prohibition, depending on the circumstances. Good lawyering and artful drafting may go a long way towards avoiding some firearms disabilities in appropriate cases. Anyone facing such a legal action should consult with a competent, experienced attorney and should never attempt to represent oneself.

How Do I Remove a Legal Disability?

See ***Appendix I*** of this book.

Chapter 4
Concealed Weapons Permit

Introduction

South Carolina's concealed weapons law helps you protect yourself and others from deadly attacks. The law provides for a permitting system that gives private citizens a license to carry firearms in public. The law also created a major exception to South Carolina's general handgun prohibition. *See* Section 16-23-20, South Carolina Code of Laws and other sections of this book.

Rep. Bobby Cox Open Carry with Training Act

South Carolina Representative Bobby Cox led the charge for a significant elimination of carry restrictions for Concealed Weapons Permit holders through the *Open Carry with Training Act (2023)*. While the changes are incorporated throughout this chapter and book, in a nutshell, the Act expands options for how a CWP holder can carry a concealable weapon (handgun) in public in South Carolina. It does **not**, however, change where a CWP holder can carry nor does it remove the ability of a business or employer to post a sign prohibiting the carrying of a concealable weapon on the premises.

What Does the Permit Allow?

Generally, the permit allows you to carry a handgun around with you. Specifically, the statute says that a permit holder can carry a concealable weapon, in a concealed or open manner, in certain places under certain circumstances. These terms will be defined in this chapter.

What does Concealable Weapon Mean?

Concealable weapon is defined as a firearm having a length of less than twelve inches measured along its greatest dimension. The statute talks about firearms and no other weapons. Also, the statute limits the overall length to ***less than*** twelve inches. So, for all intents and purposes, the statute basically allows the permit holder to carry small and medium sized handguns.

As a point of reference, small .38 Special caliber revolvers are usually about six or seven inches in overall length. Both the Ruger LCP and Kel-Tec .380 caliber automatics are about five and one-half inches long. These guns are all well under twelve inches long and are firearms so they would be legal for a concealed weapons permit holder to carry. The Smith & Wesson 327 Night Guard revolver in .357 magnum caliber is nearly eight inches in overall length. The Magnum Research Mark XIX Desert Eagle automatic pistol chambered in .357 magnum caliber is a little more than ten and one-half inches long. These guns are also well under twelve inches long and are firearms so they would be legal for a concealed weapons permit holder to carry.

On the other hand, Kel-Tec manufactures the PLR-16 Pistol. This firearm is configured like a pistol but is chambered in the .223 Remington rifle round and is over eighteen inches in overall length. This pistol is a firearm but is over eighteen inches in overall length so it does not meet the statutory definition of concealable weapon.

Those who have seen the Clint Eastwood Dirty Harry movies know that he carried a Smith & Wesson revolver chambered in the .44 magnum caliber. While there is some debate, most tend to agree that Dirty Harry was carrying a Model 29. The current Smith & Wesson Model 29 revolver is chambered in .44 magnum and has an overall length of exactly twelve inches. The statute defines concealable weapon as less than twelve inches in overall length. Therefore, if Dirty Harry was an ordinary South Carolina resident with a concealed weapons permit, he would not be able to carry his famous .44 magnum revolver concealed (nor could he carry it openly). Knowing Dirty Harry, he would follow the law and not carry the handgun even if he was "feelin' lucky" that day. Dirty Harry knows that criminal gun charges will not, "make his day."

What does Concealed Mean? (Including Open Carry Act Changes).

The Open Carry with Training Act effectively equates open carry with concealed carry. Following, if you have a CWP (or reciprocity), you can carry openly just as lawfully as concealed. Let's start with carrying concealed. Keeping in mind though, the Open Carry Act now renders the term *concealed* almost irrelevant.

Concealed is defined as, "carried in a manner that is hidden from public view in normal wearing of clothing." If a handgun is in a holster inside of your belt and fully concealed by your pants and shirt, it is concealed by your clothes. If it is fully inside of your jeans' front pocket, it is concealed by your clothes. If it is in an ankle holster and covered by your slacks, it is concealed by your clothes. However, if it is stuck halfway in your back pocket and you wear a shirt that is not designed to drop down below your back pocket, the gun is not concealed by your clothing. Similarly, if you walk around with a pistol in a holster on the outside of your hip, it is not concealed by your clothes.

Notice that I keep mentioning the idea of concealment by your clothes. The permit requires that your concealable weapon be concealed by your clothes in the normal wearing of clothes. Therefore, if you are wearing an article of clothing in the manner in which it was designed to be worn, and you are able to conceal your weapon with that article of clothing, you are concealing the weapon as contemplated in the statute. (It should be noted that a woman's purse and man's briefcase are considered articles of clothing for the purposes of the statute.)

As an example, say that you have a holster that holds a pistol in the small of your back. The pistol is concealed from public view by the normal wearing of your shirt. While in a store though, you reach high for a box and the shirt rides up your back above the pistol. As a result, a patron on the aisle sees the pistol on your back and calls the police. It can be argued that you have not violated the law because the shirt was designed to hang over the small of the back. Alternatively, the prosecution can argue that you have violated the law because reaching for a box in a store is normal activity and your gun should therefore have remained concealed. So, the best practice is to always ensure that your clothing conceals the weapon even in situations like reaching high up on a shelf. Keeping the weapon concealed might prevent an unnecessary charge and a jury determining your fate.

That all being said, the Open Carry with Training Act augments the original CWP Act to provide: "that may be carried openly on one's person." Section 23-31-210(5). Therefore, as you read through this Chapter, keep in mind that the intent of this new legislation is to allow CWP holders to carry concealable weapons ***openly*** in those places where, before, he or she had to conceal the same firearm.

What does Open Mean?

That's a good question. Whereas the original CWP Act went into detail when defining what *concealed* means, the Open Carry with Training Act is far less definitive as to what open carry means. The new act merely reads *openly on one's person*. Since there is limited express legislative intent in the Act, a Court would look at the plain meaning of *openly on one's person*. What strikes me is the language *on one's person*. That is broad. I can see arguments from a secure holster on the outside of the belt to carrying a pistol in the hand. If carrying openly though, you, the firearm carrier, must be mindful that carrying in the hand might get you a charge for brandishing or pointing and presenting. Worse, you could cause another to draw and shoot at you mistakenly in "self-defense." The crimes of brandishing or pointing and presenting are discussed elsewhere in this book. Secondly, *on one's person* differs from the term ***on or about one's person*** used when defining where a CWP holder can now carry in one's vehicle. On one's person suggests attachment to the person whereas on or about one's person suggests not attached. Following, when you are outside of your vehicle, home, or business, the pistol needs to be attached to you as opposed to simply close-by.

What Does the Permit NOT Allow?

The permit does not deputize you as a citizen's auxiliary police officer. A permit holder should not consider him or herself a law enforcement officer. Likewise, he or she should not act as an armed vigilante. The permit is designed to allow the holder to carry a weapon in case it is needed to repel a deadly or great bodily harm attack. Thing of your concealable weapon as an emergency defensive tool.

More details of where you can carry a concealable weapon, concealed or openly on your person, with the permit will follow later in this chapter. Initially though, I will explain how to get the permit.

Qualifications

First, you must be either a resident of the State of South Carolina or a qualified non-resident. The term "resident" means that you intend to make South Carolina your permanent home for now. It also includes military personnel permanently stationed in South Carolina. If you are not a resident you can still get a permit if you are a qualified non-resident. Qualified non-resident means that you reside in a state other than South Carolina but you own real estate in South Carolina.

Additionally, you must be at least 21 years of age. This might be an area ripe for a court challenge because 18 year-olds can already possess a handgun and the South Carolina Supreme Court has already ruled that it is unconstitutional to deny 18 year old adults the right to keep and bear arms. Further, 18 year-olds can buy a handgun from a private (non-FFL-licensed) individual. The legislature should create a permit that fills this gap. However, for now, you must be at least 21 to get the permit.

Also, you must not suffer from a physical infirmity that would prevent you from passing the range qualification portion of the concealed weapons permit course. Alternatively, you must not suffer from a physical infirmity that would prevent you from completing one of the alternate proofs of training discussed later in this chapter.

Finally, you must be able to legally possess handguns. This means that you must not be a convicted felon or have any other firearms disability (see our chapter on Legal Disabilities). Also, one can also be legally disqualified for certain misdemeanors like criminal domestic violence. There is an exception to this requirement for those who have received executive clemency.

The Application Process

Obtaining a concealed weapons permit is a fairly simple process. You must provide a complete and accurate application and provide proof of training. SLED has created a checklist for completion of the application on their website.

You can save a tremendous amount of time, energy and hassle by signing-up for your required training with an instructor that provides most of the other application requirements also. In other words, some training instructors and programs offer only the training while others offer the complete service of application, fingerprints, etc. It is a great convenience to have all the application requirements assembled by your instructor on the day of your concealed weapons permit class.

WAYNE PUTMAN
Summerville, SC
SLED Certified CWP Instructor
NRA Pistol Instructor
SC Constable

The Application Form

However, if you want to apply on your own, you get started by fully completing a South Carolina Concealed Weapons Permit Application Form R-078 (Revised 3/27/09). The application form itself is available to the public on the SLED website. Go to SLED's website at: www.sled.sc.gov and click on "Concealed Weapons Permit Program" on the left side of the website and thereafter click on "Concealed Weapons Permit Application." The form allows you to type in the information but be careful about losing information that you type in. Many applicants report that they are unable to "save" the completed form. To be safe then, complete the form and print immediately. The form is good for both new and renewal permits.

Online Application and Communication with SLED

Under South Carolina Code of Laws Section 23-31-215(H), applications may be made online. Formerly, an applicant was only allowed to either mail the application or delivery in-person to SLED. If the applicant chooses to apply online, SLED may continue to make all contact with the applicant through online communications (i.e. email). Some people prefer emails as opposed to phone calls and letters so this is a welcome addition.

The application requires that you give your name, date of birth, place of birth, sex, race, height, weight, eye color, hair color, current residence address (if you are a qualified non-resident you will also have to give the address of the property that you own in the state. We will talk about proof of qualified non-residency a little later in this chapter.) Additionally, you must certify that you are not prohibited from possessing a weapon under state or federal law. You must also certify that you understand that, should you later become prohibited from possessing a weapon, your permit is automatically revoked and you must surrender it immediately to SLED. If you choose to qualify through a SLED approved instructor, there is a place on the form where your training instructor must include the training date and instructor certification. Alternatively, if you choose to qualify through one of the alternatives to the class for proof of training, you will need to provide the proper documentation. Finally, you must then certify that all of the information that you have provided is true and correct to the best of your knowledge.

Arrests, Pleas, Convictions and Traffic Tickets

The application form no longer asks: *Have you **ever** pled guilty, been found guilty, paid a fine, forfeited bond, been jailed or placed on probation for any offense? If yes, furnish details on another sheet.* SLED no longer requires that you list these. Alternatively, SLED accesses your records and uses anything it finds to base its approval or denial.

The background check that SLED conducts usually uncovers all run-ins you have had with the law. I routinely have clients who have been denied a CWP for some minor misdemeanor they did as a younger person. Some charges from the 1950's. We are generally able to appeal the denial successfully after providing SLED with additional information from the Clerk of Court but there is a delay none-the-less. Generally, what is needed is a certified copy of the *Final Disposition* of the offense. Sometimes SLED will also insist upon an expungement of the charge. An expungement merely removes the record from most law enforcement records but has no affect upon firearms disability. However, SLED still insists upon it. If the charge did create a firearms disability, then a pardon is required (see the chapter on firearms disabilities).

Speeding tickets and minor traffic infractions typically have no effect upon your application. Only if there are multiple infractions in a relatively short period of time do they become an issue with an application.

Residency

You are no longer required to provide proof of residency as of February 11, 2014. However, if you are seeking a CWP as a qualified non-resident, you will be must also submit proof of residency or qualified non-residency. First, let's figure-out if you are a resident, qualified nonresident, or a non-resident. Remember, permits are only legal for residents and qualified non-residents.

CWP for a South Carolina Resident

Section 23-31-210(1) of the S.C. Code of Laws defines resident as:

> an individual who is present in South Carolina with the intention of making a permanent home in South Carolina or military personnel on permanent change of station orders.

In general, you are a resident if you have your residence in South Carolina as opposed to visiting. A South Carolina driver's license is further evidence that you “live” in South Carolina. If you live close to a bordering state, it is not a problem that you work or otherwise have significant contacts with the neighboring state. Primarily, the South Carolina Code of Laws and SLED are interested in your physical residence. Section 23-31-215(3) of the S.C. Code of Laws requires that you provide proof of residence or qualified non-residency.

There is one additional classification of resident. If you are a member of the military of the United States and stationed in South Carolina or on permanent change of station orders, you qualify as a resident.

Picture Identification

For residents, you must send picture identification. Section 23-31-210(3)(a) of the S.C. Code defines picture identification as a photocopy of your valid driver’s license or photographic identification card issued by your state of residence. Alternatively, Section 23-31-210(3)(b) of the S.C. Code allows for a photocopy of a valid: voter’s registration card, South Carolina Department of Revenue ID, any state or federal law enforcement agency ID, US Department of Defense ID, or US State Department ID. It can also be satisfied by the presentation of a certified copy of any other document which SLED determines satisfies the requirement. If you have a document other than a driver’s license or DMV ID card, always contact SLED first to see if they will accept it. Even if they say yes on the phone, there is no guarantee that they will actually accept it with your application. Why not just give them a driver’s license or DMV ID card in the first place? No need to re-invent the wheel here unless necessary.

SC CWP for Non-US Citizens

There are special requirements for residents who are non-US citizens. Additionally, non-US citizens must mark additional boxes on the Form R-078 and provide additional information. Discussing the requirements for non-US citizens is beyond the scope of this book and those applicants are encouraged to have an attorney assist them with the application.

SC CWP for a Qualified Non-Resident

If you do not reside in South Carolina, you can still get a permit if you qualify as a *qualified non-resident.* The S.C. Code of Laws define qualified resident as an individual who owns real property in South Carolina, but who resides in another state. See 23-31-210(2). To meet this qualification, you must own real estate in South Carolina. Ownership means that you must have, at least, a partial legal ownership interest. So, for example, if you live in Alabama but you inherited a ¼ interest in a parcel of land in Waterloo from your great grandfather, you can apply as a qualified non-resident.

As proof of ownership of South Carolina real estate, you must submit a completed and signed SLED Form R-168 (South Carolina Non-Resident Concealed Weapon Permit (CWP) Real Property Tax Form). This form must be completed by the county assessor of the county in which the property is located in South Carolina. This completed form verifies your ownership. You can obtain the form online at SLED's website: www.sled.sc.gov, or by calling SLED at: (803) 896-7014. You must also send in a photocopy of your valid out-of-state driver's license, DMV issued ID card or other ID from the list above for residents.

In the past, SLED has issued permit cards for qualified non-residents that are not the same dimensions and quality as the resident card. (The card traditionally issued to residents is the same size and quality as a South Carolina driver's license.) Qualified non-residents may be issued a $4^{5/8}$ inch-wide by $2^{7/8}$ inch high card. Those dimensions are considerably larger than the regular permit card and are not within the statutory parameters of 3½ inches by 3 inches. Further, the qualified non-resident cards appear to have been simply printed from a color desktop printer. The photo provided with the application is then cut with scissors and the entire card is hand-laminated. Overall, the qualified non-resident card is bulky and does not look like a permit issued by a governmental entity. It looks homemade and does not fit in a standard wallet. If you want to push the issue, contact an attorney to file a friendly suit against SLED to get the card down to the right size.

Getting Qualified Non-Resident Paperwork

If you are a qualified non-resident, your completed SLED Form R-168 must be signed by the county assessor in which your South Carolina property is located. Please refer to Appendix II for information about getting this paperwork.

Photographs and Picture Identification

If you are a resident, SLED's practice has been to electronically import South Carolina driver's license pictures into the new concealed weapons permits. Therefore, the picture on resident's concealed weapons permits is the exact same digital picture that appears on the driver's license. Non-residents, resident aliens, and military have different requirements like sending a photocopy of a valid driver's license or picture identification. See Section 23-31-215(2) of the S.C. Code.

Proof of Adequate Vision

You must also present proof that you have at least 20/40 vision. This can be natural 20/40 or it can be with glasses, contacts, or surgery, or whatever. If you are a South Carolina resident, your valid South Carolina driver's license satisfies this requirement. If you have one, you will not need any additional proof. See Section 23-31-215(4) of the S.C. Code.

Proof of Firearms Training

You must also submit proof of training. This means that you must provide an original or a certified copy of a document that certifies that you have fulfilled one of the six statutory alternatives for training. S.C. Code of Laws 23-31-210(4)(a)(i-viii).

Basic Training Provided by CWP Class

If you have not completed one of the other proof of training alternatives, the best way to fulfill this requirement is to simply take a concealed weapons class from a SLED approved instructor. By getting your training this way, you are almost guaranteed that you have fulfilled the statutory requirements for training.

The reason we say "almost" is that ***you*** are ultimately responsible for ensuring that your instructor is teaching the course to SLED specifications. The best way to ensure your instructor is teaching the course to SLED specifications is to investigate the record and history of the teacher and request proof from your instructor that his or her course meets or exceeds the SLED approved syllabus. See Section 23-31-210(4) of the South Carolina Code of Laws.

A very small number of students over the years have found out the hard way that their instructor was cheating them of the required course content. There have been several arrests of instructors who were not teaching all of the material required by SLED's syllabus. All of the students of these instructors were affected when the discrepancy came to SLED's attention.

As a side note, a SLED approved basic or advanced handgun education course offered by a state, county, or municipal law enforcement agency or a nationally recognized organization can potentially fulfill the training requirement. Again, the main requirement is that the South Carolina statutory and case law is included and the course covers the syllabus established by SLED. To be sure a course meets or exceeds SLED specifications, the instructor's syllabus is reviewed and approved by SLED prior to conducting the course.

Pursuant to South Carolina Code of Laws Section 23-31-210(4)(a)(i-viii), For a course to fulfill the statutory requirements and be SLED-approved, it must include the following:

(i) information on the statutory and case law of this State relating to handguns and to the use of deadly force;

(ii) information on handgun use and safety;

(iii) information on the proper storage practice for handguns with an emphasis on storage practices that reduces the possibility of accidental injury to a child;

(iv) the actual firing of the handgun in the presence of the instructor, provided that a minimum of twenty-five rounds must be fired;

(v) properly securing a firearm in a holster;

(vi) "cocked and locked" carrying of a firearm;

(vii) how to respond to a person who attempts to take your firearm from your holster; and

(viii) de-escalation techniques and strategies

The course (usually completed the same day) must include both a SLED approved written test and a firing range test after that day's instruction. The applicant must achieve at least a minimum score of seventy (70%) percent correct on the written test and a minimum score of seventy (70%) percent on the firing range qualification. These are SLED regulations found in South Carolina Code of Regulations Chapter 73-320.

If the instructor is SLED certified, he or she must use a SLED approved syllabus so everything on the written test is covered in the course. (Mark Bilicki, pictured here, designed the SLED-approved syllabus and has taught over 32,000 CWP students!). Therefore, you need not worry that you will be asked about topics that you have not been exposed to. A good instructor will make every effort to ensure his students are well prepared for the written test.

MARK BILICKI
Aerotech Firearms in Piedmont
NRA Master Training Counselor
SLED Certified CWP Instructor

The range test determines if you are minimally competent with the handgun that you test with that day. Most instructors allow you to bring your own handgun. If you don't have one, they will usually provide a handgun for you. Do not go to the course without being sure that you either have your own functioning defensive handgun or that the instructor will have one that you can use that day.

On the day of the course, you will be required to shoot at a target from varying distance. You will shoot at a large human-size silhouette target from 3 to 15 yards, firing a total of 25 rounds. If you don't feel confident that you can get 19 of your 25 rounds into such a target, practice at the gun range before taking the course. Safety is paramount during the range test so be keen to listen to every instruction. In general, instructors are very concerned that their students have every opportunity to pass every portion of the class.

Pursuant to 23-31-210(4)(a) of the S.C. Code of Laws, you must have completed the course within the three years prior to your application. Again, please save yourself grief and use a reputable trainer. Get assurance from the school that your training meets the requirements for a South Carolina Concealed Weapons Permit. Also, it might seem like a silly question to ask of the instructor, but make sure to verify that you will receive written evidence of completion of the training. It would be a shame to pay good money and go through training only to be snookered by someone who cannot provide the right training or proof of training.

Possible Effect on Reciprocity

The 2014 change in "proof of training," brings up the issue of CWP reciprocity. The passage of the 2014 bill did not change the minimum requirements of a background check, firearm training, and safety. If another state wants reciprocity with South Carolina, that state's CWP scheme must have equal or greater minimum requirements. Therefore, there are no changes made that could bring in new states. But, if another state's requirement for reciprocity is that the other state have CWP issuance standards "equal to or greater than" their own issuance standards (just as SC had until 2008), the fact South Carolina no longer requires an 8-hour minimum course in handgun education could cause the loss of some CWP reciprocity states. More recently though, the US Supreme Court *Bruen* has forced some states to adopt CWP programs and this has led to South Carolina having new reciprocity states. It was a shock to see we now have reciprocity with states like Illinois, Delaware, and Maryland.

CWP Instructor Exemption from Liability

Section 23-31-215(G) of the S.C. Code of Laws provides an exemption from liability to CWP instructors. However, to be protected by the exemption, the instructor must follow the syllabus approved by SLED. If an instructor wishes to reduce the number of course hours in response to a 2014 change in the law, the instructor should first submit a new syllabus to SLED and get it approved prior to reducing the course hours. Failure to get a reduced-hours of course training syllabus approved by SLED could well expose the instructor to liability for any harms caused by one of his students in a class taught to a syllabus not approved by SLED.

Alternative Proof of Training

There are other ways to fulfill the statutory proof of training requirement. *See* 23-31-210(4)(b)-(g). **All** alternatives to a basic CWP course **must** include information on the statutory and case law of South Carolina relating to handguns and the use of deadly force. *See* South Carolina Code of Laws Section 23-31-210(4)(a)(i) and 23-31-210(4)(b).

Military Training

One alternative is for former military personnel. Under 23-31-201(b)(i), a person who demonstrates the completion of basic military training provided by any branch of the United States military who produces proof of his military service through the submission of a DD214 form has met the requirement. However, that person must also show that his or her training included instruction on the statutory and case law of South Carolina relating to handguns and to the use of deadly force. *See* South Carolina Code of Laws Section 23-31-210(4)(a)(i) and 23-31-210(4)(b).

Active Military CWP

SLED is not requiring active duty military personnel stationed in South Carolina to provide any proof of training. An active duty military person stationed in South Carolina must just fill out the application form; provide a copy of his or her orders detailing them to South Carolina and military ID card, provide proof of residence within the state, provide finger print cards, and supply payment of $50. Active duty military get a special class of CWP that must be shown with his or her military ID (as a civilian would show an SC driver's license or ID).

Retired South Carolina Law Enforcement

Alternatively, under Section 23-31-210(4)(b)(ii), retired South Carolina law enforcement officers can qualify as having the required proof of training. However, under this subsection, the retired law enforcement officer must be a graduate of the Criminal Justice Academy (presumably the South Carolina Criminal Justice Academy – although that is not specified in the statute). However, law enforcement officers who are retired, but who were an officer before the requirement that officers graduate from the Criminal Justice Academy, are "grandfathered-in." He or she must also show that his or her training included instruction on the statutory and case law of South Carolina relating to handguns and to the use of deadly force. *See* South Carolina Code of Laws Section 23-31-210(4)(a)(i) and 23-31-210(4)(b).

Retired Federal and Out-of-State Law Enforcement Training

Under Section 23-31-210(4)(b)(iii), retired federal and out-of-state law enforcement officers can also qualify as having the required proof of training. However, under this subsection, the retired law enforcement officer must be a graduate from a federal or state academy that includes forearms training as a graduation requirement. He or she must also show that his or her training included instruction on the statutory and case law of South Carolina relating to handguns and to the use of deadly force. *See* South Carolina Code of Laws Section 23-31-210(4)(a)(i) and 23-31-210(4)(b).

NRA or Other National Organization Certified Instructor

Under South Carolina Code of Laws Section 23-31-210(4)(c), certified firearms instructors can qualify as having proof of training. Instructors must be certified as an instructor by the NRA or other SLED approved national organization that promotes the safe use of handguns. You will have to contact SLED directly for a current list of approved organizations. He or she must also show that his or her training included instruction on the statutory and case law of South Carolina relating to handguns and to the use of deadly force. *See* South Carolina Code of Laws Section 23-31-210(4)(a)(i) and 23-31-210(4)(b).

Demonstration of Proficiency to SLED

Under South Carolina Code of Laws Section 23-31-210(4)(d), applicants can satisfy the training requirement if he or she can demonstrate to the director of SLED that he or she has a proficiency in the use of handguns and a thorough knowledge of South Carolina law pertaining to handguns. This method seems very uncommon and mysterious. If you want to try to satisfy the training requirement this way, you must contact SLED and petition to see if the administrator will accept the proof of that training that you are offering. Approval under this alternative is done on a case-by-case basis. As with all other alternatives, applicants are statutorily required to show that his or her training included instruction on the statutory and case law of South Carolina relating to handguns and to the use of deadly force. *See* South Carolina Code of Laws Section 23-31-210(4)(a)(i) and 23-31-210(4)(b).

Active Duty Police Handgun Instructor

Section 23-31-201(4)(e) of the South Carolina Code of Laws provides and alternative for Active duty police handgun instructors. This category does not need any further explanation. You know if you are an active duty police handgun instructor or not. As with the other alternatives, applicants are statutorily required to show that his or her training included instruction on the statutory and case law of South Carolina relating to handguns and to the use of deadly force. *See* South Carolina Code of Laws Section 23-31-210(4)(a)(i) and 23-31-210(4)(b).

SLED Certified or Approved Competitive Shooter

Section 23-31-201(4)(f) of the South Carolina Code of Laws provides yet another alternative for those with a SLED certified or approved competitive shooting classification. These designations are sanctioned and awarded by governing bodies like the United States Practical Shooting Association (USPSA), the International Defensive Pistol Association (IDPA), and the National Rifle Association (NRA). You must contact SLED directly to see if your handgun classification qualifies you for the proof of training required by the statute. Again, applicants are statutorily required to show that his or her training included instruction on the statutory and case law of South Carolina relating to handguns and to the use of deadly force. *See* South Carolina Code of Laws Section 23-31-210(4)(a)(i) and 23-31-210(4)(b).

Active or Reserve Military Training for CWP

Certain military experience can provide proof of training under South Carolina Code of Laws Section 23-31-201(4)(g). In general, you submit proof that you are an active or reserve member of the military (including National Guard) and have had official military handgun training from your branch of service (Coast Guard, Air Force, Army, Marines, Navy). There is ***no longer*** a requirement that the training occur in the three (3) years prior to CWP application. Once again, it's probably worthwhile to call SLED prior to applying to see if your military training qualifies for the exception. Like with the other training exceptions, applicants are statutorily required to show that his or her training included instruction on the statutory and case law of South Carolina relating to handguns and to the use of deadly force. *See* South Carolina Code of Laws Section 23-31-210(4)(a)(i) and 23-31-210(4)(b).

SLED Regulations for Proof of Training and Instructors

SLED has been given statutory authorization to promulgate general guidelines for CWP applicant *proof of training* course requirements and for the qualifications for instructors. *See* the last paragraph of South Carolina Code of Laws Section 23-31-210 (after Subsection (4)(g)). SLED has generally codified these guidelines through regulations found in the South Carolina Code of Regulations Chapter 73-300. Further regulations regarding course guidelines, instructor qualifications, and CWP denials based upon unqualified instructors are found in Chapter 73-310, 320, 330, and 340.

Fingerprints

You must submit two complete original sets of fingerprints. You can get your fingerprints taken at any law enforcement agency or any other SLED approved fingerprint technician. A non-law enforcement trainer can be a SLED approved fingerprint technician.

South Carolina Code of Laws Section 23-31-215(A)(7) provides that a law enforcement agency cannot charge you more than $5 for fingerprints associated with an application for a concealed weapons permit. If the officer demands more, the statutes do not authorize or support him. If you give the officer more, you could be contributing to his unofficial "lunch fund."

It is important that you use the fingerprint cards that SLED provides. To get your cards, call SLED at: (803) 896-7014. Note that this is a different number from other SLED numbers. Again, make sure that you get at least two cards because you will need to submit two original fingerprint cards with your application.

If you never had your fingerprints taken, it is simple. Appendix III discusses the process of getting your fingerprints in greater detail.

Exception to the Fingerprint Requirement

There is a very narrow exception to the fingerprint requirement. The fingerprint requirement can be waived if you have a valid reason that it is impossible for you to produce a full set of fingerprints. Maybe you do not have ten fingers or you have a prosthetic or other condition. In this case, you must submit whatever fingerprints you can produce with a written statement from a licensed medical provider specifying the reason that a full set of your fingerprints cannot be taken.

Application Fee

The 2021 Open Carry Act prohibits SLED from collecting an application fee. **There is currently no application fee**. The former $50 application fee in Section 23-31-215(A)(6) South Carolina Code of Laws has been deleted.

The Role of SLED in Approval or Denial

Once you submit your application, SLED will begin conducting a multi-jurisdictional fingerprint review. *See* Section 23-31-215(B) South Carolina Code of Laws. They will also commence a criminal background check with input from the Sheriff of the county in which the applicant resides or owns property is owned. The sheriff may submit a recommendation to SLED (favorable or unfavorable) on your application within ten working days.

If the fingerprint and background check are "favorable," SLED must issue the permit. As it stands now, what constitutes "favorable" is up to the discretion of SLED. If SLED denies your application, they must give you a written statement within 90 days from the date of the application specifying the reason for the denial. If they fail to give you the written denial within the 90 days, SLED must issue the permit by default. Be aware that that, due to administrative constraints, an approved CWP might not arrive at your mailbox for up to 120 days. If you got your CWP by default because SLED missed its deadline, permit may be revoked upon written notification from SLED that sufficient grounds exist for revocation or initial denial. See 23-31-215(A) and (D).

Denial of CWP Application

We are routinely contacted by clients who have been initially denied because encounters with the law in the past. These encounters range from minor theft and youthful mischief to DUIs to felonies. Some have been done over 50 years ago and the applicant can barely remember what was involved. The applicant is often not prohibited from possessing a firearm. Further, the applicant does not show up in NICS instant firearms background checks for firearms purchases from a gun dealer (FFL). In any case, most criminal run-ins will be found during a SLED fingerprint/background check and will result in an initial CWP application. However, many of these initial denials are overturned by SLED once the applicant timely appeals and provides SLED with additional information.

If SLED does deny you your permit, you can appeal the decision. You have 30 days from the date you receive the denial notice to file a written appeal specifying the basis for your appeal. This appeal is submitted to the chief of SLED (the denial will give you who and where to send the appeal). SLED will then have 10 days from receiving your written appeal to issue a written decision. This written decision will either reverse the denial (granting you a permit) or uphold the denial. If the decision is to uphold the denial, SLED must specify the reasons why your denial is being upheld.

Generally, so long as your prior run-in with the law was a non-violent misdemeanor, you have a good chance of being issued the CWP after a timely appeal. SLED is mainly looking to see that the potential penalty for the crime did not make you a person prohibited from possessing firearms. SLED will require you to provide a ***certified copy*** of the ***final disposition*** of your case from the Clerk of Court of the tribunal (court) where your case was processed. So, if your case was a Union County case, you must contact the Clerk of Court for Union County. If it was a Liberty County, Florida case, you must contact Liberty County, Florida. If the case is so old that it was before the Court issued final dispositions, SLED will require that you get a certified letter from that Court stating so much. SLED seems to also require that you get the record expunged. Expungement paperwork can be found for free through most county prosecutors in the county in which you case was prosecuted.

If your appeal results in SLED standing by its original denial, you then have the option of petitioning for review by an Administrative Law Court (ALC). You must file your petition for ALC review within 30 days of receiving your SLED appeal results. We will not get too in depth with the intricacies of administrative law here (the procedures are set out in South Carolina Code of Laws 1-23-380.) However, you should know that an appeal to an ALC is limited in the scope. Basically, the administrative law judge can review only the record before him or her. The judge cannot substitute his or her own judgment for SLED's with respect to the weight of evidence or questions of fact. Even if the judge would have decided the case in your favor, he is required to uphold SLED's decision unless one of the following listed causes for *reversal* are involved. The judge may affirm SLED's decision or send your application back to SLED for further proceedings. Further, the judge may reverse or modify SLED's decision in narrow circumstances where substantial rights have been prejudiced because SLED's findings, inferences, conclusions, or decisions are:

- in violation of constitutional or statutory provisions;
- in excess of the statutory authority of the agency;
- made upon unlawful procedure;
- affected by other error of law;
- clearly erroneous in view of the reliable, probative, and substantial evidence on the whole record; or
- arbitrary or capricious or characterized by abuse of discretion or clearly unwarranted exercise of discretion.

If you want to appeal at this level, the administrative courts allow for you to represent yourself. You can save attorney's fees by organizing your appeal and presenting your case yourself. The administrative courts are generally held in a smaller courtroom with only the judge, the judge's assistant and the parties (with their attorneys if represented), and security. The rules of procedure and evidence are a little more relaxed than in a civil court of law.

The risk of representing yourself on your appeal is that you might not present your best case to the court. However, many people can organize and present their case very well without an attorney present at the hearing. Each individual appellant must make a cost/benefit analysis when deciding to hire an attorney for the appeal. If you are unsuccessful with your appeal, you can reapply for your CWP and start the process all over again. As a final note, if you want legal help, you should talk with an administrative law attorney or gun rights attorney WELL BEFORE your 30-day appeal window closes.

Once You Get Your Permit

Your permit will be valid statewide until it is revoked or expires. It will be revoked if you become prohibited from possessing a weapon, move to another state or no longer own property in the state. If you voluntarily surrender the permit or get charged with a crime that will make it illegal for you to possess a firearm the permit will be revoked. If your permit is revoked because you are charged with a crime that will make it illegal for you to possess a firearm, and you are later found not guilty, your permit must be reinstated at no charge. If revoked, it must be surrendered to a sheriff, police department, or SLED agent. Alternatively, you can send by certified mail to the chief of SLED. If you fail to surrender the permit for the above reasons, you have committed a misdemeanor. Remember also that, if your permit is revoked because you have become a person prohibited under state law from possessing a weapon, your name, address, and reason for revocation will be published in an annual report by SLED (S.C. Code 23-31-215(T)(7)).

What if I Am Approached by a Law Enforcement Officer?

At first glance, South Carolina Code 23-31-215(K) appears to provide that you must carry your permit card with you whenever you carry a concealable weapon, concealed. Additionally, it appears to require that if you have a concealable weapon, concealed, and a police officer identifies himself as a police officer and then asks for your identification or driver's license, you must inform the officer that you have a permit and present the permit to the officer. Failure to comply with this section is a misdemeanor. However, there is an important distinction that you must make with respect to this section.

Carrying Under an Exception vs. with your CWP

The statutory provision above is qualified with the words: [w]hen carrying a concealable weapon *pursuant to* [the concealed weapons permit statute]. So, what about if you are carrying a concealable weapon, concealed or openly, **not** *pursuant to* the concealed weapons permit statute? In other words, what if you are legally carrying a concealable weapon under one of the handgun exceptions? For instance, there is a handgun exception allowing a handgun in your car glove box. The answer can only be found by conceptualizing two different ways to legally carry a concealable weapon.

You will learn in the next chapter that the general rule is that it is illegal to carry a handgun openly or concealed in South Carolina. There are, however, exceptions to that general rule that permit you to legally carry a handgun. In fact, there are such large exceptions that they almost swallow-up the entire rule. One is with the concealed weapons permit (explained in this chapter) and the other is under one of the statutory exceptions (explained in the next chapter). If you want to legally carry a handgun, you must determine for yourself, "Am I carrying legally under the CWP statute or am I carrying legally under another statutory exception?"

Carrying Under the CWP Statute

This chapter explains how and where you can carry if you have a concealed weapons permit. The law of carrying with a CWP is one of the statutory exceptions. But even though you can carry one way by having your CWP, you might also be able to alternatively carry pursuant to one of the other statutory handgun exceptions. This concept will be explained with an example shortly.

Carrying Under a Statutory Exception

Another way to legally carry a handgun is under one of the other statutory exceptions. The next chapter explains the other statutory exceptions. So, a person without a CWP can carry a handgun if he or she does so under an exception. The important point here though, is that, even if you **do** have a CWP, you can none-the-less carry under one of the statutory exceptions.

Now, let's look at an example of how these handgun carry concepts work with each other in the context of a vehicle. Say, for instance, that you are speeding in your car in South Carolina. Say also that you have a CWP and you are carrying a handgun in your front pocket that meets the definition of a concealable weapon. You also have your CWP (card) with you. At that point, you are legally carrying a handgun under the CWP statute.

You look in the rear-view mirror and there is a police car with flashing lights behind you. You pull over and the police officer asks you for identification. Because you are carrying the handgun pursuant to the CWP statute, you are required to inform the officer that you have a concealed weapons permit.

Alternatively, what if the facts are the same except that the handgun has been in the glove compartment the entire time? One exception to the general prohibition on handguns allows handguns to be carried in the glove compartment or console of vehicles. Therefore, in this example, you are carrying pursuant to the statutory glove compartment exception and not pursuant to the CWP statute. Remember that the requirement to inform an officer exists only if carrying pursuant to the CWP statute. Following, there is no requirement that you VOLUNTEER to inform the officer that you have a CWP or that there is a handgun in the glove compartment. If the officer happens to ask if you have weapons in the car, you should tell the officer that you have a handgun in the glove box.

You can envision other instances where you must conceptualize whether you are carrying under a CWP or a statutory handgun exception. For instance, there is a statutory exception that permits licensed hunters and fishermen to carry a concealed handgun when hunting or fishing. If a person is a licensed fisherman and carrying a concealed handgun while fishing, he does not have to show a law enforcement officer his CWP permit card if asked for identification. Why not? He is carrying under a statutory exception and not under the CWP statute.

What if I Have a Concealed Weapon When My Buddy is Pulled Over?

What do you do if you are a passenger in a car and the driver get stopped by a police officer? If you are carrying a concealable weapon, concealed or openly, under the CWP statute, and the officer asks you for your identification, you are only required to inform the officer that you have a CWP and then be able to present it. If the officer asks only the driver for his identification, you are not required to volunteer that you have a CWP. However, if the officer then turns to you and asks you for identification, you are required at that point to disclose that you have a CWP. If all handguns are in the glove box or otherwise carried under another statutory exception, nobody has to volunteer to the officer that they have a CWP when asked for identification. Again, because the firearms are in the glove compartment and that is allowed under a statutory exception.

The Practical Elements of a Law Enforcement Officer Road Stop

If ever stopped by a law enforcement officer while in your car, sit in your seat and keep your hands on the steering wheel. In most cases, the officer will approach you. Never make a move to get out of the car or reach for anything in the car. Simply sit in your seat with your hands on the wheel or otherwise in plain view. The first thing that the officer should do is identify him or herself. If the officer does not ask for driver's license or other identification, you do not have to volunteer that you have a concealed weapons permit. However, the officer is likely to ask for your driver's license, vehicle registration and proof of insurance. At that point, if you are carrying a concealable weapon, concealed, pursuant to the CWP Statute, inform the officer that you have a concealed weapons permit. The officer might then ask where the weapon is located. Inform the officer where the weapon is located but do not reach for it. The officer should then instruct you as to retrieving your license and paperwork.

Alternatively, if you have your CWP but are legally carrying a handgun in the glove box pursuant to the statutory exception, you do not have to volunteer to the officer that you have a CWP or that there is a handgun in the conveyance. But what if the officer asks for registration paperwork and the paperwork is in the same location as the weapon? Should you open the glove box and reach for the registration without first telling the officer that you have a handgun in the glove box? While there is no statutory provision requiring you to volunteer that you have a handgun in the glove box, not informing the officer could result in the officer drawing his weapon on you out of safety for his own self. So, you should inform the officer that you have the firearm in the glove box. As before, in any case, if the officer asks if you have a weapon in the conveyance you should disclose to the officer that you have a firearm in the glove box.

The main point is that you might not be required to produce your CWP or volunteer that you have a handgun if you fall under one of the other handgun exceptions. However, you must weigh that right against the possibility of causing the officer to draw his weapon out of a perceived need for self-defense. Also, there is always the possibility that an officer does not fully understand the law and might arrest you even though you were carrying legally under a statutory exception. Police are people too and they make mistakes. It is up to you to know your rights and balance your rights against the practicalities of a police stop.

Traffic Stop from a Police Perspective (Maj. Mike Nunn, Esq.)

One of the most dangerous activities in which a police officer engages is a traffic stop. A traffic stop constitutes a seizure under the Fourth Amendment and at a minimum must be based on reasonable suspicion of a violation of law. A suspected moving violation is all that is necessary to justify an officer activating the blue lights and the law obligates the motorist to stop. Traffic stops are intended to be educational and to correct improper or dangerous driving.

For the officer, there is no such thing as a "routine traffic stop." Each one is unique based on its own peculiar circumstances, including the personalities of the persons involved. We know that a traffic stop can cause some anxiety for the motorist and it causes anxiety for the officer as well. Police officers are trained to recognize two distinct types of traffic stops; "high risk," where the officer knows that the person being stopped is armed and/or dangerous; and "unknown risk," where the officer is unaware of a specific risk, but must be prepared for any risk. There are different practices and protocols for each of these types of stops.

With a "high risk" stop, sometimes called a "felony stop," the officers suspect that the occupant of the vehicle is or has been involved in some sort of criminal activity and reasonable suspicion exists that he/she is armed and/or dangerous. This stop usually involves at least two officers and the location of the stop is generally selected by the officers to place them and the public at the best strategic advantage.

Depending on the circumstances, from a position of relative safety the officers may call the driver and/or passengers to exit the vehicle in such a manner as to be able to observe their access to weapons until the suspects are secured. In this case, a "contact officer" handles all of the communication with the vehicle occupants and the "cover officer" observes the behavior of the suspects, paying close attention to the hands and waist areas while remaining ready to respond to any threat. A stolen vehicle, an escaped inmate, kidnapper, or armed robbery suspect are examples of a "high risk" or "felony traffic stop."

The overwhelming percentage of traffic stops are "unknown risk" stops. In this type of stop, the officer typically has no knowledge of the person being stopped other than what he/she observed that gave rise to the stop in the first place. Usually this is an observed moving violation. In the case of this category of stop, the officer is at a distinct disadvantage compared to the driver or occupants of the vehicle. The driver knows the status of his privilege to drive, whether he just committed a crime, and whether he is carrying contraband or a weapon. More importantly, the driver knows his intentions regarding the officer. The driver knows whether he intends to flee, fight, or harm the officer. The officer does not. That is why it is called an "unknown risk" stop as the officer must be prepared to react immediately to any perceived threat to his/her safety. The police officer is at a distinct tactical disadvantage because of the "perception and reaction" time lag. In addition, an "unknown risk" stop can escalate into a "high risk" stop depending on the circumstances such as failure to stop for the blue light or an attempted assault on the officer. Fortunately, in the vast percentage of stops, the officer and the vehicle occupants exercise their respective duties and ultimately everyone goes safely on their way.

Beyond the initial reason for the stop, if the officer notices behavior or indicators that suggest there may be other criminal activity afoot, he may have reasonable suspicion to extend the stop to investigate that suspicious activity. Officers involved in narcotics and contraband interdiction are trained to recognize criminal indicators which are inconsistent with the typical law-abiding motoring public and can often lead to the search of vehicles suspected of containing contraband. For instance, it is well known that drug traffickers often use rental vehicles rented by others not there to haul their contraband. They also often attempt to mask the odor of the narcotics they are transporting from the officer or narcotics sniffing canines by using air fresheners. To blend in with the law-abiding motoring public, drug traffickers will often display pro-law enforcement or "Terrific Kid" bumper stickers on the rental vehicles. While it is common to travel in a rented vehicle, it is not common for the person renting the vehicle not to be present, for air fresheners to be used or for the rental vehicle, or to have personal or family oriented bumper stickers. This is a presentation not consistent with the general traveling public.

However, the most important indicator is simply the behavior of the driver and occupants of the vehicle. While everyone is a little nervous on a traffic stop initially, the level of apprehension normally subsides as the stop progresses. Not so with the smuggler. His freedom hangs on not being detected. Excessive perspiration, nervousness, heavy breathing, shaking hands, distracted looks and responses are all involuntary physical indicators that the person is under stress and there is likely something else going on. This too, is not typical of the law abiding traveling public. Couple all that with conflicting stories of departure and destination between the driver and passengers of the vehicle and the officer may have sufficient reasonable suspicion of criminal activity to seek consent to search the vehicle for contraband. If consent is denied, the officer can have a canine conduct a free air sniff around the exterior of the vehicle. A positive canine alert establishes probable cause to search the vehicle for narcotics anywhere in the vehicle where narcotics could be hidden, which is just about anywhere. With either consent or probable cause to search, any contraband discovered in the vehicle can be seized and criminal charges may be filed.

None of these indicators (and there may be more) in and of themselves or in isolation are necessarily indicative of criminal activity. To the trained officer however, the presence of multiple indicators can lead to reasonable suspicion justifying an extension of the traffic stop to investigate further. The courts have consistently held that there is such a consistent and pervasive nexus between drugs and guns that officers have reasonable suspicion to conduct a frisk for weapons on a traffic stop where narcotics are detected. The same nexus is not however, justified in cases involving driving under the influence.

Having reviewed the two types of traffic stops from the officer training standpoint, how should the motorist respond to make the stop go as smoothly as possible? First, when the blue lights appear in your rear- view mirror, drive your vehicle to nearest safe place onto the right shoulder that is completely off the roadway. If you are in fear because of location or you are alone, see a special procedure later in this section.

When you stop, stay in your vehicle, shift the gear into park and place your hands on the steering wheel in full view of the officer. If at night, cut on the dome light for illumination. When the officer approaches, roll down your window, put the cigarette out, cut off the music and end any telephone conversation or texting. This encounter requires your full attention, so you will want to eliminate any distractions for you and the officer. The officer should identify him/herself and briefly explain the reason for the stop. You will probably be asked for your driver's license, registration and proof of insurance and state law requires you to produce them. If you have a Concealed Weapons Permit (CWP) and are carrying pursuant to the permit law, you are required to notify the officer when you are asked for your driver's license. Passengers carrying pursuant to a CWP are required to disclose when the officer asks for their license or identification. Even if you are not a CWP holder, if there is a weapon in the vehicle it is a good idea to notify the officer of its location. No one likes a surprise on a traffic stop, especially if it involves a firearm. At this point, you should listen closely to and follow the instructions of the officer, keep your hands where they can be seen and do not make any sudden movements or gestures toward the weapon. Most officers will tell you that when encountering a CWP holder on a traffic stop, their anxiety level goes down as the permit holder is known to be complying with the law and has been through training and a background check.

Most officers will not ask you to exit your vehicle unless it becomes necessary to do so. This is for your safety as well as the officer. State law requires officers to issue some writing for each citizen encounter, either a citation (ticket) or a written warning, so there will be a record of each stop even if it does not result in a citation.

If you feel unsafe at night stopping for the blue light at the location, turn on your hazard lights, reduce your speed to below the speed limit, illuminate your dome light and drive to the nearest safe and well lighted location. By doing so, the officer will know that you have acknowledged the requirement to stop and are just looking for a safe place. If you have a cell phone, you can call 911 to advise that you intend to stop at the first safe location and they will pass that information along to the officer.

For the officer, the stop is not personal; it's just business (and no, there is no ticket quota and the Sheriff's Office is not dependent on citations for revenue.) You may disagree with the officer's decision to issue a citation, which is your right, but the side of the road is not the place to argue your case. The courthouse is that place. Regardless of whether you agree with the ticket, if you believe you have been treated unfairly, don't argue with the officer, but contact a supervisor. Likely, the stop is being both audio and video recorded for everyone's safety.

Finally, regardless of any problem you may be having when stopped by the police, whether it be an expired or suspended license, an outstanding warrant, possession of contraband, or you are just having a bad day, resisting, running or fleeing will not improve your circumstances. It will only make things worse and your chances of getting away are slim to none. You will also be placing yourself, the officer and the public at great risk. Being honest and owning up to any problems is the best way to handle these situations and most officers will be as polite and understanding as you allow them to be.

The overwhelming percentage of traffic stops are handled courteously and professionally, with both the driver and officer going safely on their way. Observing these common-sense suggestions will reduce anxiety and enhance safety for everyone.

CWP vs. Exception Flow-Chart

Following is a CWP vs. exception flow-chart that helps organize the differences between carrying a concealed weapon, concealed under the CWP statute versus carrying a handgun under another statutory handgun exception. This chart is limited to a typical carry situation from your dwelling property, into your vehicle, and possibly getting pulled over by a law enforcement officer for speeding. The chart assumes that you are not legally disqualified from owning or possessing a firearm and that you are not fleeing after committing a crime.

(Remainder of page intentionally blank.)

Do you have a South Carolina Concealed Weapons Permit (CWP)? (or Reciprocity)

YES
You can choose to carry under the CWP Statute <u>**OR**</u> a another statutory handgun exception.

You can have and carry any legal handgun - concealed or openly - in your home or on your private property.
See Sections 16-23-20(8) and (12).

You can carry a concealable weapon, concealed or openly, from your dwelling place to your conveyance (vehicle) and make a diversion to the mailbox, etc. You **MUST** have your CWP card with you.
See Section 16-23-20(12).

Once in your conveyance (vehicle), you can carry the concealable weapon, concealed, or open on or about your person (i.e. in your clothing, purse, etc.) or under a seat or in any open or closed storage compartment within the vehicle's passenger compartment or in the luggage compartment in a closed container w/fastener.
See Section 16-23-20(9)(a).

If stopped by a law enforcement officer and an officer asks <u>**YOU**</u> for identification, you **MUST** show the officer your CWP card. If YOU are in the conveyance and not asked for YOUR ID, you do not have to show your CWP. (**ONLY** the person asked by a law enforcement officer for ID must produce his or her CWP card.) Also, there is no statutory requirement for anyone to volunteer to the officer that there is a firearm in the vehicle.

NO
You can **ONLY** carry a handgun under a handgun exception.

You can have and carry any legal handgun - concealed or openly - in your home or on your private property. See Section 16-23-20(8).

<u>**OR**</u> ↓

You can carry any legal handgun, openly or concealed, directly from your dwelling place to your vehicle (including motorcycles) under 16-23-20(15).

<u>**OR**</u> ↓

Once in your vehicle, handguns **MUST** be stored in a closed glove box, closed console or in a secured container in the luggage compartment of the vehicle under 16-23-20(9)(a). (Saddlebags for motorcycles). Exception for hunting, fishing or target/shows under 16-23-20(3), (4), and (7).

<u>**OR**</u> ↓

If you have a CWP but choose to carry under the 16-23-20(9)(a) or (16) handgun exception (i.e. handgun is in the glove box, console, saddle bags or in a secured encasement in the luggage compartment), you **DO NOT** have to show the officer your CWP card. Also, there is no statutory requirement for anyone to volunteer to the officer that there is a firearm in the vehicle.

Carrying without the CWP Card on your Person

What if you are carrying a concealable weapon, concealed or openly, and you have a CWP, but you do not have the CWP identification card with you? Your CWP can be verified through the SLED computer over the dispatch. But even if the officer verifies that you have one, you are still in violation. You can be arrested and charged. Theoretically, the officer can let you go based upon verification through dispatch. But you should never take that risk. It is the law that you always carry the CWP card with you whenever you have a concealable weapon, concealed with you. Carrying the card with you is required by Section 16-23-215(K). Failure to have the card is a misdemeanor carrying a fine of $25.

Be aware that Section 16-23-460 could also apply. This Section, not even in the CWP Statute, creates an additional penalty for carrying a concealed weapon not in compliance with the CWP Statute. The additional penalty is that your weapon must be forfeited and you either pay up to a $500 fine or serve 90 days in jail.

What if an Officer Wants to Check You for Weapons?

What if an officer wants you to get out of the car to check you for weapons? At any time, and even with no suspicion, an officer can pat you down to check for weapons. An officer always has a right to look after his or her own safety by patting you down for weapons. The officer can even handcuff you briefly while he or she pats you down. Just because you are being patted down or briefly handcuffed while the officer checks you does not mean that you are under arrest. If you are being placed under arrest, the office will inform you that you are being placed under arrest. If you are placed under arrest, you have a right to remain silent and you should always exercise that right until you have an attorney counseling you.

Police Searches

What if the police officer asks to search your car? An officer has a right to search your car if he or she has ***reasonable suspicion*** that you or your passengers have been involved in criminal activity. The officer can search not only your car but also your person and objects belonging to you or any passengers. If an officer has a reasonable suspicion that you or your passengers have been involved in criminal activity, you are subject to search whether you have given permission or not. However, if the officer does not have reasonable suspicion, he or she cannot make a search **without your permission**. Whether an officer has reasonable suspicion is ultimately up to the courts and not you.

What is Reasonable Suspicion to Search?

Reasonable suspicion, in its most basic sense says that "*an officer has reasonable suspicion to believe that a crime has been committed.*" While this standard may seem simple, reasonable suspicious contains other rules that must also be met. A more extended definition of reasonable suspicion, and the one that a court would use to determine if a police officer has the right to stop your vehicle, requires that a reasonable officer, when considering the *totality of the circumstances*, has some objective reason to believe that a crime or misconduct has been or will be committed.

Standards Law Enforcement must Follow

The first standard that we must understand is the reasonable officer standard, which is a specific case of the reasonable person standard. It is the easiest to understand, but also the vaguest to apply. The reasonable person standard does not have an exact legal definition. However, it usually means that another reasonable person in similar circumstances would have acted or believed similarly. The precise application of this standard changes with the situation, but officers are usually expected to behave how another officer would respond.

The second standard that is critical to reasonable suspicion is "the totality of the circumstances". The entirety of the circumstances means that an officer must consider all available facts when determining reasonable suspicion. This standard holds that there is no single element that an officer must consider when determining reasonable suspicion. Instead, the officer must consider all aspects of the circumstance, even if those individual elements are not suspicious or illegal.

For example, it is not illegal to have a bloody knife sitting in your car or for you to be wearing a bloody jacket, but these things might be enough to make an officer suspect that you committed a crime. This suspicion cannot be based merely on hunch or intuition but must be specific and articulable, meaning that the officer should be able to state what objective set of circumstances made them suspicious enough to stop the car.

Reasonable Suspicion vs. Probable Cause

As stated above, the only justification that a police officer needs to stop your car is reasonable suspicion, but you also might have heard that police need probable cause to search your vehicle. What is probable cause, how is it different from reasonable suspicion, and when can police search my car? While reasonable suspicion only requires that the officer has some specific reason to suspect that a crime has been committed, probable cause is a higher standard and requires that the officer has some specific knowledge that a crime has likely taken place at a particular location or by some specific person. The higher standard for probable cause is essential for traffic stops because while there are some areas of your car that an officer can see when near your vehicle, other areas are hidden. The probable cause standard determines if they can search your car, and what areas they are allowed to look in.

When Can my Car be Searched?

If a police officer pulls you over, do they have the right to search your car? The standards required for an officer to search your vehicle are much lower than what would be required to search your house; some parts can be searched during a traffic stop, other parts require that an officer believes that some crime has been committed. If an officer pulls you over during a routine traffic stop and sees something like drugs or a weapon sitting in plain view on your seat, then they likely have enough information to take any illegal items and search the rest of your car.

An officer can also search areas of your vehicle where a weapon could be hidden if they have reason to believe that you might be armed or dangerous. Similarly, an officer can also search your car if they have probable cause to believe that you have committed a crime or if the officer has enough evidence to arrest you. In these cases, the officer can search the rest of your vehicle for other contraband. The other situation which an officer has the right to search any part of your car is when you **give permission**. This means that even if he doesn't have a reason for the search, if you give a police officer permission to do so, he or she may search every part of your car.

When Can I be Searched?

What if you are not in a car but rather stopped on the street while carrying a concealable weapon, concealed with a CWP? If approached by an officer on the street, you have no legal duty to inform the officer that you have a CWP or a weapon unless the officer asks you for identification. If the officer does ask you for ID, immediately inform the officer that you have a permit. As a practical matter, tell the officer exactly where the CWP and weapon is located. Don't reach or grab for your permit or the weapon. Resist the tendency to touch your weapon because people have a natural tendency to touch a weapon when they are indicating its location. Keep your hands away from your weapon and simply tell the officer where the weapon is located.

Again, the officer can pat you down for safety. Similarly, the officer can search you and your belongings if he or she has a reasonable suspicion that you have been involved in criminal activity. However, if the officer has no reasonable suspicion, he or she can only search with your permission. As before, if you have a weapon and do not have your permit on you, the officer can arrest you and charge you.

A law enforcement officer can search you, your vehicle, and your belongings without your permission if the officer has reasonable suspicion that you have been involved in criminal activity. If the officer has no reasonable suspicion, the officer can only search with your permission. If you give permission for a search, any evidence found is admissible in court even if it would not have been admissible if permission had not been granted.

Therefore, **you should NEVER give a law enforcement officer permission for a search**. If the law enforcement officer has probable cause, the officer needs no permission.

South Carolina not a "Stop and ID" State

Officers are prohibited by the Constitution of the United State and South Carolina from simply going around and stopping and "IDing" people. To do so is a "search and seizure" and officials cannot search you and seize things or information from you absent well-established exceptions. Any searches and seizures without first getting a warrant from a judge is presumed a violation of the 4th Amendment and the violation must be overcome by the officer relying upon exceptions. The South Carolina Constitution goes even further than the US Constitution by establishing a "privacy right." In all cases, government officials must have reasonable suspicion that you have or are in the process of committing a crime in order to stop and "ID" or search you without being able to reasonably articulate the crime that you have committed or are about to commit. An officer cannot pat you down for weapons unless he or she has already stopped you and able to articulate facts that establish reasonable suspicion that you have committed or are in the process of committing a crime. While well-established rights exist, this area of law can get pretty tricky so please educate yourself further about *Terry v. Ohio* and other controlling cases before testing the limits of reasonable suspicion as it relates to police stops and searches.

Especially if you want to test legally carrying a concealable weapon, concealed under your CWP and challenge a police request for ID on grounds of no articulable reasonable suspicion.

With reasonable articulable suspicion (slang "RAS"), a law enforcement officer can stop and possibly search you, your vehicle, and your belongings without your permission if the officer is convinced and can articulate facts that you have been involved in criminal activity. If the officer has no reasonable suspicion, the officer needs your consent to stop, communicate and search. If you consent to the conversation, stop and/or search, any evidence found is admissible in court even if it would not have been admissible if permission had not been granted.

Therefore, you should be cordial to officers but generally avoid consensual conversations, stops, and/or searches and seizures unless lawfully detained or arrested. Most Americans have constitutional rights that they are not aware of and generally "comply" with whatever is asked for by law enforcement. "Compliance" is not required in many instances and even unadvised many times. However, you need to have a firm understanding of the basics of Terry Stops, Stop-an-ID, Fourth Amendment search and seizure, and First and Second Amendment protected activity. Do not try to assert the finer points of your rights during a police encounter unless you have at least a basic understanding.

Law Enforcement Officers Can Be Wrong

The authors of this book have the utmost respect for law enforcement officers. In fact, one of the authors is a law enforcement officer. Law enforcement officers go through tremendous training and continuing education. Like the rest of us, however, they are not perfect and they can make mistakes.

Even though you might be legally correct in a situation involving firearms, there is plenty of room for error on the part of the officer. You might still be stopped, interrogated, searched, harassed, or even arrested for carrying a firearm or other dangerous weapon. Legal questions can be left to a judge to sort out. So, get your CWP and follow the law but also be aware that having a CWP and following the law is not an absolute guarantee against a misunderstanding that results in embarrassment, discomfort, or an expensive legal headache.

Unlawful Places to Carry Even with a Concealed Weapons Permit

Even with a permit, the South Carolina Code of Laws makes it a crime to willfully carry a handgun into certain places. Do not knowingly bring a handgun into:

- A business that sells alcoholic beverages for onsite consumption, ***if you are also consuming alcoholic liquor***, beer or wine (unless you are an owner or person in legal control of that business as discussed later in this chapter; **or** a business that has properly posted a legally sufficient sign; **or** a business that has warned you to leave the premises or remove firearms from the premises, *See*

16-23-465 S.C. Code of Laws and further explanation in this chapter;

- A law enforcement, correctional, or detention facility, 23-31-215(M)(1) S.C. Code of Laws;

- A courthouse or courtroom, 23-31-215(M)(2);

- A polling place on an election day, 23-31-215(M)(3)

- The office of, or the business meeting of, the governing body of a county, public school district, municipality, or special purpose district, 23-31-215(M)(4)

- school or college athletic event not related to firearms (without the express permission from school authorities), see *The Rules for Schools* in the chapter on *Possessing and Transporting a Gun without a Permit* for a more thorough discussion of weapons on school grounds or activities, 23-31-215(M)(5);

- A daycare facility or pre-school facility (without permission), 23-31-215(M)(6);

- A place where the carrying of a firearm is prohibited by Federal Law like federal buildings, federal lands, military bases, (without permission), 23-31-215(M)(7);

- A church or other established religious sanctuary unless you have express permission of the appropriate church official or governing body, 23-31-215(M)(8);

- A hospital, medical clinic, doctor's office, or any other facility where medical procedures are performed unless you are authorized by the employer, 23-31-215(M)(9); or,

- A place clearly marked with a sign prohibiting the carrying of a concealable weapon on the premises. The sign must be of the exact specifications set forth in S.C. Code of Laws Section(s) 23-31-22 or 21-31 235. See the section of this book on *Places that Don't Want You to Carry.*

Even with a CWP, if you willfully carry into one of these places you can be charged with a misdemeanor and the punishment is a fine of at least $1,000 or a jail sentence of up to one (1) year, or both, in the discretion of the court. See S.C. Code of Laws Section 23-31-215(M)(10). Also, your permit is automatically revoked under S.C. Code of Laws Section 215(J).

If you bring your handgun into a business that sells alcoholic beverages for onsite consumption, **and consume alcoholic liquor, beer, or wine**, the crime is also a misdemeanor but the possible penalty is a fine of not more than $2,000 or jail for not more than two (2) years, or both. Also, your CWP will be automatically revoked under S.C. Code of Laws Section 215(J). This crime and penalty does not apply if you are the owner or person in legal control of the business or have the written permission from the owner or person in legal control of the premises. The rules for business owners or those in legal control are discussed in another section of this book.

There is more bad news. The offenses in this section are subject to the additional penalties created in Section 16-23-460. These penalties arise if convicted of carrying a concealed weapon not in compliance with the CWP Statute. The additional penalty is that your weapon must be forfeited and you either pay up to a $500 fine or serve 90 days in jail.

Permission from the Person in Charge

A *September 25, 2018* South Carolina Attorney General Opinion supports that you can get special permission to possess firearms from

authorized individuals at places like schools, hospitals, doctor's offices, and churches. However, you must get the express permission of the presiding officer of the institution to be exempted. Express permission means a positive offer and acceptance of permission. As a rule of thumb, you will want this permission in writing on the official letterhead of the institution. Make sure the permission is from the presiding officer or presiding body. Examples would be the university president and university chief of police, hospital physical plant chief, doctor who owns the medical clinic, or church pastor, deaconate or presbytery.
Notwithstanding the list, it appears that you can get a form of "special permission" to carry concealable weapons and other handguns onto and into places like military bases and state and local government buildings. Getting "special permission" from the person in charge of the institution is not a part of the concealed weapons permit statute but, instead, seems to have informally evolved from the college handgun exception found in Section 16-23-420 and the exceptions in the preceding paragraph that arise from the concealed weapons permit statute.
Where does this exception come into play? Sometimes you will see gun shows in public buildings or county fairgrounds facilities. Also, some military bases sponsor shooting competitions. Beyond these events, there might be instances where the city building official or base commander thinks it appropriate to allow certain individuals the ability to have concealable weapons or other weapons on the premises. The simple rule is to always get written permission from the presiding official on the letterhead of the institution. If you feel comfortable with, or can only get verbal permission, that is your call. Just remember to make certain that you have official permission and that the person who gave you permission will back you up in court if it comes to that. If not, you are risking serious consequences to your ability to lawfully possess and carry a gun.

Take special note that there are virtually no instances where non- law enforcement officials can carry handguns (or any firearms) into courthouses. South Carolina law prohibits firearms in courthouses and federal law prohibits firearms in federal courthouses. 18 U.S.C. 930(g)(3) defines a "Federal Court Facility" as the courtroom, judges' chambers, witness rooms, jury deliberation rooms, attorney conference rooms, prisoner holding cells, offices of the court clerks, the United States attorney, and the United States marshal, probation and parole offices, and adjoining corridors of any court of the United States.

Churches with Church School Facilities

South Carolina Senators Tom Corbin and Ronnie Cromer, as well as Representative Nathan Ballentine, requested an attorney general opinion on whether a person holding a Concealed Weapons Permit ("CWP") who has the express permission of the appropriate church authorities to carry a concealed weapon on the premises is nevertheless barred from carrying by the fact that the church also operates a daycare and a preschool at the same location. SC Attorney General Alan Wilson's office responded with a *June 28, 2018 South Carolina Attorney General Opinion*. That opinion concludes that a court would conclude that where a person has the express permission of the appropriate official or governing body of a church which owns or has legal possession or control of the church's real property, and where that person is not otherwise prohibited by law from possessing a concealed handgun, that person may lawfully carry on the premises consistent with such permission even when the church also operates a daycare or preschool on the same premises. Remember that an attorney general opinion, while highly instructive and weighty, is not law and law enforcement and the courts are not bound by it.

Churches that Lease Facilities from Schools

As part of the 2021 Open Carry with Training Act, Section 23-31-232 South Carolina Code of Laws, CWP holders, if given express permission given by the appropriate church official or governing body, may carry a concealable weapon, concealed or openly, on the leased premises of an elementary or secondary school. The CWP may carry only during "church" times and only in the areas leased (including parking lots and walkways). The school districts may require that the church official disclose that its congregants might be carrying during those times. Carry under this provision is suspended if the school district is carrying on curricular or extra-curricular school activities on the premises at the same time. Last, the provision fixes a possible conflict with the Federal Gun-Free School Zone Act (18 U.S.C. Section 921(a)).

Added Privileges for Some Office Holders with a CWP

Certain people can carry their concealable weapons, concealed, anywhere in the state if they have a concealed weapons permit and are carrying out the duties of their office. Privilege holders include: most judges; prosecutors and assistant prosecutors; and worker's compensation commissioners. The 2021 Open Carry Act expanded this list to include the South Carolina Attorney General and assistant attorney generals.

If you are one of these folks and have a permit, you can carry a concealable weapon into courthouses or wherever else your official duties take you.

There are two issues involved in analyzing this provision. The first is whether you are one of these special people. If you are one of these people, you know it. The second issue is whether you are carrying out the duties of your office. It is clear a judge sitting on his or her bench during a trial is carrying out official duties. Likewise, an assistant prosecutor interviewing a witness in a government building is carrying out his or her official duties. (Prosecutors must follow individual jail, prison, or other incarceration facility rules though).

Say, though, that a worker's compensation commissioner is investigating a case and is required to talk with someone in a business that serves alcoholic beverages. That would seem to fall under official duties and the commissioner's carry is legal. Likewise, what if a prosecutor is investigating the facts of a case and is required to inspect areas of a school? That too would seem to fall under the exception and the concealed carry would be legal. A search for case law on this issue turned up nothing, probably because the type of people who are the subject of this provision do not get arrested for carrying concealed weapons very often. If this provision applies to you, you likely have legal education and experience. Therefore, all we can say is use your best judgment in determining the extent of this provision.

Elected Officials (City Commissioners, County Council, etc.)

Just like any other person with only a CWP, an official elected to a governing body of a county, public school district, municipality, or special purpose district with only a CWP is limited from carrying a concealable weapon, concealed or openly, into an office or meeting of the body he or she is elected to. This is the conclusion of a *South Carolina Attorney General in an Opinion dated April 2, 2012.* South Carolina Code of Laws Section 23-31215(M)[a](5) expressly limits a person with only a CWP from carrying in the office of or business meeting of a government body.

Similarly, Section 16-23-420 of the South Carolina Code of Laws prohibits handguns in public buildings with the express permission of the person or authority in charge of the building. To try to get around both these limitations, elected officials have suggested enacting a local ordinance specifically exempting or authorizing elected officials. However, the same Opinion goes on the conclude that any ordinance passed by a local government body exempting any persons from these limiting Code sections would be found invalid by a Court under the South Carolina firearms law preemption statute (§ 23-31-510 South Carolina Code of Laws). So, some enumerated elected officials with only a CWP are not permitted to carry into a meeting of the body they are elected to nor are they even able to carry into their own official office. To get around this, those elected officials will need to have some other exception like being a constable.

Elected Officials (Treasurers, Register of Deeds, Tax Collector, etc.)

Some elected officials with only a CWP are not prohibited from carrying at their offices. The prohibited offices and meetings enumerated in Section 23-31215(M)[a](5) do not include elected local officials like Treasurers, Register of Deeds, and Tax Assessors. Further, that official is generally the chief officer of the building in which his or her office located. Therefore, under 16-23-420, he or she can give himself or herself (and anyone else) permission to be in the government building with a handgun. This is supported by a South Carolina Attorney General Opinion dated June 6, 2016.

U.S. Post Offices

With or without a CWP, you are prohibited from bringing a handgun into a U.S. Post Office building under South Carolina Code of Laws Section 16-23-420. That statue makes it a crime to carry a handgun into a publicly owned building. The crime is a felony that carries a prison term not to exceed five (5) years and a fine of no more than $5,000 or both. Conviction on the charge also burdens you with a lifetime federal firearms disability. Don't forget the additional penalties of Section 16-23-460 (weapon must be forfeited and you either pay up to a $500 fine or serve 90 days in jail). This South Carolina prohibition is to the buildings only and not the post office parking lot.

U.S. Post Offices must have a sign posted that cites 18 U.S.C. 930(a) and postal regulation 39 CFR 232.1(l). The sign is posted pursuant to 18 U.S.C. 930(h). In a nutshell, 930(h) provides that a person is not guilty of carrying in a government building - i.e. 930(a) - unless the sign is conspicuously posted. Section 930(a) prohibits a person from knowingly possessing, or causing to be present, a firearm or dangerous weapon, or attempts to do so in a federal facility. Federal facility is generally defined as buildings where core governmental functions take place. See Doe v.Wilmington Housing Auth., 880 F. Supp. 2d 513, 532 (D. Del. 2012).

As to post office parking lots, there is reason to consider those areas safe for firearm possession. A recent federal court decision in Colorado provides the reasoning. The court ruled in favor of a Colorado man holding that a Postal regulation barring firearms in its parking lots violates his right to keep and bear arms under the Constitution. However, the facts in the case were favorable for the plaintiff. The man, Mr. Bonidy, who has the equivalent of a CWP and regularly carries a handgun for self-defense, drives several miles from his home to the post office to collect his mail. Mail delivery is not available to his rural home. On arrival at the postal property though, he was barred from carrying a firearm or keeping a firearm in his parked vehicle by 39 C.F.R. 232.1(l).

Mr. Bonidy wrote a letter to the postmaster asking that the regulation be withdrawn but the Postal Service refused. Mr. Bonidy and the National Association for Gun Rights then filed suit.

Section 39 C.F.R.232.1(l) provides:

Notwithstanding the provisions of any other law, rule or regulation, no person while on Postal property may carry firearms, other

> *dangerous or deadly weapons, or explosives, either openly or concealed, or store the same on Postal property, except for official purposes.*

This regulatory prohibition, that carries a fine, imprisonment for 30 days, or both, is broader than 18 U.S.C. 930(a), which prohibits private possession of firearms inside federal facilities. The total ban impairs the right to keep and bear arms when individuals are traveling to, from, or through Postal property to get their mail. Anyone with a hunting rifle or shotgun in his car, or a handgun in his glove compartment for self-defense, violates the regulation simply by driving onto Postal Service property.

In this case, the Court distinguished the parking lot from other "sensitive places" like the inside the building or in the employee parking area. The Court ruled that the public parking area is not a sensitive place and the defendants failed to show that an absolute ban on firearms is substantially related to their important public safety objective. Further, that the public interest in safety and Mr. Bonidy's liberty can be accommodated by modifying the regulation to permit Mr. Bonidy to "have ready access to essential postal services" while also exercising his right to self-defense. The Court ordered the postmaster at that location to permit Mr. Bonidy to use the public parking lot with a firearm secured in his car.

With this ruling, the court balanced the interests of the post office with that of Mr. Boniday and concluded that the postmaster must make reasonable accommodations for each person as opposed to adhering to a broad "one size fits all" firearm prohibition.

The USPS appealed the decision of the Colorado District Court to the Tenth Circuit Court of Appeals (Federal) and that held that the ban on carrying or storing firearms on Post Office property does not violate the 2nd Amendment. The Court affirmed the district court order upholding the constitutionality of 32 C.F.R. § 232.1(1) as applied to the post office building and reversed the district court order invalidating the regulation as applied to the parking lot.

The case has been appealed to the United States Supreme Court and the Supreme Court has not yet acted on the petition.

It is important to note several things about this ruling. For one, it is the 10th Circuit Court of Appeals decision as opposed to the Supreme Court. Therefore, it is not the law of the land or an ultimate decision on the Constitutionality of the postal regulation. Second, it is specific to the facts of the case. Mr. Boniday has some favorable facts in his favor like the absence of mail delivery at his home. With respect to complying with the law, the best practice is to assume that all USPS property has an enforceable regulation prohibiting possession or storage of firearms anywhere on the premises.

Retail Mail Stores

Retail mailing stores that sell stamps, packaging materials, mailbox services, and shipping services are an alternative to U.S. Post Offices. Typically, these stores are located at shopping centers, malls, or in stand-alone buildings. They are generally classified as *contract post offices* under 39 Code of Federal Regulations 241.2. Because they are wholly private, they are not considered federal property and you are not prohibited from carrying a concealable weapon, concealed or openly into those stores.

Carrying at a Bank or ATM Machine

Because banks are highly regulated by the federal government, many people confuse banks for federal property. Banks are private companies that are insured and heavily watched by the federal government but are not owned by the federal government (at least not yet) and are not federal property. You are not prohibited from carrying a concealable weapon, concealed or openly, into a bank if you have your permit. Be on the lookout, however, for banks that post a statutorily compliant "No Concealable Weapons" sign discussed later in this chapter. If that sign is up and it conforms to the statute, you cannot bring your concealable weapon, concealed into the building. You can still use the outside ATM and not break any law though.

No Drinking at Businesses That Serve Alcohol on the Premises

If you are carrying a concealable weapon, concealed or openly, you must be careful not to drink in a business that sells alcoholic liquors, beers or wines for on-premises consumption. If you have a CWP, you are permitted to carry a concealable weapon, concealed or openly, into an establishment that sells alcoholic liquors, beer, or wine for onsite consumption under 16-23-465(B)(1). However, you cannot consume alcoholic liquors, beer, or wine on the premises. So, you can be on the premises carrying a concealable weapon, concealed or openly, but you cannot drink while carrying. A violation is punishable by a fine of not more than $2,000 and a jail sentence of not more than two (2) years, or both. Further, a CWP holder must have his or her permit revoked for a period of five (5) years. See Section 16-23-465(A), South Carolina Code of Laws.

For business owners, employees, and those in legal control of a business, this topic is explored in greater detail later in this chapter and in the chapter on *Possessing and Transporting* handguns without a concealed weapons permit.

Remember that this prohibition prohibits drinking while carrying a pistol or other firearm into a business that sells alcohol for on-premises consumption. It does not prohibit you from drinking while carrying another type of self-defense item (like a Byrna®) or up to 50cc of pepper spray concealed or open. CWP holders are not prevented from carrying a concealable weapon, concealed or openly, into a package liquor store, convenience store or bulk store if alcohol is not served for on-site consumption in that business.

Sometimes, upscale groceries stores will have wine sampling. Technically this would trigger the prohibition if the store is selling the samples for onsite consumption. However, if the store is giving the samples with the hope that you will purchase a bottle to take out of the store to drink, the statute appears not violated. Regardless of whether a business technically serves alcohol or not though, always be on the lookout for a "NO CONCEALABLE WEAPONS ALLOWED" sign on the storefront. We will talk about that sign next.

Premises That Don't Want You to Carry.

Even though the state provides for the issuance of concealed weapons permits, it also protects the rights of businesses, employers, and property owners. A CWP holder can be prohibited from carrying a concealable weapon, concealed or openly, on a property. An owner, holder of lease interest, or operator of a business can prohibit CWP holders from carrying concealable weapons, concealed or openly, upon the property.

To prohibit a CWP holder from carrying on their property, the owner, holder of lease interest, or operator of a business must give proper notice. The notice can be actual or *constructive* notice.

Owner or Agent Requests That You Leave (Actual Notice)

Actual notice is where the owner, holder of lease interest, or operator of a business simply requests that the CWP holder carrying a weapon either leave the premises or remove the weapon off the premises. *See* Section 16-23-465(B)(3) of the South Carolina Code of Laws. If the CWP holder violates this section of the CWP law at a business that sells alcoholic liquors, beer, or wine for onsite consumption, he or she may be charged with violating Section 16-23-465(A), a misdemeanor carrying the potential penalty of a fine up to $2,000, imprisonment for not more than 2 years, or both. If the premises are not a business that sells alcoholic liquors, beer or wine for onsite consumption, the violation can be Section 16-11-620 of the S. C. Code of Laws, criminal trespass with a potential penalty of a fine of up to $200 or imprisonment for up to thirty (30) days. See Section 23-31-15(M)(10) and Section(s) 16-23-465(A) and (B)(3) of the South Carolina Code of Laws. The holder is also subject to the additional penalties of Section 16-23-460 (i.e., the weapon must be forfeited and you either pay up to a $500 fine or serve 90 days in jail).

Required Sign (Constructive Notice)

Constructive notice means legally sufficient notice by a conforming sign. A sign that meets the statutory requirements for dimensions, etc. imputes *constructive notice* upon every person who enters the building. A sign that reads, "NO CONCEALABLE WEAPONS ALLOWED" provides legally sufficient constructive notice. The sign **must** be in both written language and in ***universal sign language***. Braille is not required, presumably because all permit holders have met the SLED 20/40 vision requirement. *See* South Carolina Code of Laws Section 23-31-220 and 23-31-235. However, have you ever seen one of these signs with universal sign language? What is universal sign language? Do we have a "problem" in this state that none of the signs provide constructive notice? A brief internet search revealed that there is no universal sign language and that there are over 300 sign languages across the globe. So, if there is no universal sign language, and none of the signs have sign language on them anyway, is there no constructive notice and can we pretend like the signs don't exist? My colleagues and I explore questions like this each year at my *Shaw's Annual South Carolina Gun Law Seminar* held each year in Charleston and Spartanburg.

A conforming sign must be posted at each entrance where a concealed weapons permit holder might enter. It must be clearly visible from the outside of the building with a width of eight (8") inches and a height of twelve (12") inches. The words "NO CONCEALABLE WEAPONS ALLOWED" must be included, typeset in black, and one (1") inch tall. The letters must be all uppercase type and placed at the bottom of the sign and centered between the lateral edges of the sign.

Additionally, the sign must have a black silhouette of a handgun inside a circle which is seven (7") inches in diameter with a diagonal horizontal line that runs from the lower left to the upper right at a forty-five degree angle. The Code of Laws specify that the circle "must have a diameter of a circle." This seems to suggest that the circle must be a perfectly round circle and not a fancy oval or elliptical orbit shape. Finally, the sign must be placed not less than forty inches and not more than sixty inches from the bottom of the entrance door. If the place where concealed weapons are prohibited does not have doors, the signs must be bigger. To be specific, thirty-six (36") inches wide and forty-eight (48") inches tall. Again, it must contain the words "NO CONCEALABLE WEAPONS ALLOWED" in black three-inch-tall uppercase type at the bottom of the sign and centered between the lateral edges. It must have a black silhouette of a handgun inside a circle which is thirty-four (34") inches in diameter with a diagonal line that is two (2) inches wide and runs from the lower left to the upper right at a forty-five degree angle. The circle portion must be two inches wide just as the diameter is two inches wide. The sign must be placed not less that forty (40") inches and not more than ninety-six (96") inches above the ground. The purpose of these specifications is to standardize the signs. Therefore, a sign **must meet these specifications to be legal and enforceable against CWP permit holders**. The sign must also be posted in sufficient quantities to be clearly visible from any point of entry into the area where concealable weapons are prohibited.

Sign Unique to the Business

The 2021 Open Carry Act further convoluted the sign requirement by adding the language, "*[n]othing in this section prevents a public or private employer or owner of a business from posting a sign . . . which may be unique to that business.*" (South Carolina Code of Laws Section 23-31-235(D)). Wait . . what?!?!? Does this this nullify all of the stringent sign requirements and allow an owner or authorized person to post any sign it deems appropriate? That is a question for the courts to determine if a challenge arises. As it stands, we've got longstanding strict statutory sign requirements, but then a new "catch all" provision that directly conflicts with those strict requirements. Hopefully, the South Carolina General Assembly will correct this untenable contradiction during the current term.

Penalty for Carrying into a Prohibited Business

If a CWP holder ignores a legally correct/properly posted sign and carries a concealable weapon, concealed or openly, onto the premises, the holder can be punished in accordance with Section 16-11-620 of the S.C. Code of Laws. The charge is basically trespassing. You could be fined up to $200 or jailed for up to 30 days. Additionally, if you are charged a second or subsequent time, your permit will be revoked for one (1) year. These prohibitions do not apply to law enforcement officers. *See* Section 23-31-15(M)(10) of the South Carolina Code of Laws.

If the CWP holder violates this section of the CWP law at a business that sells alcoholic liquors, beer, or wine for onsite consumption, he or she may be charged with violating Section 16-23-465(A), a misdemeanor carrying the potential penalty of a fine up to

$2,000, imprisonment for not more than 2 years, or both. *See* Section(s) 16-23-465(A) and (B)(3) of the South Carolina Code of Laws. Don't forget the additional penalties of Section 16-23-460 (i.e., the weapon must be forfeited and you either pay up to a $500 fine or serve 90 days in jail. Forfeiture of weapons is discussed in depth in another section of this book).

That being said, why would you want to do business at a place that actively opposes your right to keep and bear arms anyway? Plus, criminals might target businesses where they think there is less of a chance to encounter armed resistance from a CWP carrier. Therefore, take your business elsewhere.

Lawsuit Protection for Business Owners

If you own a business which is open to the public, you might be thinking about the liability involved in having people coming into your business with concealed weapons. You might think that if you don't have a sign prohibiting people from carrying concealed weapons into your business, you will be opening yourself up to civil liability if a patron with a concealed weapon uses it on a criminal. The legislature has anticipated scenarios where injured criminals or their families attempt to sue a business owner simply because the owner allowed the legally armed patron to carry concealed in his or her store. The South Carolina Code of Laws provides that businesses that allow their patrons to carry concealed weapons cannot be sued simply because the business allowed the armed patrons.

As a side note, business owners should be aware that they face potential liability for shootings on other legal theories and causes of action. Mainly, business and property owners face liability if they knew of a history or propensity for violent attacks on the premises and failed to protect patrons. For instance, a person shot in a store by an armed robber might argue that the business knew about prior attacks and did nothing to warn customers about the prior attacks. Similarly, a plaintiff could argue that the business failed to provide security or failed to provide enough light in the parking lot. Business owners should carefully follow all recommendations from their risk management office or liability insurance carrier regarding risk minimization and preventative best practices. Insurance companies are usually eager to give advice about risk management or to send out one of their agents to conduct a risk assessment. If your carrier does not gladly offer such a service, look for a better carrier.

It should also be noted that prohibiting or discouraging armed CWP holders on your property might create an attractive environment for criminals. If a business exercises the NO CONCEALED WEAPONS ALLOWED sign, a criminal might see that business as an attractive place to commit a crime. If a criminal or deranged gunman has a choice of operating in a gun free zone as opposed or one that welcomes CWP holders, logic says he will choose the gun free zone. Therefore, it could easily be argued that a business owner created an unsafe environment for the patrons of the business by posting such signs prohibiting CWP carry and the business should be held legally responsible for the additional danger created by the posting of the signs prohibiting CWP carry.

Business Owners, Managers, and Employees

With or without a permit, a business owner, or the person in legal control of the business, may possess any legal firearm while on the premises of the business. The owner or person in legal control can carry a firearm either concealed or openly. This is true even if the business serves alcohol on the premises. This is because of an exception to the general handgun prohibition and has nothing to do with CWP law. *See* 16-23-20(13) of the South Carolina Code of Laws. Further, the owner or person in legal control of the business may grant permission to his employees to carry firearms openly or concealed while in the business (with the sole exception of businesses that sell alcoholic beer, wines, and liquors for on-site consumption).

In order for employees to carry while at work, they must determine whether they can legally carry pursuant to their concealed weapons permit or pursuant to an exception to the general statutory handgun prohibition. In other words, there are two ways for an employee to legally carry at work but the employee must make sure that he or she falls under one of the two statutorily created exceptions.

One way an employee can legally carry at work is by carrying under a concealed weapons permit pursuant to South Carolina Code of Laws Section 16-23-20(12). Under this provision of the concealed weapons permit law, an employee can carry a concealable weapon, concealed or openly, into his work without first obtaining his employer's permission (and even knowledge). However, the employee cannot carry pursuant to a concealed weapons permit if the business sells alcoholic beer, wine, or liquors for on-site consumption. Likewise, an employee cannot carry under the concealed weapons permit statute if the employer has erected a proper NO CONCEALED WEAPONS ALLOWED sign on the premises.

Another way an employee can carry at work is under the South Carolina Code of Laws Section 16-23-20(13) exception. Under this exception, an employee can carry any legal firearm at work, open or concealed, so long as the employee has the permission of the owner or person in legal control ***and*** has a concealed weapons permit. Even under this permissive exception, though, employees of a business that sells alcohol for on-site consumption cannot carry a pistol or firearm while on the business premises. Note that, even though carrying at work under this exception requires an employee to have a CWP, the employee is not carrying pursuant to the permit but pursuant to the statutory exception. Therefore, the employee may carry openly and may carry firearms different from those defined previously in this chapter as "concealable weapons." Further, an employee carrying under this statutory exception may carry at a business that posts the NO CONCEALED WEAPONS ALLOWED sign because the employee has the business owner's (or the person in legal control's) permission. Confused? You should be, this type of confusing drafting should be eliminated by the General Assembly.

Company Vehicles and Machinery

Finally, a business can prohibit its employees from carrying on business property like company machinery or vehicles. For example, say that you work as a repairman for a power company. Say also that the company chooses to prohibit guns at work under both the CWP Statute and also by a policy or condition of the workplace. The company provides you a vehicle and sends you to locations away from the office to repair power lines that the company owns. You are doing offsite repairs and driving a company vehicle to and from the offsite location. In this case, the employer can prevent you from carrying under your CWP the entire time that you are at work because the company owns or controls the office, the vehicle that you use to get to and from the offsite location, and the offsite location. Therefore, you can face both criminal liability under the CWP statute and private employment action by your employer if your employer for violating the policy or condition against carrying guns at work.

Next, let's look at a pizza delivery person using his personal vehicle to deliver pizzas for a company that chooses to disallow guns at work under both the CWP Statute and a policy or condition of the workplace. While picking up a pizza at the store, the driver is prohibited by the *business property* language of the statute. While at the property of a customer, the driver would probably be prohibited by the *work place* language of the Statute. But, while driving his personally owned vehicle between the work place and the property of delivery, he would be free to carry pursuant to the CWP law even if he was on the clock. The way to accomplish this is to carry the handgun under one of the handgun exception (i.e. glove box or console) while on work property and carry according to the CWP Statute (i.e. on, or about, the person) when inside the private vehicle. As in the previous example, the employer could still take employment action against him if it was discovered he had guns at work in violation of a company policy or condition. However, the employer could not invoke the police powers of the state to further punish the delivery person with a crime.

(Remainder of Page Intentionally Blank.)

Guns at Work Chart

	Owner	Person in Legal Control of Business	Employee
Do I need a CWP to carry any legal firearm at the business or store where I work (not including offsite work areas)?	No	No	**Yes,** whether carrying under S.C. Code 16-23-20(13) or carrying under 16-23-20(12).
Can I carry any sized firearm at a business or work?	Yes	Yes	**Yes,** if carrying under S.C. Code 16-23-20(13). Need Employer's Permission. NO, if carrying under S.C. Code 16-23-20(12) can only carry a concealable weapon as defined by the CWP law.
Can I carry at a business or work that sells beer, wine or alcoholic liquors for on-site consumption?	**Yes.** Drinking OK.	**Yes.** Drinking OK.	**Yes,** if CWP holder 16-23-20(12) and employer has not posted sign or given actual notice to not carry. No drinking.
Can I carry openly (i.e. on my hip) at a business or work?	Yes	Yes	**Yes,** can carry openly or concealed if carrying under S.C. Code 16-23-20(13) – read it though! **No,** can only carry concealable weapon, concealed, if carrying under 16-23-20(12).
Can I carry a handgun, openly or concealed, to and from the business and my vehicle under the Section 16-23-20(15) exception?	Yes	Yes	**Yes,** can carry openly or concealed under S.C. Code 16-23-20(15), directly to or from vehicle **IF** it is legal for you to have gun in the business.

It is important for an employee to recognize the difference between the legal and business policy rules for guns at work. The above two statutory exceptions are legal rules for carrying a firearm at work. An employee's failure to carry properly pursuant to one of those two exceptions exposes the employee to criminal arrest and prosecution. Alternatively, the employee should also determine if the company has a firearm policy that would prevent him or her from possessing guns at work. If the company has a policy against employees carrying guns at work, the employee could face discipline or be fired regardless of what the statutes say about employees carrying firearms at work.

Other People's Homes or Dwellings

Permit holders may not carry a concealable weapon, concealed or openly, into the residence or dwelling of another person without the express consent of the owner or tenant. If you do, you can be charged with a misdemeanor and can be punished by a fine of not less than $1,000 or up to one year in jail or both. Also, your permit will be revoked for 5 years. (*See* SC Code of Laws Section 23-31-225). Don't forget the additional penalties of Section 16-23-460 (weapon must be forfeited and you either pay up to a $500 fine or serve 90 days in jail). Do not go to someone else's place with a concealed weapon unless they give you their permission or you are sure that they do not have a problem with you carrying on their premises.

From Car to Home and Vice Versa with a Permit

With or without a CWP, you can carry a handgun, concealed or not, from your car to your house or apartment and from your house or apartment to your vehicle. Same with a hotel room (discussed elsewhere in this book). If you have your CWP, this provided in SC Code of Laws Section 23-31-230. If you do not have a CWP, you are carrying under a handgun exception (South Carolina Code of Laws Section 16-23-20(15)), as opposed to CWP law, and you must go directly from your home to your vehicle or vice versa. Having the CWP additionally allows you to take a diversion to the mailbox, walk around the neighborhood, talk with the neighbors, etc. if your handgun is a concealable weapon. If you do not have a CWP, this provision is dealt with in more detail in the chapter on possessing and transporting handguns without a concealed weapons permit.

Partial Exception for CWPs on the Capitol Grounds

Section 10-11-320 of the South Carolina Code of Laws makes it unlawful to carry a firearm while on the capitol grounds or within the capitol building. The section defines capitol grounds as, "that area inward from the vehicular traveled surfaces of Gervais, Sumter, Senate and Assembly Streets in the city of Columbia."

There is somewhat of an exception for CWP holders though. Section 10-11-320(B) provides that a CWP holder who is authorized to park on the capitol grounds or in the parking garage below the capitol grounds may have a firearm in the vehicle. However, the firearm must remain locked in the CWP holder's vehicle while on or below the capitol grounds and must be stored in a place in the vehicle that is not readily accessible to any person upon that person's entry to or below the capitol grounds. The best practice here is to place the firearm in the trunk or luggage compartment of the vehicle before entering the capitol grounds and then return it to any other legal location on your person or in the vehicle after you leave the capitol grounds. See the *Can I Carry on the Capitol Grounds* section in the *Possessing and Transporting Guns without a Permit* chapter for more information about the prohibition and the penalties for violations.

Permit Reciprocity with Other States

If you have a valid permit from another state that has a reciprocal agreement with South Carolina, you can legally carry a concealed weapon just as if you have a South Carolina permit. As of September 8, 2022, the states with South Carolina reciprocity are: Alaska, Arizona, Arkansas, Delaware, Florida, Georgia, Illinois, Idaho (Enhanced Only), Iowa, Kansas, Kentucky, Louisiana, Maryland, Michigan, Minnesota, Missouri, Nebraska, New Mexico, North Carolina, North Dakota (Enhanced Only), Ohio, Oklahoma, South Dakota (Enhanced Only), Tennessee, Texas, Virginia, West Virginia, and Wyoming. Check the SLED website periodically for the most current list of reciprocal states. Also, see the websites for the states that you travel to. Reciprocity is somewhat complicated in that sometimes the reciprocal states will only recognize resident permits as opposed to resident or non-resident permits. Also check popular concealed carry websites found through searching the web.

Carrying in North Carolina and Georgia

Because North Carolina and Georgia border South Carolina, you might need to know if and how you can carry in these states. This section is not comprehensive but gives a quick general guide. For complete information about carrying in these neighboring states, you must read the statutes and cases for a given state. However, a "shortcut" is to check with each state's law enforcement agency, attorney general, and/or "carry" organizations' websites.

As a quick thumb-nail though, we can look at both state's general rules. If you have a South Carolina permit, you can carry a concealed handgun in North Carolina. You must always carry your permit with you and, if stopped by a law enforcement officer, you must indicate to the officer that you have a permit and indicate where the weapon is located. You should follow the same prohibitions as if you were in South

Carolina with respect to government property, federal buildings and businesses that post a no weapons or firearms sign. Additionally, you cannot carry at schools, events that charge an admission fee like sports and theaters, and any place that sells alcoholic beverages. As in South Carolina, you specifically have the right to take your concealed weapon with you into highway rest area bathrooms. Different from South Carolina is that you cannot carry at financial institutions like banks. Different also is that you cannot carry at a parade, funeral procession, picket line or political protest.

Georgia and South Carolina recently agreed to reciprocity. If you have a South Carolina permit, you can carry a concealed handgun in Georgia. You must always carry your permit with you if carrying. You should follow the same prohibitions as if you were in South Carolina with respect to government property and federal buildings. There is no law providing for businesses to post a no weapons or firearms sign but any business owner can ask a carrier to leave because of carrying. Failure to leave after being asked is a trespass crime. You can carry at schools but only while dropping off or picking up a student and you may also may keep a firearm in an unoccupied motor vehicle while parked on campus. As in South Carolina, you specifically have the right to take your concealed weapon with you into highway rest area bathrooms. You can carry at public gatherings but you cannot carry in a church sanctuary if the church does not have a policy of allowing carry. You can also have a firearm in your vehicle in a church parking lot. Georgia law does not prohibit concealed carry in restaurants or even bars.

When traveling from South Carolina to any other state, the general rules for transporting and possessing a weapon out of state are reviewed in the *Possessing and Transporting a Handgun without a Permit* chapter.

Renewal of the South Carolina CWP

Your permit is good for five (5) years. *See* South Carolina Code of Laws Section 23-31-215(P). You can renew the permit online or by completing SLED application Form R-078 (check the "Renewal" box instead of "New Application" box this time) and paying a $50 renewal fee. You will need to send along a picture ID or paper or electric copy of your ID. As with the original application, if you are a disabled veteran or a retired law enforcement officer, the $50 fee will be waived. However, to get the veteran rate, you must provide SLED with your DD-214 and evidence of receipt of VA disability payments. Section 23-32-215(Q) provides that SLED must conduct or facilitate a state and federal background check of the applicant. If the background check is *favorable*, SLED must renew the permit. There's that fuzzy term "favorable" again.

At least thirty (30) days before your permit expires, SLED is required to mail or email you an expiration notice with information about how to renew. If you let your previous permit expire for longer than sixty (60) days, SLED might require proof of new training and will make you apply by mail.

Trouble with the Law before CWP Renewal

If you are seeking renewal online, you will be required to certify that your circumstances have not made you ineligible for renewal. There is a list of circumstances like change of citizenship, arrests, domestic violence, etc. One of the questions asks if you, *"were arrested or charged with an offense for which you plead guilty; were found guilty, paid a fine, forfeited bond, were placed in jail or placed on probation since your last CWP Application."*

Make sure that you do not attempt to renew online if you have had **any** run-ins with the law since you were approved for your first CWP. If you do not, the background check will probably find them. If you are found to be dishonest on the application, SLED has a reason to prevent you from ever getting a permit in South Carolina. Not the least of which, you can be found to have committed perjury, which is a terrible charge to carry around with you because it involves fraud, deceit and moral turpitude. So, if you had a run in with the law since you were approved for your original CWP, do not apply for renewal online. Further, make sure you mention the nature of the run-in on your written application package.

This means traffic (moving violation) tickets also. So, even if you got a traffic ticket from the time you were approved for a CWP, you should not apply for renewal or replacement online and mention the ticket on the written application.

Again, all applications, online or paper, subject the applicant to a new background check. *See* South Carolina Code of Laws Section 23-31-215(Q).

Carrying with an Expired CWP

If a CWP holder is carrying with an expired CWP, that person will not be charged with unlawful carry under Section 16-23-20 of the South Carolina Code of Laws so long as the CWP has been expired no more than one year. Alternatively, the holder may only be fined no more than $100 under Section 23-31-215(U) of the South Carolina Code of Laws.

CWP Remains Valid While Renewal is Pending

Provided you are otherwise qualified, and you are properly applying for renewal or replacement, your license cannot be suspended during the renewal or replacement. As a small part of a large 2013 appropriations bill, the South Carolina General Assembly enacted the following temporary statute:

A concealed weapons permit may not be suspended by a state official, agent, or employee supported by state funds if the permit holder has initiated a renewal or replacement application and the processing and issuance of a renewal or replacement permit is delayed for administrative reasons. A concealed weapons permit remains valid during the pendency of the renewal or replacement process so long as the application for replacement renewal is submitted prior to the expiration of the permit. (Section 62.22, 120th Session, 2013-2014, H. 3710).

This temporary statute is good through June 30, 2014 but is subject to reenactment. Check SLED's website for the current status of the temporary statute.

Renewal of a Non-Resident CWP

If you are a qualified non-resident, you've got a little more work on your hands. In addition to the application and fee, you must submit a photocopy of your valid driver's license or identification card from your state of residence. You must also send a new photo of your face. The photo can be no larger than 3" X 5". Just like when you originally applied, you must again submit a newly certified SLED Form R-168 (South Carolina Non-Resident Concealed Weapon Permit (CWP) Real Property Tax Form). This lets SLED know that you still own real estate in South Carolina.

Once you submit these things, SLED will again conduct a federal, state and local fingerprint review. If the background check is favorable, the permit will be renewed. SLED indicates that it will take about thirty (30) days to process your renewal.

Be mindful of your residency or qualified non-residency status. If you move to South Carolina, you are now a resident and should apply for a resident concealed weapons permit. If you retain an ownership interest in South Carolina real estate, you are still a qualified non-resident. If you sold your interest in South Carolina real estate, your permit became void at that point and you should have surrendered your qualified non-resident permit.

Lost or Stolen Permit

If your permit is lost or stolen, tell SLED immediately. Section 23-31-215(L) of the South Carolina Code of Laws provides that failure to tell SLED immediately is a misdemeanor with the penalty of a $25 fine. You apply for a replacement using SLED Form R-022 available from SLED's website. The replacement fee is $5.

There's really no reason not to notify SLED considering that, when you notify them, they will issue a replacement permit. Further, you are deemed to still have a valid CWP while waiting for SLED to issue you a replacement under Section 16-23-215(L).

Change of Permanent Address

If you change your permanent address, you must notify SLED in writing within 10 days. Along with your written notification, you must send a $5 replacement CWP fee. SLED will then issue a new permit that includes your new address. Like before, Section 23-31-215(L) provides that your old CWP with the old address remains valid until you get the new one. When you get the new permit, you must send the old permit back to SLED.

If you are stopped and the officer discovers that the address on your permit is incorrect, you are subject to a misdemeanor with a fine of $25. The misdemeanor on your record stinks and so does a $25 fine but don't forget the additional penalties of Section 16-23-460 (weapon must be forfeited and you either pay up to a $500 fine or serve 90 days in jail). If you are abiding by the change of address law, however, and are doing so within the time limits set by that statute, you should not be subject to the original misdemeanor or the additional penalties of Section 16-23-460.

Grounds for Revocation of CWP

Your CWP is valid statewide unless it becomes revoked. The reasons for automatic revocation are set forth in South Carolina Code of Laws Section 23-31-215(J). If you move your permanent residence to another state or no longer own property in the South Carolina your license is automatically revoked. Also, if you voluntarily surrender the CWP it is automatically revoked.

Two other reasons for automatic revocation are if you become a person prohibited from possessing a firearm under South Carolina law or if you are ***charged*** with a criminal offense that would subject you to potential a South Carolina or federal firearms disability. (*See* the chapter on firearms disabilities).

Notice this second condition is that a person becomes merely ***charged*** with certain crimes as opposed to ***convicted*** of those crimes. If you are merely charged with an offense that, upon conviction, would prohibit you from possessing a firearm, you must immediately surrender your CWP to a sheriff, police department, a SLED agent, or by sending the CWP to the Chief of SLED by certified mail. We discuss in the Firearms Disabilities Chapter how to determine if a given charge carries with it the potential of a firearms disability. Generally, if the offense has a potential penalty of more than 2 years in jail for a state crime or one year in jail for a federal crime, there is the potential for a firearms disability.

In addition to these statutory grounds for revocation, SLED has issued additional grounds through regulations. These regulations are promulgated under South Carolina Code of Regulations Chapter 73-

60(6). SLED may revoke or suspend a CWP if the permit holder has violated any SLED firearms or CWP rules in the Code of Regulations, when SLED has good reason to believe the holder might have violated rules or statutes related to the CWP program (pending hearing), or if SLED determines that the CWP holder abused any privileges afforded by the CWP.

Permit Holder List is Not Public Information

Can the public find out that you have a concealed weapons permit? For most folks . . . no. SLED maintains a list of all permit holders and the current status of each permit. In the spring of 2008, the South Carolina legislature passed H3528 which amended Section 23-31-215 of the South Carolina Code of Laws. The amended statute now requires SLED to keep the list from free from public inquiry except under very limited circumstances. The practical effect of this legislation is to keep the identity of concealed weapons permit holders from the public eye. Be cautioned that permit holders who have their permit taken away because of a lifetime federal firearms disability or South Carolina Code of Laws Section 16-23-30(B) will be subject to public inquiry and disclosure.

Reciprocity with a Utah CWP

Utah allows non-residents to apply for and receive a Utah CWP. If you are a South Carolina resident and you get your Utah permit, you will be recognized as having a valid permit by more states than a South Carolina permit allows. Notably, the South Carolina resident will gain recognition from Georgia with the Utah permit. See: http://dps.georgia.gov/georgias-firearm-permit-reciprocity.

It is important to note though that a South Carolina resident cannot simply get a non-resident Utah CWP and use it for South Carolina. South Carolina does not have reciprocity with Utah, therefore,

South Carolina residents must get a South Carolina CWP to carry concealed in South Carolina.

The Utah CWP is good for 5 years and the current fee is $51.00 for non-residents. Instruction is required. The instruction time is about 3.5 hours with no shooting and no written test.

To get the most authoritative and updated Utah reciprocity information, please visit: http://bci.utah.gov/concealed-firearm/reciprocity-with-other-states/

Chapter 5
Possessing and Transporting Guns without a Permit

Whether you are a weekend shooter, gun collector, or have a weapon for self-defense, there is a good chance that you will transport or carry the weapon outside of your home. If you do not have a concealed weapons permit, it is essential that you know the rules for transporting or carrying a weapon with or without a permit. This chapter deals with possessing and transporting without a concealed weapons permit.

If you get any lesson from this chapter, it should be to always assess the legality of your gun's location. You should also see the value of getting a concealed weapons permit if you are eligible for one. The permit allows you to legally carry in many more situations than without one.

Handguns

So, where and when can you carry your gun? First let's start with the general rule. The general rule is that you cannot legally possess or carry a *handgun*, openly or concealed, unless you fall within a statutory exception to the general rule. Violation of this rule is a misdemeanor that carries a potential penalty of $1,000 and up to 1 year in jail under South Carolina Code of Laws Section 16-23-50(A)(2). If you have the handgun concealed, you are also subject to prosecution under South Carolina Code of Laws Section 16-23-460 that is a misdemeanor with the potential penalty of a fine between $200 and $500, a jail stay between 30 and 90 days, and the mandatory forfeiture of your weapon to the government. One bright spot is that a conviction will not burden you with a Federal firearms disability.

So, you cannot walk around with a pistol on your hip or concealed in your clothes unless you legally possess and carry under an exception. In general, possession is a broader category that extends from having the handgun in the building or vehicle that you occupy whereas carrying is narrower such as in your clothes or purse/backpack.

A handgun is described as, "any firearm designed to expel a projectile and designed to be fired from the hand, but shall not include any firearm generally recognized or classified as an antique, curiosity, or collector's item, or any that does not fire fixed cartridges." That sentence is a mouthful. Generally, it means pistols and revolvers that you would have on hand to shoot and not collect as a hobby. This chapter, and a good portion of this book, is designed to explain the exceptions.

Handguns in Your Home

Under South Carolina Code of Laws Section 16-23-20(8), you can carry a handgun, concealed or open, in your home. The main restriction is that it must be legal for you to own the gun in the first place. So, if you are legally entitled to own a handgun, you can watch TV or cook dinner inside your home with that gun on your hip or in your pocket. You can also carry the same handgun, concealed or not, on your entire outside premises if you own the land and buildings around your home. Also, even if you do not own the dwelling you are in but have legal control of that dwelling, you have the same right to carry as if you were the owner. For instance, if you have a valid lease at an apartment complex, you have legal control over your dwelling unit.

If you live in an apartment, condominium or similarly attached residential dwelling unit, you are only entitled to carry in your unit and not around the common areas. There is one exception to the *common areas* prohibition though. You can carry a handgun in the common areas if you are walking *directly* from your dwelling to your vehicle. This privilege stems from South Carolina Code Section 16-23-20(15) that allows carry between a vehicle and a place where you are legally entitled to possess a handgun.

If it is safe to do so, you can even fire guns on your property. In fact, a case interpreting the Shooting Range Protection Act found that an area customarily used for shooting at a person's home property was protected from legal actions based upon nuisance for noise. Of course, always follow gun safety rules when shooting on your home property. Pay special attention to the chapter on common gun crimes and lawsuits so that you understand possible criminal and civil liability regarding discharging guns.

Handguns and Firearms in Foster Homes

If you have foster children in your home, there are special rules for you. Section 114-550(H)(18) of the South Carolina Code of Regulations require that firearms (including handguns) and any ammunition shall be kept in a locked storage container except when being legally carried upon the foster parent's person. There are other exceptions also. A firearm and ammunition can be out of the locked storage container if it is being used for educational, recreational, or defense of self or property purposes by the foster parent. A foster parent can also have the firearm out for cleaning. Note that this provision applies whether the foster parents have a concealed weapons permit or not.

Handguns in Other People's Homes with Permission

Under South Carolina Code of Laws Section 16-23-20(8), you can carry a handgun on the premises and inside of other people's homes if you have their permission to be on the premises and have their permission to possess a handgun on the premises. So, if you are at your grandparent's beach house on Edisto Beach and want to have a handgun there, you fall within the exception and can carry on the premises or inside the beach house. This assumes that you have your grandparent's permission to be on the premises and their permission to possess a handgun on the premises. Similarly, if you regularly go to a friend's apartment and he allows you to be on the premises and to have a handgun there, you are within the exception and can possess. Again, this applies whether you have a concealed weapons permit or not.

Group Child Care Homes

Group child homes are private homes designed and licensed to provide education or supervision of children. South Carolina Code of Regulations 114-517(E)(3) requires that firearms, weapons, and ammunition are to be kept in a locked drawer or cabinet.

Child Care Centers

With or without a concealed weapons permit, you cannot bring a firearm to any child care center. It makes no difference if the child care center is public, private or connected to a religious institution. Treat those places like you would a school. For all child care centers, 114-507(E)(3) provides that firearms, weapons, and ammunition are not permitted in the center or on the premises without the express permission of the authorities in charge of the premises or property. This does not apply to a guard, law enforcement officer, or member of the armed forces, or student of military science. Review the "Rules for Schools" section of this chapter for further clarification.

Business Owners Bringing Handguns to Work

(See the Guns at Work Chart in the Concealed Weapons Permit chapter for an easy reference guide for carry at work questions.)

Under Section 16-23-20(13) of the South Carolina Code of Laws, a business owner can carry a handgun, concealed or not, on the premises of his or her business. So, a baker can have a handgun on his hip while on the premises of his bakery. If he thinks wearing a handgun on his hip will scare-off customers, he can carry a handgun concealed, with or without a concealed weapons permit, on his premises. If he is in the suburbs and has a parking lot on his premises, he can carry in the parking lot. Alternatively, if his shop is downtown and he has only a city sidewalk outside of his door, his privilege ends at his door threshold.

There are two different definitions for a business owner under this business owner privilege. First, as discussed in the paragraph above, the privilege exists for the actual owner of the premises. Therefore, if you own the building and surrounding premises where you actively conduct your business, you have the privilege for the building and surrounding premises.

Second, the privilege exists for the person who has legal control of the business. Therefore, if you are leasing the building and premises from a landlord, the privilege exists for you in the building and the premises. For business owners who lease in a community commercial space such as malls, shopping centers and strip centers, the more restrictive rules that apply to the common areas for apartments controls. Therefore, business owners in stores with common areas like shopping centers should assume that their privilege stops at the front door threshold. These business owners should also be aware of lease provisions that may prohibit business owners from having guns on the premises. But while breaking terms or conditions of a lease might bring a breach of contract action against a business owner, the owner is not open to criminal prosecution by the government because of solely breaking the terms or conditions of a lease.

The second definition of business owner allows another possible privilege holder. Dr. Robert Butler, assisted in drafting the business owner privilege legislation. He indicates that the intent of the legislation is to extend the definition of "legal control of a business" to include the on-site manager or supervisor (if the business is owned by a corporation) since corporations are not human and can only act through humans.

The privilege seems to cover only one manager or supervisor at any given time on the premises.

Defining Fixed Place of Business

South Carolina Code Section 16-23-20(13) provides for the foregoing privilege. However, that section also restricts the privilege to fixed places of business. Stores, restaurants, offices, manufacturing plants, malls, gas stations, and shopping centers are fixed places of business. Kiosks in malls are probably fixed if the business generally occupies the kiosk in the same place from day-to-day. Similarly, semi-permanent fruit stands and food huts are probably fixed if the stand generally occupies the same place from day-to-day and leases the land.

It is less likely that a court would find that wheeled businesses like boiled peanut trailers or barbeque smokers are fixed places of business unless they occupy the same place day-after-day. On the other hand, ice cream trucks that move through neighborhoods probably do not pass statutory muster for a fixed place of business. However, the ice cream man inside his truck is still privileged under the exception for vehicles. Although, if he is using the vehicle exception, he needs to have it in the glove box or other encased areas discussed below under the automobile exception. He cannot carry it as if it were a fixed place of business. The ice cream man scenario can be extrapolated for any similar mobile business arrangement that you can think of. Likewise, the semi-permanent fruit stand or food scenarios can be extrapolated for other similar business arrangements. We are not aware of cases determining what is, or is not, a fixed place of business for the purposes of Code Section 16-23-20(13). Therefore, we can only try to envision business arrangements that probably fall on one side or the other. For your practical purposes in trying to obey the law, the more that you attempt to stretch the meaning of "fixed place of business," the more chance you have of ending up a test court case on the subject. You do not want to be a test case under a criminal statute such as section 16-23-20(13) because conviction means jail time, fines, and confiscation of the handgun.

Employees Bringing Handguns to Work

(See the Guns at Work Chart in the Concealed Weapons Permit chapter for an easy reference guide for carry at work questions.)

For employees of a business, other than a manager or supervisor of a corporation discussed above, the rules are different for handguns at work. As described in the CWP chapter, for employees to carry while at work, they must determine whether they can legally carry pursuant to their concealed weapons permit or pursuant to an exception to the general statutory handgun prohibition. In other words, there are two ways for an employee to legally carry at work but the employee must make sure that he or she falls under one of the two statutorily created exceptions.

One way an employee can legally carry at work is by carrying under a concealed weapons permit pursuant to South Carolina Code of Laws Section 16-23-20(12). Under this provision of the concealed weapons permit law, an employee can carry a concealable weapon, concealed or openly, into his work without first obtaining his employer's permission (and even knowledge). This is true even for businesses that sell alcoholic liquors, beer, or wine for onsite consumption so long as the employee has a valid CWP and is carrying under the provisions of the CWP statute. Even if the owner, leaseholder, or business operator has erected a proper NO CONCEALED WEAPONS ALLOWED sign on the premises, the employee can get written permission to ignore the sign from his or her employer. *See* 23-31-215(M)(10).

Another way an employee can carry at work is under the South Carolina Code of Laws Section 16-23-20(13) exception. This is slightly different from the previous exception found in 16-23-20(12) above.

Under this exception, an employee can carry any legal firearm at work, open or concealed, so long as the employee has the permission of the owner or person in legal control ***and*** has a concealed weapons permit. Even under this permissive exception, though, employees of a business that sells alcohol for on-site consumption cannot carry a pistol or firearm while on the business premises. Note that, even though carrying at work under this exception requires the employee to have a CWP, the employee is not carrying pursuant to the permit but pursuant to the statutory exception. Therefore, the employee may carry openly and may carry firearms different from those defined previously in this chapter as "concealable weapons." Further, an employee carrying under this statutory exception may carry at a business that posts the NO CONCEALED WEAPONS ALLOWED sign because the employee has the business owner's (or the person in legal control's) permission.

It is important for an employee to recognize the difference between the legal and business policy rules for guns at work. The above two statutory exceptions are legal rules for carrying a firearm at work. An employee's failure to carry properly pursuant to one of those two exceptions exposes the employee to criminal arrest and prosecution. Alternatively, the employee should also determine if the company has a firearm policy that would prevent him or her from possessing guns at work. If the company has a policy against employees carrying guns at work, the employee could face discipline or be fired regardless of what the statutes say about employees carrying firearms at work.

Handguns at Businesses that Serve Liquor, Beer, and Wine

Regardless of whether a business owner (or the person in legal control of a business as described above) has a permit or not, he or she can carry a handgun, openly or concealed, at his or her place of business. This privilege comes directly from South Carolina Code Section 16-23-20(13) and is not abated by additional language in the section, any other code section, or case law. For more analysis on guns and businesses that serve alcohol, see the concealed weapons permit chapter.

For businesses that sell liquor, beer, or wine for on premises consumption, employees of that business can use the employee privilege of Section 16-23-20(13) and the general CWP privilege given by 16-23-20(12). Remember that Section 16-23-20(13) gives employees the privilege to carry a concealable weapon if they have a concealed weapons permit and the permission of the owner. Again, the rules for carrying guns at work are organized in the "Guns at Work" chart in chapter 5.

Again, the business owner or person in legal control of the business, concealed or not, with or without a permit. The same person can even drink alcohol while possessing the handgun. Further, the owner or person in legal control can lawfully use the handgun while intoxicated if the handgun is used in self-defense as described in the chapter on self-defense. Employees con carry concealed without express permission by the employer under Section 16-23-20(12) or with permission from the employer under Section 16-23-20(13), South Carolina Code of Laws.

South Carolina state, local and reserve law enforcement officers can carry a weapon, concealed or not, onto a business that serves alcohol for consumption on the premises. According to an *Attorney General Opinion dated May 12, 2006*, the officer does not have to be uniformed or furthering his or her official duties. However, federal or out-of-state law enforcement officers must be furthering official duties. Every officer, though, should check with the policy of their department regarding carrying off-duty.

Automobiles and Other Private Conveyances

If you do not have a concealed weapons permit and you are traveling within South Carolina, you can have a handgun in your car or other conveyance under the handgun exception found in Section 16-23-20(9)(a) of the South Carolina Code of Laws. A conveyance is any vehicle used to get you down the road. Traveling in a car or other conveyance from one location in South Carolina to a destination in South Carolina keeps you under the state law that we are discussing here. For traveling between states, we discuss the interstate rules a little later in this chapter.

The basic rule is that you can carry a loaded handgun in your vehicle if it is secured in a closed glove compartment, a closed console, or in the trunk. You may also transport the handgun if it is in a closed container secured by an integral fastener and if that container is in the luggage compartment. It is legal to open the glove compartment, console, or trunk to retrieve a driver's license, registration, or proof of insurance for a law enforcement officer. Again, be very careful if you have a gun in your vehicle and stopped by a law enforcement officer. The first thing that you should do (before reaching for anything) is inform the officer that you have a firearm and tell him or her where it is located. Ask the officer if he or she would like for you to get your license and registration or if the officer would like to retrieve it. Let the officer direct you on how to act.

Vehicle Trunks vs. SUV Luggage Compartments

Many automobiles built today do not have a trunk but, rather, have a luggage compartment towards the rear of the vehicle. For instance, most SUVs have a storage area behind the last row of seats towards the rear of the vehicle. The statutes provide that a handgun may be kept in a vehicle if it is secured in a closed glove compartment, closed console, closed trunk, or in a closed container secured by an integral fastener and transported in the luggage compartment of the vehicle. You might ask, what is the luggage compartment? Thankfully, the statutes answer that question.

Luggage compartment means the trunk of a motor vehicle which has a trunk; however, with respect to a motor vehicle which does not have a trunk, the luggage compartment is the area of the motor vehicle in which the manufacturer designed that luggage be carried or to the area of the motor vehicle in which luggage is customarily carried. In a station wagon, van, hatchback vehicle, or sport utility vehicle, the luggage compartment is the area behind, but not under, the rearmost seat. In a truck, the luggage compartment is the area behind the rearmost seat, but not under the front seat.

If you keep the handgun in the luggage compartment, it must be in a closed container secured by an integral fastener. A closed container is best defined as a relatively strong container that is capable of fully encasing the handgun and closing completely with a handgun inside. Integral fastener is a latch or lock that is designed to be a functioning element of the container and capable of keeping the container closed and the contents inside the container. Think of a closed container with an integral fastener in terms of a commercially available clasping case. The case does not need to be locking in the sense of a padlock or combination lock but, rather, clasping in the sense of gun case latches, fishing tackle box clasps, or an ice cooler snap straps. At the subcommittee hearing where this issue was discussed, it was determined that a zippered gun rug (or nylon case) and a hard plastic gun case with clasps are good examples of qualifying containers. The easiest way to ensure compliance is to buy a commercially available gun container at your local gun store.

Guns on the Seat, Floor, or Door Pocket of a Car

For convenience or whatever reason, some people might be inclined to leave or place a handgun on the seat or the floor of his or her car, boat, or other conveyance. With a CWP, you are given great latitude of where you can store a concealable weapon (i.e. pistol) in your vehicle (or other conveyance). *See* SC Code of Laws Section 16-23-20(9)(a)&(b).

Without a CWP though, except for possibly under the Fishing or Hunting exceptions found in Section 16-23-20(4), it is not lawful in South Carolina to have a handgun under the seat of a vehicle. Also, without a CWP permit, you cannot keep a handgun on the seat or in a door pocket of the vehicle. Without a CWP, you can only have handguns in the closed glove compartment, closed console, or in the trunk (or luggage area of and SUV or pickup) or in a closed container with an integral fastener. See 16-23-20(9)(a). The best way to stay safe from criminal and civil liability is to keep handguns in safe containers like holsters, purses, pockets, cases or glove compartments. Setting the criminal penalty aside, why leave handguns lying around the car anyway? Treat handguns like the deadly weapons that they are and not like a stray bag of cheese doodles.

Traveling Out of South Carolina

Say that you want to travel outside of the State of South Carolina for a family reunion. If your family gatherings are anything like ours, you will want to take your gun to defend your plate of food. Seriously though, gun owners want to bring their gun with them always and traveling is no exception. The problem is that different states have different laws about to guns. Slightly out of character, the Federal Government has provided some gun protection for interstate travelers. 18 USC Section 923(A), also known as the Firearm Owners' Protection Act or "FOPA," provides:

> *Notwithstanding any other provision of any law or any rule or regulation of the State or any political subdivision thereof, any person who is not otherwise prohibited by this chapter from transporting, shipping, or receiving a firearm shall be entitled to transport a firearm for any lawful purpose from any place where he may lawfully possess and carry such firearm to any other place where he may lawfully possess and carry such firearm if, during such transportation the firearm is unloaded, and neither the firearm nor any ammunition being transported is readily*

> *accessible or is directly accessible from the passenger compartment of such transporting vehicle: provided, that in the case of a vehicle without a compartment separate from the driver's compartment the firearm or ammunition shall be contained in a locked container other than the glove compartment or console.*

Does the Federal FOPA Protect You?

So, FOPA sounds pretty good, but before you throw the gun into the car and take off, consider the limitations of this law. First, you must be a person who is not otherwise prohibited from transporting, shipping, or receiving a firearm. In other words, that you are not prohibited from possessing a firearm. We help you determine whether you are prohibited from possessing a firearm in several other parts of this book so we will not revisit any of those analyses here.

If you are not prohibited from possessing a firearm, you move on to the next phase of analysis. You must determine if it is legal for you to both possess AND carry the firearm in both the departure state AND the destination state. To simplify this analysis, you can focus on the carry portion of the analysis. This is true because, to carry a gun, you must also possess the gun. This means there is no instance where you could carry a gun without possessing it. Therefore, if it is legal to carry it, then it is also legal to possess it.

Be extra careful though, of relying upon FOPA when inside jurisdictions that historically have less regard for citizens exercising their natural right to keep and bear arms. Even though you are "legal" and covered by FOPA, some draconian jurisdictions have arrested firearms possessors none-the-less. If possible, avoid traveling through large Northeastern or west coast jurisdictions with firearms anywhere in your vehicle or on your person.

Carrying Pursuant to a CWP and Reciprocity

Before going further, now is a good time to discuss another benefit of getting your concealed weapons permit (CWP). You do not have to worry about the rules of the FOPA if you have a South Carolina CWP and you are in a state with reciprocity. If you have your CWP and are in a state that has reciprocity with South Carolina, you can carry your gun concealed so long as you carry under the rules of that state's CWP law. If you are traveling through several states, all of which have reciprocity with South Carolina, you do not have to mind the provisions of the FOPA because you will be carrying pursuant to your permit. However, you must know and follow the rules for concealed carry in each individual state. In general, most states have minor differences in concealed weapons permit rules but you are responsible for the difference none-the-less. To understand the differences in reciprocity states, check each state's website or law enforcement agency.

Interstate Travel Scenarios Under the FOPA

To help you understand how to best travel interstate under the FOPA, it is helpful to discuss scenarios that you might encounter. An easily understood scenario is one in which you have a South Carolina CWP and you are traveling from a point of origin in South Carolina, though one or more reciprocity states and ultimately to a state that has reciprocity with South Carolina. As discussed in the previous section, it is legal for you to possess and carry the gun in your departure state (South Carolina) and it is legal for you to possess and carry the gun in accordance with each state's CWP rules in each state that you travel through and in the destination state. You do not have to mind the FOPA rules under this scenario, only the rules for carry under a CWP for each state that you are in. Alternatively, you can choose not to carry under the CWP rules but, rather, follow the FOPA rules. The advantage of traveling this way is that you only need to know how to travel pursuant to the FOPA and you are not required to know the CWP carry rules for each state of travel. The disadvantage is that you will probably not be able to have your firearm on or about your person during travel and possibly when you get to your destination state.

Another easily understood scenario would be where you are not allowed to possess and carry a firearm at all in either the state of origin or the destination state. If it is unlawful for you to possess and carry the gun in both the departure state and the destination state, you cannot transport firearms under the FOPA.

A slightly more complicated scenario would be that you have a South Carolina CWP and are traveling to a destination state that has reciprocity with South Carolina. However, you are also traveling through one or more states that do not have reciprocity with South Carolina. Under this scenario, you are only allowed to carry under your CWP in the reciprocity states but must travel under the rules of the FOPA in the non-reciprocity states.

Scenarios other than those described above are less clear-cut and place you in a legal grey area. Questions arise if you are legal to carry the gun under limited circumstances in either the departure state or the destination state. Typical examples are that many states allow you to carry a gun if you are hunting, fishing, or going to a shooting range or other lawful shooting function. If you are not going to one of these activities in the destination state, this can make the FOPA inapplicable. Further complicating the analysis is the fact that generally, this federal law will be interpreted by a state court. The way that the FOPA normally comes up is where someone is traveling and gets stopped by a member of the state or local police force. The person is charged on state gun violations and gets tried in a state court. Because of our judicial structure under Federalism, unless the United States Supreme Court steps in, the provisions of FOPA will be decided by state courts. State courts may view some of the nuances of FOPA differently. Therefore, the following information can be used to make the best choice on whether you can transport your gun and, if so, under what circumstances.

To illustrate the difficulty of determining what a court will decide when it comes to state guns laws and FOPA, let us look at a case out of the State of New York. Beach v. Kelly involves the interpretation of FOPA by a New York state court. This case involves a citizen of New York (Beach) who worked in private security and obtained a license which is known as a *Premises Resident Pistol License*. This is a restricted license that applies only to a specific location. It also allows the person to transport the pistol so long as it is unloaded, secured in a locked container, and transported only to and from authorized small arms ranges and shooting clubs. (This same freedom to exercise the natural right to keep and bear arms exists in many states without any licenses at all.) Through an unrelated investigation, the licensing body in New York learned that Mr. Beach transported his gun to the State of Nevada for a security officer convention. New York used Beach's action as a basis to revoke his Premises Resident Pistol License.

Mr. Beach appealed the decision to a New York court and initially won. The trial court found that the word *carry* as used in the FOPA should not be construed so narrowly as to undercut the Act's basic objective. The court was following the guidance provided by the U.S. Supreme Court case Muscarello v. United States. The trial court further noted that in City of Camden v. Beretta, the US Supreme Court determined that the basic objective of the FOPA was to allow law abiding citizens the right to transport their firearms in a safe manner during interstate travel.

Unfortunately for Mr. Beach, the decision of the trial court was overturned on appeal. The New York Supreme Court determined that Mr. Beach's license allowed him to carry the firearm on the specific premises listed in the license. The Court found that the license only allowed Mr. Beach to carry the firearm away from that location if he was going to a small arms range or shooting club or hunting area. The New York Supreme Court determined that, since Mr. Beach was not taking the gun to a small-arms shooting range, shooting club, or hunting area, it was not legal for him to leave the premises with the gun. Further, since it was not legal for him to leave the premises with the gun, under the circumstances at the time he left the premises, the FOPA did not apply.

While that is a lot to digest, the main point is that you should be careful if you plan to travel interstate under the FOPA. There are technical requirements to be protected by the act and state courts sometimes stretch the act's plain meaning. However, the following section should give you enough information to analyze your travels and determine if the act will protect you.

Defining Destination States

For the Act to apply, you cannot be prohibited from possessing and carrying the gun in the destination state. More accurately, you must not be prohibited from possessing and carrying a firearm in *every* destination states. Yes, you can have more than one destination state. So, what is a destination state?

The answer is easy to determine if you drive non-stop from your state of origin to your destination state, stay in the destination state for a week and then drive non-stop back to your origin state. In that scenario, your destination states are clearly defined. It becomes less clear if you make any legally significant stops in any of the states between those states. Courts have determined that stopping for gas and food in a non-destination state does not create a sufficient intent to make that state a destination state. Likewise, courts have determined that renting a motel for the night in a non-destination state is not evidence of intent to make that state a destination state. However, if you stop and visit a theme park in what you consider a non-destination state, courts are likely consider that stop sufficient evidence of an intent to make that a destination state. Similarly, meeting a client or doing any business in a state will almost certainly be sufficient evidence of intent to make that state a destination state for purposes of the FOPA.

Rules for Transporting Interstate under the FOPA

Once you have determined each destination state and that you are not prohibited from possessing and carrying in that state, you can then legally transport firearms under the FOPA. To be protected by the act, you must transport firearms unloaded AND both the firearms and any ammunition must not be readily accessible from the passenger compartment. In plain English, you should keep the unloaded firearms and ammunition in the trunk. If the vehicle does not have a trunk, the unloaded firearms and ammunition should be kept separate in locked containers in a place *other than* the glove compartment or console.

Also, it must be legal for you to possess and carry the gun in your *destination* state. Notice that it must be legal for you to possess a gun in the state you are going to and not just South Carolina. Again, the gun must be unloaded and both the gun and the ammo must be stored in such a way that they are not directly or readily accessible. In other words, the gun should be unloaded and carried in your trunk. If your vehicle does not have a trunk, and no other section that is separate from the passenger compartment, it must be stored in a locked container but not the glove box or the console. Locked here does not mean padlocked or combination locked but rather that the integral locking mechanism is closed. Again, a better word to describe a locked integral locking mechanism might be *latched*.

Federal law allows you to transport your gun *through* whichever states in the United States that you want. As you travel through each state, you are free to carry your weapon to the extent that state permits. For example, if you are traveling through a state with the same possession laws as South Carolina, you can take your gun out of the trunk and put it into your glove box or console. When you get to the next state line, you must reevaluate where you are permitted to keep the gun.

Motorcycles

Without a permit, the most important thing to remember about motorcycles is that the handgun must be secured inside of a compartment. Under Section 16-23-20(16) of the South Carolina Code of Laws, you can legally carry a handgun inside a saddlebag, side compartment, or rear compartment so long as the compartment can be securely closed.

Private Boats

The best way to possess or carry a firearm on a boat is by using the hunting and fishing exception found in Section 16-23-20(4) of the South Carolina Code of Laws. That section provides an exception for "licensed hunters or fishermen who are engaged in hunting or fishing or going to or from their places of hunting or fishing while in a vehicle or on foot." Therefore, you can possess or carry a handgun, whether openly or concealed, so long as you have a fishing license and are fishing or going to or from a place of fishing. If you want to carry or possess under this exception while going to or from a place of fishing, make sure that you are going *directly* to or from the place of fishing. Remember that this exception applies to and from a place where it is legal to possess or carry a handgun (such as your home or vehicle) to the place of fishing. This exception only applies if the person possessing or carrying the handgun has a valid hunting or fishing license AND is engaged in hunting or fishing at the time of possessing or carrying the handgun. The Section 16-23-20(4) exception is applicable to all rivers, lakes, ponds and water bodies that you will encounter in or abutting South Carolina lands.

While the authors have not been able to find a definitive legal authority on this, the best practice is to assume that South Carolina law applies at least three (3) miles out into the Atlantic. After that, you are in international waters and there are no gun restrictions against most common semi-automatic rifles, pistols, and revolvers. Be careful, though, if you plan to arrive at a foreign nation like Bermuda or the Bahamas with your vessel. Once you get into their waters, you are under their laws. Also, make sure your guns are legal before you come back into the waters of the state of South Carolina. A detailed discussion of firearms on the seas is beyond the scope of this book so you are advised to look for more resources if you plan to be on the seas with a firearm.

Aircraft and Airports

Your ability to carry a firearm onto an aircraft depends upon variables such as your destination, whether the flight is private or commercial, the place in which you must embark and disembark the aircraft, the manner you carry the firearm, and whether you have a CWP. We will first look at how you intend to carry the firearm. Remember that this discussion assumes that you are otherwise lawfully entitled to possess a firearm. Also, remember that the regulations that we discuss here originate in federal law so violations are federal offenses.

We can start by determining whether you plan to be in the sterile area or only in non-sterile areas of the airports. Several different federal statutes and regulations apply to transportation of firearms on aircraft, depending upon the type of aircraft and aircraft operation and where you board the aircraft.

The so-called *sterile area* of an airport is defined in 49 Code of Federal Regulations (CFR) 1540.5 as *a portion of an airport defined in the airport security program that provides passengers access to boarding aircraft and to which the access generally is controlled by TSA, or by an aircraft operator under part 1544 of this chapter or a foreign air carrier under part 1546 of this chapter, through the screening of persons and property.* So, the sterile areas are those places beginning at the entrance to the security checkpoints and up to, and including, the gates to the aircraft. The sterile area is easy to recognize because you first must subject yourself and your carry-on luggage to search and inspection before entering.

Upon entering the sterile area, you are subject to the prohibitions of 49 CFR 1540.111. This section prohibits carrying weapons on your person or in carry-on luggage or otherwise accessible. The section also prohibits weapons on board the aircraft that you board from a sterile area.

The section does provide a general exception for law enforcement officers that are required to carry firearms or other weapons while in the performance of law enforcement duties at the airport and virtually all other sworn law enforcement officers (49 CFR 1540.111(b)(1) and 1544.219). Other specific exceptions include law enforcement officers accompanying prisoners (49 CFR 1544.221), air marshals (49 CFR 1544.223), and employees of qualified private security service companies. Additional information regarding these exceptions is beyond the scope of this book so it is important for those seeking to carry under these exceptions to find materials that thoroughly discuss these sections of the CFR and federal statutes.

When it comes time to board an aircraft after leaving the sterile area, it does not matter whether the aircraft that you board is a commercial, charter, freight, or private aircraft as a result of the broad prohibition from carrying a weapon onto the plane found in 49 CFR 1550.5. So, even if you are boarding a friend's private Cessna and you have the pilot's permission, it is unlawful for you to carry a firearm onto the plane if you enter through the sterile area.

Just because you cannot carry any weapon on your person or in your carry-on luggage, you still can take your firearm on your travels if it is otherwise legal to do so. Section 49 CFR 1540.111(c) permits passengers to pack firearms into checked luggage. You must first unload the firearm and declare the firearm to the airline or aircraft operator. You must keep the firearm locked in a hard-sided container and you must be the only person with the key or combination while in the sterile area or on the plane.

You can carry ammunition in checked-in luggage inside the locked hard-sided container with the firearm or on its own 49 CFR 1540.111(d). More specific information regarding carrying ammunition is contained in 49 CFR 175.10(a)(8). That section provides that ammunition must be securely packaged in boxes or other packages specifically designed to carry small amounts of ammunition and that ammunition clips and magazines must also be securely boxed. If you are flying a commercial airline or charter, you should check with that individual operator to get information about possible additional policies regarding firearms and ammunition.

Under Section 49 CFR 175.10(a)(9), you can carry mace or similar pepper spray onto commercial aircraft but you can only have one container and the container cannot hold more than 4 fluid ounces in volume. Further, the container must have a positive means to prevent accidental discharge and must be checked-in so that the aircraft operator can store the container in the luggage area of the aircraft.

A detailed discussion of the penalties for violations of these regulations is beyond the scope of this book. However, 49 USC §46505 makes it a crime, subject to fine and jail time for not more than 10 years, or both, when an individual on, or attempting to get on, an aircraft in, or intended for operation in, air transportation or intrastate air transportation, has on or about him a concealed dangerous weapon that is or would be accessible in flight. Additionally, 49 USC §46303 provides for a civil penalty of $10,000 for having a concealed dangerous weapon that is or would be accessible to the individual in flight.

Carrying a firearm in the non-sterile areas is less burdened with federal regulations than in sterile areas but there are some significant rules that you are required to follow under federal law. In the non-sterile areas, your ability to possess a firearm will depend upon factors like way you are carrying the firearm, the size of the aircraft, your destination, and whether the flight is commercial or private. As before, you must be otherwise carrying lawfully under South Carolina law as explained in other sections of this book.

While 49 USC §46505 above seems to criminalize firearms on virtually all aircraft, the definitions of *air transportation* and *intrastate air transportation* found in 49 USC §40102 limit the applicability of the statute to *commercial air carriers*. Air carriers are defined as individuals or businesses that provide transportation for hire either between 2 states or within 1 state using a turbojet aircraft with more than 30 seats. So, for the most part, these definitions limit the applicability of this statute to the airlines and charter businesses that are conducting flights between states or flying with 31 seat and larger turbojet aircraft.

In concert with 49 USC §46505, 49 CFR 1550.7 provides a blanket prohibition of firearms (except for the previously discussed exceptions) on aircraft weighing more than 12,500 pounds and where the aircraft's operation is not otherwise subject to the statutes and regulations addressed above. Under this regulation, the aircraft operator must conduct a search of the aircraft before departure and screen all passengers, crewmembers, and other persons and their carry-on items before boarding regardless of whether boarding and loading occurs from a sterile area.

Under 14 CFR 135.119, charter flights have specific firearms restrictions. Under this regulation, you may not, while on board an aircraft being operated by a [charter flight] certificate holder, carry on or about you a deadly or dangerous weapon, either concealed or not concealed. This section does not apply to many law enforcement officers or to crew members who have their company's permission to carry firearms. So, while this regulation appears to limit the possession of firearms, if the charter operator grants you permission, either directly or through their general policy, you are excepted from the regulation and able to carry firearms onboard.

You are under no federal regulations if you are flying in a private aircraft not being operated by a common carrier within South Carolina. If you are flying between South Carolina and another state, you are subject to 18 USC §926(A) just as if you were driving or otherwise traveling interstate. For a more detailed description of interstate travel under 18 USC §926, see the *Traveling Out of South Carolina* section earlier in this chapter.

Public Transportation

If you have your Concealed Weapons Permit, you can carry in accordance with the CWP Statute. However, if you do not have a CWP, the rules are different for you. You are prohibited from carrying a concealable weapon, concealed (see definition in the Concealed Weapons Permit Chapter) in public. Therefore, you cannot carry a handgun either on your person or in your bags if using public transportation.

Rifles, shotguns, and other weapons are different. For those, you can treat public transportation just like any other place in public because there is no South Carolina Code of Laws specific to public transportation.

If you are traveling to another state, federal rules apply and you need to have the weapon unloaded and in a locked container. You must also declare the weapon to the carrier company and deliver it to the possession of the carrier for transportation. You must also comply with the FOPA law discussed earlier in this Chapter.

The Rules for Schools

In the past, it was virtually impossible to be on any school premises with a firearm. Parents dropping-off kids for school, students at colleges, teachers going to work, and anybody else required to be on school property had a problem. The problem was that the South Carolina Code of Laws made it illegal to have a firearm on any grounds owned, operated or controlled by a school. There was an exception if you had permission from the authorities in charge of the premises or property but getting that permission was rare. So, for instance, while parents might have otherwise been legal possessing a firearm (either on his or her person with a CWP or in the glove compartment or console) while driving the children to school, the same firearm became illegal once the parent drove onto school premises. Further complicating the process was that it is often difficult to determine where school premises begin and end. This situation left the parents in the unfortunate position of having to choose between breaking the law by entering school property with a firearm or leaving the firearm at home. Similarly, teachers and college students who could otherwise lawfully carry a firearm off campus were required to forfeit their right to keep and bear arms the instant that they crossed onto school premises.

The legislature amended South Carolina criminal law to provide an exception to the prohibition against certain weapons on school grounds under certain circumstances. Specifically, it amended Sections 16-23-420 and 16-23-430. Firearms on school grounds were decriminalized if the possessor satisfies two conditions:

1. have a valid Concealed Weapons Permit (CWP); <u>**AND**</u>,

2. the firearm is kept in:

a. a closed glove compartment;
b. console; or,
c. trunk or in the luggage area of the vehicle so long as the firearm is inside of a closed container that has an integral fastener. Also, the vehicle must be attended or locked.

Following, let's look at each element of the law as well as potential questions and problems that may arise.

Weapons on School Premises

Section 16-23-430 prohibits "***weapons***" on ***elementary*** and ***secondary*** school premises (elementary, middle, and high schools). The section specifically defines a firearm as a weapon. Violations are a felony carrying a potential penalty of $1,000 fine and five (5) years in jail, or both, as well as confiscation of the weapon and a lifetime federal firearms disability. However, the section provides an exception for CWP holders:

> *(B) This section does not apply to a person who is authorized to carry a concealed weapon pursuant to Article 4, Chapter 31, Title 23 when the weapon remains inside an attended or locked motor vehicle and is secured in a closed glove compartment, closed console, closed trunk, or in a closed container secured by an integral fastener and transported in the luggage compartment of the vehicle.*

Likewise, Section 16-23-420 provides:

> *The provisions of this subsection related to any premises or property owned, operated, or controlled by a private or public school, college, university, technical college, or other post-secondary institution,* ***do not apply*** *to a person who is authorized to carry a concealed weapon pursuant to Article 4, Chapter 31, Title 23 when the weapon remains inside an attended or locked motor vehicle and is secured in a*

> *closed glove compartment, closed console, closed trunk, or in a closed container secured by an integral fastener and transported in the luggage compartment of the vehicle.*

For the most part, these sections eliminate criminal liability for CWP holders possessing a weapon on elementary through high schools, as well as colleges, so long as the weapon remains inside a closed glove compartment, closed console, closed trunk (or in the luggage area as long as the weapon is in a closed container secured by an integral fastener) and the vehicle itself is locked or attended. However, there are important distinctions that you need to be aware of. Further, there are other laws that apply to firearms on school grounds.

South Carolina Issued CWP vs. Out-of-State CWP

To be able to bring a firearm onto school premises under those conditions, you must have a valid ***South Carolina issued*** CWP. If you do not have a South Carolina issued CWP (either resident or qualified non-resident), this new law does not apply to you. If you do not have any CWP, you are still prohibited from bringing a firearm of any kind onto school premises (S.C. Code of Laws Section 16-23-420 (A)) (unless you fall under an exemption like police officers or you have permission from the authorities in charge of the school).

If these Sections were to stand alone, a person with an out-of-state CWP asserting reciprocity would benefit the same as would someone with a South Carolina issued CWP. But, these sections do not stand alone. Out-of-state CWP holders are burdened by the federal Gun Free School Zones Act.

Gun Free Schools Act of 1996

Under the federal Gun Free Schools Act of 1996, Without a South Carolina issued CWP, you are prohibited from knowingly possessing a firearm in a "school zone" (basically within 1,000 feet of an elementary, middle, or high school with some exceptions). The Gun Free Schools Act is interpreted by the Bureau of Alcohol Tobacco and Firearms to require that the individual carrying the firearm must have a CWP ***issued by the state that the school is in.*** This distinction is important because there are many instances where out of state parents might have to travel to a South Carolina school for student competitions or events. To insure compliance with the Gun Free Schools Act, holders of out-of-state CWPs (with S.C. reciprocity) should park off elementary, middle, or high school premises with any firearms stored in the closed glove box, closed console, closed trunk, or in a closed container with an integral fastener in the luggage area of the vehicle.

Before we move on, let me mention that you should consider the federal Gun Free School Zone Act to also within 1,000 feet of an **off-site event** sponsored by one of these schools. The act defines a *school zone* as:

> *[I]n, or on the grounds of, a public, parochial or private school; or within a distance of 1,000 feet from the grounds of a public, parochial or private school (18 U.S.C. 921(a)(25)).*

The Act goes on to define a *school* as:

> *[A] school which provides elementary or secondary education, as determined under* ***State law*** *(18 U.S.C. 921(a)(26)).*

So, to fully define school under the act, we must look at South Carolina law. With respect to firearms, the South Carolina Code of Laws defines *schools* as:

> *[P]roperty owned, operated or controlled by a public or private school (S.C. Code of laws 16-23-420(a)).*

Therefore, you should consider the federal Gun Free School Zones Act not only applicable to within 1,000 feet of all public and private schools but also within 1,000 feet of all premises where any school sponsored or controlled activity is occurring. If this law seems burdensome, it is, and it should be struck down for several reasons. However, at this point, it is the law and you can incur criminal liability if you are found in violation of it.

Possessing at Schools with a South Carolina Issued CWP

If you have a valid South Carolina CWP, the new law provides an exception to the prohibition against firearms on all school premises or areas controlled by schools without getting special permission from the authorities in control of the school. The firearm can be loaded and chambered. Again, to fall within the exception, the CWP holder must have the firearm in a closed glove box or console, closed trunk, or in the luggage area of vehicle so long as the firearm is in a closed container with an integral fastener.

Brief Definitions for School Terms

We go into further detail explaining the terms as this chapter goes on. For convenience though, we give brief definitions here:

Schools – Public and private preschools through Colleges including technical schools.

School Premises – Inside the real estate boundaries of the school property and any other premises that the school is controlling (i.e. off campus ball games or competitions).

Console – There exists reasonable debate amongst gun owners as to the definition of *console*. There is no case defining console so I can only give my reasoned opinion. A factory installed console between the front seats is clearly a console. Aftermarket consoles that attach to the floor between the front seats or the front seat itself might likely be ruled a console also. It is also reasonable to think that consoles between the rear seats would be included in the definition but you can't be sure. However, the more that the console gets away from a factory installed or permanently attached aftermarket console between the two front seats, the more wiggle-room a court must find that the console is not a console under the Section.

Luggage Area - The luggage area of a vehicle is that area designed for storage of luggage. In a typical SUV, the luggage area is behind the last row of seats.

Closed Container - A container that is capable of fully closing so that items inside the container cannot be seen (i.e. a gun case, tackle box, or gun rug).

Integral Fastener - A device, designed as part of the container, that is capable of positively keeping the container closed (i.e. a metal or plastic clasp on a gun case or tackle box or the zipper on a gun rug).

The above definitions are important because, even though CWP holders will now be legal carrying onto school premises and events, the CWP holder cannot carry as typically allowed under the permit. The CWP generally allows the holder to carry a handgun in a concealed holster on the person, in a pocket, around an ankle, or in a purse or briefcase. For schools though, the CWP holder cannot carry a concealable weapon, concealed on school premises. Alternatively, the CWP holder can only possess a firearm on school premises if the firearm is in the vehicle's closed glove box, closed console or closed trunk or in the luggage area in a closed container with an integral fastener. So, if the CWP chooses to carry his or her concealable weapon, concealed, on or about his person on the way to a school, the CWP holder must remove the handgun from its concealed location and place it into one of the listed areas of the vehicle ***before*** entering the school premises or event. While it seems illogical to move a safely holstered firearm to one of the areas of the vehicle listed, that is the law and a violation will subject you to criminal prosecution. (We will discuss the legality of transitioning from concealed carry to one of the vehicle areas later in this section.)

Another requirement is that the vehicle must be locked or attended. So, if you simply drop children off at school, you remain in the vehicle and the vehicle remains attended. Also, if you stand alongside of your vehicle or nearby the vehicle, you could probably successfully argue that the vehicle is attended under the meaning of the law. If, however, you leave the car in the school parking lot and walk the child to the first class or assembly, you must lock the vehicle before leaving it in the parking lot. Since there is no court case defining the term "attended vehicle" under this section, the best practice is to lock your vehicle if you are not in it or standing very nearby to it.

The South Carolina CWP holder should pay special mind to the concepts of *attended vehicle* and *person in possession* of the firearm if leaving the vehicle on school premises. For instance, what if the husband has a South Carolina issued CWP and leaves his handgun in the glove box to walk his child to first period class after locking the vehicle. In that instance, he complies because the firearm is in a legal place and the vehicle is locked when he walks away. However, say that wife is also in the vehicle on the school premises but she does not have a South Carolina issued CWP. The firearm is now in the possession of the wife who does not have a South Carolina issued CWP so she is not legal. But, what if the husband locked his wife in the car before leaving the car? Has the husband complied with the law because he left the firearm in a legal place in the locked vehicle? This issue might eventually require court interpretation or a modification of the law. For now, the best practice is to ensure that anyone left in the vehicle with a firearm has a valid South Carolina issued CWP.

Once the South Carolina issued CWP holder is off the school or school event premises, the weapon can be retrieved from its storage in the vehicle and returned to the place of concealment on or about the person. Or, if the CWP holder wants to leave the handgun in the glove box, console, trunk, or luggage area, he or she can because those areas fall within an existing exception to the general prohibition against handguns (Section 16-23-20(9)(a)).

Transitioning from concealed carry to one of the vehicle areas is protected by a different section of the Code. South Carolina Code of Law Section 16-23-20(12) makes it legal for a CWP holder to transition between his person and a closed glove compartment, console, or trunk or in a closed container with an integral fastener in the glove compartment. Notice the Section says ***between*** the CWP holder's person and those specified areas of the vehicle so it is legal to transition both to and from concealment on your person.

Employer Liability vs. Criminal Liability for School Staff

Teachers, administrators, professors, and staff with CWPs can keep firearms in their attended or locked vehicles, in the specified areas of the vehicle on school premises, without criminal liability. Undoubtedly, some authorities in charge of the school or school premises might try to institute a policy of "no guns on the premises" as a condition of employment. This issue has already been addressed in a South Carolina Attorney General's Opinion dated March 1, 2000. The Attorney General concluded that a Department of Corrections policy could not prohibit that which state law allows. Therefore, the Department of Corrections could not prevent employees from having guns in their vehicles. Before going on, it is important to note that the Attorney General Opinion is applicable to ***state-run*** school facilities and possibly not private facilities.

In his opinion, the Attorney General discussed a Department of Corrections policy that prohibited employees, including guards, from having a firearm in their vehicles. The policy provides that any employee violating the rule would be fired. Citing case law from as far back as 1928, the Attorney General opined the long-established precedent that a state agency is powerless to prohibit that which the State authorizes, directs, requires, licenses, or expressly permits. He then went on to note that, because the General Assembly specifically granted, through Section 16-23-20, the right to carry a firearm in the closed glove compartment, closed console, or closed trunk of an automobile, the Department of Correction's prohibition against an employee's having a weapon in his locked motor vehicle would be without authority and inconsistent with state law. Sections 16-23-420 and 430 expressly permit a CWP holder to have firearms on school premises in his vehicle in the specified vehicle areas and either attended or locked. So, CWP holders are not prohibited for having a firearm in the vehicle despite any state-run school's policy against firearms on school premises.

Private schools and colleges are not agencies of the state so the same analysis above cannot be strictly applied to those institutions. Private schools are private organizations operating on private property and are not state agencies. So, teachers, staff and administrators might face employment sanctions if the institution has a policy against employees having firearms on the premises. Likewise, visitors and students of private universities are subject to the rules and regulations of each private institution. While violators of such institutional policies would not face criminal liability, they are none-the-less subject to any penalties applicable for rule violations.

Students on College Campus

Some students can possess firearms on campus without any special permission. The first thing that a student must do is determine whether it is legal for him or her to possess a firearm in general. Under South Carolina law, with some exceptions, the minimum age for possessing a handgun is 18 years of age. Remember, though, that a campus possessor must have a valid South Carolina CWP (or reciprocity from another state pursuant to the federal Gun Free School Zones Act). The minimum age to get a South Carolina CWP is 21 years of age.

States other than South Carolina might issue CWPs to persons under age 21 (18 to 20-year-olds). If the student is relying upon a CWP from a reciprocal state, the student should be aware that South Carolina Code of Laws Section 23-31-215(N) requires a CWP holder from a reciprocal state to abide by South Carolina law. An 18-year-old can possess a handgun in South Carolina but cannot get a South Carolina CWP until he or she is 21 years old. Thus, it appears that an 18 to 20-year-old CWP holder from a reciprocal state would **not** be legal. However, this issue has not been determined by a court. To ensure compliance with the law, holders of out-of-state CWPs, relying upon reciprocity, must be 21 years of age when bringing handguns onto campus.

If the student has a CWP, the student must remember to leave the handgun in an attended or locked vehicle in the specified areas as discussed previously. Again, the federal Gun Free School Zones Act is not applicable to colleges, community colleges, technical schools or any similar educational institution that is not an elementary or secondary school.

Private College vs. State College

As a final note, students should be aware of differences between public and private universities. As stated earlier in the section regarding employee liability, private universities and colleges are not agencies of the state. Private universities and colleges are private organizations operating on private property and are not state agencies. However, they remain schools and so the student must consider these criminal laws. Additionally, students and visitors on private university premises might face non-criminal sanctions if the institution has a policy against having firearms on the premises. So long as a person follows the rules for schools in general, however, a "no weapons on school property sign" only creates a possible trespass charge but no criminal firearm infraction. Remember to that even outdoor "No Concealable Weapons" signs must be the statutory size to create legal notice. *See* the Concealed Weapons Permit chapter.

Rifle or Shotgun on School Premises

Some have suggested that the language of the Code allows CWP holders to have not only concealable weapons (most handguns) in vehicles on school grounds, but ***any*** type of weapon. This interpretation is based upon language in Section 16-23-430 never referring to "firearms" or 'handguns" but only **weapons**. Under this interpretation, a CWP holder is allowed to have any type of weapon on school grounds so long as it is stored in a closed glove compartment, console, or trunk, or in the luggage area in a closed container with an integral fastener.

The benefit under this interpretation is that weapons larger than those that qualify as *concealable weapons* under the CWP Section would qualify as weapons. The CWP Section defines concealable weapons as *a firearm having a length of less than twelve inches measured along its greatest dimension*. Because legal rifles must have a barrel length of at least 16 inches and shotguns must have a barrel length of 18 inches, rifles and shotguns do not fall within the definition of a concealable weapon. So, if the new law is interpreted to mean *weapons* and not *concealable weapons*, CWP holders would not be prevented from having rifles and shotguns so long as they are stored in the allowed areas of an attended or occupied vehicle. Obviously most glove compartments and consoles are not able to contain a rifle or shot gun, however, most trunks and luggage areas are.

There are not yet any court cases interpreting the meaning of weapon under this new law. If a CWP holder chooses to carry a rifle or shotgun under this interpretation and is later arrested for possession of firearms on school grounds, that individual might well be the "test case" for the issue. Because the new law specifically cites carrying pursuant to the CWP Section, the most conservative way to approach interpreting *weapon* is to define it the same way the CWP does. To carry a weapon pursuant to the CWP Section, the weapon must be a concealable weapon. Therefore, the best practice is to only store concealable weapons in the allowed areas of attended or locked vehicles. In general, concealable weapons are handguns less than 12 inches long.

Note: if you want to keep a long gun on campus for hunting or target practice, several colleges are known to provide gun lockers at the campus police station. Ask your campus police department before bringing a firearm on campus if you want to use this option.

Motorcycles on School Premises

Section 16-23-20 of the S.C. Code of Laws spells out the general handgun prohibition and the exceptions. That Section of the Code of Laws differentiates motorcycles from vehicles. Subsection (9)(a) provides the exact language upon which the new law (S. 593) gets its language (i.e. [there is an exception to the handgun prohibition if] the person has the handgun *in a vehicle* and the handgun is in the closed glove compartment, console, etc.) Later Section 16-23-20, Subsection (16) grants a separate and distinct exception for a person *on a motorcycle* if the firearm is secured in a saddlebag. So, it can safely be said that the legislative intent of Section 16-23-20 is to view vehicles separately from motorcycles. It is also significant that the Subsections refer to an exception of the person is ***in*** a vehicle or ***on*** a motorcycle.

So, when we you think about guns on campus, you should assume that the legislature had the same intent. Sections 16-23-420 and 430 track the language of 16-23-20(9)(a) which provides for an exception if the gun is ***in*** *the vehicle* in one of the legal areas. The new law makes no provision for a person ***on*** *a motorcycle*. You should assume that if the legislature wanted to include an exception for motorcycles, it would have included an exception for them as it has in section 16-23-20. Therefore, the best practice is to not assume that the campus exception applies to motorcycles.

School Premises without a CWP

If you don't have a CWP do not carry a handgun, or any firearm, onto a school, college, or university campus. South Carolina Code of Laws Sections 16-23-420 generally prohibits firearms on school grounds and events. All levels of schools from kindergarten to universities are included in that section's prohibition. Further, all areas of the school, not only inside the buildings, are no gun zones. Be aware that the prohibition is for private schools as well as public schools and even extends to preschools. If a facility resembles an institution for teaching and learning, treat it like it is a school and do not bring a firearm with you unless you have the correct permission (discussed later).

Criminal Penalties for Guns on School Grounds

The prohibition against guns at schools found in South Carolina Code of Laws Sections 16-23-420 and 16-23-430 are virtually identical yet are two separate offenses. Section 16-23-430 is somewhat broader in that it prohibits all weapons which may be used to cause bodily injury or death (guns certainly) but narrower in that it only applies to elementary and secondary (middle and high) school grounds. Therefore, if you bring a gun onto elementary or secondary school grounds, and you do not fall within one of the exceptions, you can be charged under **BOTH** Section 16-23-420 and 16-23-430. A violation of Section 16-23-420 is a felony with the penalty of a fine of not more than $5,000 or imprisonment of not more than 5 years, or both. A violation of Section 16-23-430 is a felony with the penalty of a fine of not more than $1,000 or imprisonment of not more than 5 years, or both. Under Section 16-23-430, the arresting agency can confiscate the gun. A conviction under either of these sections subjects you to a lifetime federal firearms disability. If the gun is concealed you can tack on a Section 16-23-460 violation that is a misdemeanor with the penalty of a $200-$500 fine or a jail term of 30-90 days and a mandatory forfeiture of the gun to the government. Section 16-23-420 is explained in greater detail below in the *No Deadly Weapons on Elementary and Secondary School Grounds* section later in this chapter.

Be cautioned that this prohibition extends to ***any*** properties owned by the school or university, too. So, if a tract of land somewhere in the boonies is donated or willed to a college, innocent hunters or explorers that may traipse across the land are committing a felony. There is no requirement that the person with the firearm know the unimproved land he is on is owned by a school.

Off Campus Events

You are also prohibited from possessing a firearm at off-campus events sponsored by the school. Therefore, firearms are prohibited at school sponsored ball games, exhibitions, events, and programs. The prohibition applies even if the school does not own or lease the property on which the event is taking place. A school could be holding games on a privately-owned field and you are prohibited from possessing a firearm at the event or in the parking area of the event. What you must keep in mind is, if the event that you are going to is a school sponsored event, without a concealed weapons permit, you cannot bring a firearm on your person or in your vehicle. If you do have a CWP, you can follow the CWP rules for schools discussed previously in this chapter.

Driving Through a Campus Without a CWP

Even without a CWP, you are entitled to transport or possess firearms and any other legal weapons on major state, county or city streets through or adjacent to school properties and events. Be aware though that, as soon as you pass over from the major street into a school road or parking lot, the rules for schools apply.

Section 16-23-420(E) indicates that the road must be open "full-time" to public vehicular traffic. So, a road that is not open to public vehicular traffic 24 hours a day is technically off-limits to firearms possession or carry.

Be careful about state and local roads through campus that are not open 24 hours a day. For instance, a school might have authority to close a major road for a certain portion of the day for student parking or passenger drop-off.

What makes this language of the statute especially troubling is the likelihood that a vehicle operator is unaware whether a road is closed for a portion of the day. For instance, a gun owner or possessor from Augusta might be required to travel to Columbia for a meeting. That traveler might be driving on a road through the University of South Carolina that is closed for a portion of the day. Technically, the traveler is violating the law and is subject to serious criminal liability.

Permission from Authority in Charge of School Grounds

Section16-23-420(A) of the Code provides another exception to the general prohibition of firearms on school premises. This exception is separate from the CWP exception discussed earlier in this chapter. If you have the permission of the "authorities in charge of the premises or property," you can lawfully possess or carry a firearm onto a school, college, or university. (This exception was probably created for school shooting matches and there are very few other instances where a school principal or president is likely to give you permission.) The statute does not explicitly define who these "authorities" are nor have the authors are to uncover any court cases that define the terminology. Therefore, we are left with simply trying to give you our best interpretation of the terms.

The term "authorities" is plural so it can be inferred that there is more than one source of authority from which to obtain the permission. Further, the statute references the authority "in charge" so some sort of administrator can be inferred. Finally, the statute specifically references "premises or property" so it can be inferred that the statute contemplates the person or persons in charge of the specific property where the firearm will be allowed.

So, we can reasonably infer that "authorities in charge" include the school president or principal, a campus police chief, grounds, or physical plant chief, superintendent of schools, school board, school board chief, or similar administrator with managerial authority.

Because the statute references the "premises or property," it can be inferred that the person that gives permission must have authority over the actual property to be entered with a firearm. So, the permission is arguably sufficient if it is obtained from an authority in charge of the property that the firearm is brought upon even if that authority is not the ultimate school authority like the president, principal or school board. For instance, a coach might have authority over a property that contains archery fields that are also sometimes used for shooting matches. The statute can be interpreted to define the coach as an "authority in charge of the premises or property."

The best form of permission is in writing so try to get that if you want to assure that you are legal. The worst type of permission would be to assume that you have permission when in fact you do not.

If you do get permission from an authority, beware that Section 16-23-420(B) makes it a crime for you to display, brandish or threaten anyone with a firearm at a school. Therefore, you could get a criminal charge for showing off or threatening someone with a firearm. While it is impossible to use a firearm at a school shooting match without displaying it or brandishing it, it seems ridiculous that you would get prosecuted under this seemingly incongruent statutory language. On the other hand, it seems very likely that you would get prosecuted under the statute if you were threatening someone with a firearm at a shooting match at school.

Law Enforcement and Guards on School Grounds

Section 16-23-420(D) exempts authorized guards and law enforcement officers. *Guard* is not defined by the statute or related case law so we will assume the statute means private *security officers* hired by the school or stationed at the school with the school official's permission. Guard probably also means armored vehicle security officers on campus to service ATMs and financial institutions. For more information on security officer definitions and licensure in South Carolina, see the chapter on miscellaneous gun laws later in this book. Notwithstanding the relatively ambiguous statutory meaning of *guard*, it is clear however that all law enforcement officers are exempted. Remember that most campus police are state pay-rolled law enforcement officers and not private security officers.

Military and Military Science on School Grounds

Less clear is the exception for members of the armed forces and students of military science found in South Carolina Code of Laws Section 16-23-420(D). In the practical sense, these students primarily exhibit firearms on campus for drills and the firearms are typically nonfunctional. Some college programs might have live-fire shooting competitions at gun ranges or remote and secured areas of the school. In an abundance of caution because of a lack of controlling court decisions, the best advice for members of the armed forces and military science on campus is to never possess a firearm on campus except when provided by your command for official purposes. Otherwise, you are risking a felony charge and all the wonderful civil rights deprivations that go along with it.

Married Students on School Grounds

Another exception is for married students found in Section 16-23-420(D) of the South Carolina Code of Laws. Married students residing in an apartment provided by the private or public school can carry a firearm in or around a particular building if authorized by the person legally responsible for the security of the buildings. Your likelihood of getting such permission is probably slim but the exception does exist in the statutes. The married exception is somewhat of a statutory oddity. Why would the legislature carve out a special exception for married people living on campus? One reason might be as an incentive for students to get married. Talk about a shotgun wedding! Another reason might be to create an incentive for married couples with guns to consider living on campus. Additionally, puzzling is that the exception is not really an exception at all. Married or not, part (A) of Section16-23-420 requires that any student desiring to have a firearm on campus first get permission from campus officials or possess under the CWP exception.

For the Military, Military Science, or married student exceptions, unless you are a law enforcement officer or qualified guard you will need written permission from the campus police chief or the university president. You will probably get denied but there is no law against asking.

If you are a hunter, many college police departments allow you to keep your hunting rifles and possibly hunting pistols at the police station. Get permission from the campus police department first though before bringing the firearm on campus.

Deadly Weapons on Elementary and Secondary School Grounds

In addition to the general prohibition of firearms on school premises and events without permission from authorities in charge of the premises, Section 16-23-430 makes it a crime to possess or carry ***any weapon*** onto the premises of any elementary or secondary school without the permission of school officials. The statute lists knives (with a blade over two inches long), blackjacks, metal pipes or poles, or any other type of weapon, device or object which may be used to inflict bodily injury or death. Therefore, just about anything that can be used as a dangerous or deadly weapon is prohibited on elementary or secondary (middle and high) school premises.

Anyone that looks at the above statute section should see that it is ridiculously over broad. Prohibited items include, "any other type of weapon, device or object that may be used to inflict bodily injury or death." Without even considering items on the school lunch menu, think of all the things students can use to inflict bodily injury or death on each other. Pens and pencils may be jabbed into the eyes. A backpack strap may be used as a garrote around the neck. A baseball bat may be cracked against the head. Quite literally, a jury could find most students, teachers, and administrators in violation of this statute on any given school day.

It is unclear if the term *school officials* used in Section 16-23-430 differs from the meaning of *authorities in charge of the premises or property* described in Section 16-23-420. The term *school officials* might encompass a broader class of administrators that have school managerial responsibilities but are not necessarily in charge of the premises or property. However, the terms might be synonymous. The authors and legislative consultant are not aware of any case law interpreting these terms so we cannot give a more definite definition. So, the "Exception for Permission from the Authorities in Charge of the Premises" section of this chapter contains the best advice that we can give now.

Deadly Weapons, Other Than Firearms, at College

The prohibition against non-firearm deadly weapons is only directed at elementary, middle, and high schools. The same prohibition does not extend to colleges and universities. Therefore, there is no specific prohibition against those non-firearm deadly weapons on college campuses. Just remember though that there is a general vague prohibition from carrying "a deadly weapon usually used for the infliction of personal injury" ***concealed*** on your person anyplace except one's own premises (*see* South Carolina Code of Law Section 16-23-460).

Expulsion for Bringing a Firearm to a Public School

Section 59-63-235 of the South Carolina Code of Laws provides for the mandatory expulsion of any *student* determined to have brought a firearm to school.

Under this section, the district board of trustees (school board) must expel the student for no less than one year if they determine that the student brought a firearm onto the school grounds or any setting under the jurisdiction of a local board of trustees. As before, this provision not only applies to school grounds but to any school-sponsored venue or activity.

For the purposes of this section, the best definition of *student* is a person enrolled in a public education institution from kindergarten through high school. The reason for this interpretation is that Section 59-1-150 defines only Kindergarten through High School and Section 59-1-160 defines School District as,

> *any area or territory comprising a legal entity, whose sole purpose is that of providing free school education, whose boundary lines are a matter of public record, and the area of which constitutes a complete tax unit.*

Colleges' and universities' sole purpose is not to provide a free education so they are not considered a part of a school district. Finally, Section 59-63-235 is in one of the Chapters (Chapter 63 specifically) specified as part of The South Carolina School Code defined in Section 59-1-10 whereas the colleges and universities chapters (Chapter 110 and beyond) do not.

The expulsion must follow the procedures established pursuant to South Carolina Code of Laws Section 59-63-240. The one-year expulsion is subject to modification by the district superintendent of education on a case-by-case basis. Students expelled pursuant to this section are not precluded from receiving educational services in an alternative setting. Each local board of trustees must establish a policy which requires the student to be referred to the local county office of the Department of Juvenile Justice or its representative.

Carry on the Capitol Grounds in Columbia

With or without a permit, Section 10-11-320 of the South Carolina Code of Laws makes it unlawful to discharge, carry, or otherwise have a firearm readily accessible while on the capitol grounds or within the capitol building. The section defines capitol grounds as, "that area inward from the vehicular traveled surfaces of Gervais, Sumter, Senate and Assembly Streets in the city of Columbia." If you violate this section you are guilty of a misdemeanor and, upon conviction, must be fined not more than $5,000 or imprisoned not more than three (3) years, or both. Because this state misdemeanor has the potential for a jail sentence over two (2) years, a person convicted of this crime will have a lifetime federal firearms disability in addition to the other penalties. Also, if the weapon was concealed, you are in violation of Section 16-23-460 and, if convicted, you will forfeit the firearm to the government forever.

There is somewhat of an exception for CWP holders. Section 10-11-320(B) provides that a CWP holder who is authorized to park on the capitol grounds or in the parking garage below the capitol grounds may have a firearm in the vehicle. However, the firearm must remain locked in the CWP holder's vehicle while on or below the capitol grounds and must be stored in a place in the vehicle that is not readily accessible to any person upon that person's entry to or below the capitol grounds. The best practice here is to place the firearm in the trunk or luggage compartment of the vehicle before entering the capitol grounds and then return it to any other legal location on your person or in the vehicle after you leave the capitol grounds.

Hotels, Motels, and Lodging

With or without a permit, if you are otherwise legally entitled to possess one, you can have your firearm in your hotel room. Further, with or without the permit, you can carry the weapon concealed from your conveyance to your room. This authorization is found in Section 23-31-230 of the South Carolina Code of Laws. You must go directly from your conveyance to the room (except for check-in). Again, it is OK to have your concealed weapon with you while you check in but do not stop at the free continental breakfast, pool, or any other area unless you have your CWP. Never go into the bar even with a CWP.

South Carolina statute 45-2-30(A)(4) gives an innkeeper the right to refuse or deny anyone accommodations, facilities, or privileges if the innkeeper reasonably believes that the guest is bringing onto the premises anything that might be dangerous to others. This statute specifically mentions firearms and explosives as potentially dangerous items. Therefore, this statue allows innkeepers to keep guests out if the innkeeper does not want firearms on the premises. This statute stands on its own and does not reference the "No concealable weapons allowed" sign discussed earlier.

However, for CWP holders, Section 45-2-30(A)(4) conflicts with Section 23-31-203. The latter contains the language *not withstanding any provision of law* which overrides 45-2-30(A)(4) for persons carrying under the CWP Statute or carrying under another exception. So, CWP holders can carry a concealable weapon, concealed, from their conveyance to their lodging room or accommodation that they have rented and paid an accommodation tax upon. If you are not carrying under the CWP statute, 45-2-30(A)(4) applies and an innkeeper might be justified in denying you accommodations, facilities or privileges if he thinks that you have a firearm and he does not want firearms on the premises. In that case, if you want to have your gun with you and the lodging business does not, just vote with your feet and check-in to a different lodging business.

There is a detail about Section 23-31-203 that you should be aware of. Again, that section reads, "any person may carry a concealable weapon from an automobile or other motorized conveyance to a room or other accommodation he has rented and upon which an accommodations tax has been ***paid***. The verb "paid" indicates past tense so you are advised to pay for your accommodations in advance before arriving at the accommodations to take advantage of the provisions of this section.

National Parks, Forests, and Wildlife Refuges

On February 22, 2010, a federal law went into effect regarding guns in units of the national park and national wildlife refuge systems. The law repealed Department of Interior rules that have long prohibited Americans from possessing readily available firearms for self-defense in these units. *Units* include national parks, wildlife refuges, battlefields, military parks, historic sites, trails, monuments, and any other area under either national system. Keep in mind that this law primarily focuses on carrying handguns for personal defense and not firearms for hunting. The law is Public Law 111-24 and is called (crazy enough) the Credit Card Accountability Responsibility and Disclosure Act of 2009. It amends the Truth in Lending Act, the Federal Trade Commission Act and the Electronic Funds Transfer Act.

People who are otherwise without a legal disability can possess, carry and transport firearms in all units, in accordance with state law. If you have a South Carolina CWP (or one from a state with reciprocity), you can carry a concealable weapon, concealed, under South Carolina CWP law. This means that you can carry a concealed handgun on or about your person. See the Concealed Weapons Permit Chapter for more details.

Alternatively, if you do not have a valid CWP (or if you chose not to carry under your CWP), you can possess firearms in accordance with applicable S.C. Law for non-CWP holders. Generally, non-CWP holders can have a handgun in their vehicle if it is stored in a closed glove compartment, closed console, or in the trunk (luggage area for SUVs and station wagons) in a closed container with an integral fastener. S.C. Law also allows a hunter or fisherman to carry a handgun (concealed or openly) while traveling to and from hunting or fishing. However, the hunting and fishing exception only protects the possessor if he has a valid license and is either hunting or fishing or going directly to or from that activity. If you want to visit a unit in another state, you must follow the law for that state.

While it is now clearly legal to carry on the *grounds* of a unit, carrying inside the *buildings* of the units is less clear. Debate exists about the definition of *federal facilities* (where firearms remain prohibited under a conflicting federal law). Without further definition, you are in a legal grey area if you carry inside the buildings. On one extreme, it's probably unlikely that a port-a-potty located in a remote area would ever be ruled a federal facility. However, what about a staffed information center? Currently, you simply must weigh the benefit of carrying your firearm against the risk of getting caught in a building that is someday ruled a federal facility.

Before you visit a unit, check the unit's website (*see* nps.gov) or call its headquarters for its policy on firearms inside buildings. National Park System units in South Carolina include: Fort Sumter National Monument, Charles Pinckney National Historic Site, Congaree National Park, Ninety-Six National Historic Site, Overmountain Victory National Historic Trail, Kings Mountain National Military Park, and Cowpens National Battlefield. National Wildlife Refuge System units in South Carolina include: Savannah National Wildlife Refuge, Tybee National Wildlife Refuge, Pinckney Island National Wildlife Refuge, Ace Basin National Wildlife Refuge, Cape Romain National Wildlife Refuge, Waccamaw National Wildlife Refuge, Santee National Wildlife Refuge, and Carolina Sandhills National Wildlife Refuge.

Existing regulations regarding the carrying of firearms remain otherwise unchanged, particularly limitations on hunting, poaching and target practice. The Department of the Interior has a very good website that has detailed information on every national park in the United States.

Carry, Shooting, and Hunting in National Forests

National ***Forests***, as opposed to National ***Parks***, are administered by the USDA through the Forest Service and are regulated differently. National Forests can have shooting ranges and hunting lands. Therefore, questions arise as to carrying to and from these areas as well as general carry.

If you are simply driving through a National Forest and only stay on the state roads, you can possess in your vehicle or on you person under the rules of South Carolina in general. If you are using the forest for shooting or hunting, however, you have some regulations to deal with.

First, each Forest is managed by a chief ranger. That Ranger has limited powers to require discharging firearms at ranges only or during hunting. The Forest Service recommends that you check with the ranger's website or call the ranger for particulars of where you can shoot. With respect to discharge in general, 36 CFR 261.10 (d) prohibits discharging a firearm or any other implement capable of taking human life, causing injury, or damaging property in or within 150 yards of a residence, building, campsite, developed recreation site or occupied area; or across or on a National Forest System road or a body of water adjacent thereto, or in any manner or place whereby any person or property is exposed to injury or damage as a result in such discharge or into or within any cave. Further, 36 CFR 261.5(b) prohibits firing tracer or incendiary ammunition anywhere in the forest.

During hunting season, you can carry a handgun in a national forest if you have a hunting license. If it is not hunting season, you must get a permit from each county in which the forest is located. To get such a permit, you will need written permission from the park ranger in charge. Remember that South Carolina Section 16-23-20(4) additionally applies. This section makes it legal for hunters to have a handgun, openly or concealed, but only if they are licensed to hunt and are engaged in hunting or fishing or going to or from their places of hunting or fishing while in a vehicle or on foot.

If you are carrying under 16-23-20(4), you can carry a handgun, concealed or not, with or without a concealed weapons permit. If you are carrying under this statute but also have a concealed weapons permit, you are not required to present your CWP to a law enforcement officer if asked for ID from the officer. This is because you are carrying under statutory handgun exception 16-23-20(4) and not under your CWP handgun exception.

State Forests and State Parks - There is a Difference!

Firearms are prohibited within all state *parks* except in areas specifically designated for firearms. If you get a concealed weapons permit however, South Carolina Statute 51-3-145(G) exempts you from the firearms prohibition so you can bring your concealable weapon, concealed, into state parks. The South Carolina Department of Parks, Recreation, and Tourism (SCDPRT) manages several quality gun ranges across the state. Obviously, firearms are allowed in the gun range areas. If you do not have a permit and want to bring a handgun to use it at the gun range, here is my analysis of the law: Section 16-23-20(14) makes it legal for a person to have and use a handgun if the person is engaged in firearms-related activities while on the premises of a fixed place of business which conducts, as a regular course of its business, activities related to sale, repair, pawn, firearms training, or use of firearms. While not a business in the classic sense, a state park gun range appears to fit the definition of a fixed place of business that conducts the use of firearms as regular course of business. So, if it is legal for you to possess a handgun, you can likewise legally possess and use that handgun at a state park gun range.

Next, Section 16-23-20(15) makes it legal for a person while transferring a handgun directly from or to a vehicle and a location specified in this section where one may legally possess the handgun. As noted above, a gun range is a place where one may legally possess a handgun. Therefore, you can legally transport a handgun, concealed or openly, directly from your vehicle to the gun range in a state park. Again, whether coming or going, you must go directly between your vehicle and the range.

After passage of the 2021 Open Carry with Training Act, as some CWP holders began to carry openly in South Carolina State Parks, some park personnel began erecting signs prohibiting carry in some of the parks. Thankfully, an Attorney General Alan Wilson Opinion was published on August 15, 2022. That opinion answered three questions:

1. Does the prohibition against firearms in public buildings (S.C. Code Section16-23-420) apply to park buildings? And if so, does the prohibition extend to cover the entire park "premises" since the purposes of the buildings and land are the same, and park premises are essentially the "campuses" on which park buildings are housed?

   ANSWER: South Carolina Park officials cannot prohibit CWP holders from carrying concealable weapons, concealed or openly, inside the parks and onto the parks grounds and areas. However, the parks officials MAY prohibit firearms inside the buildings on park grounds by using the statutory signs.

2. Does the express right to carry in S.C. Code Section 51-3-145(0) take precedence over S.C. Code Section 23-31-220 and/or S.C. Code Section 51-3-70 giving public employers and the park the right to make decisions regarding firearms and their premises?

   ANSWER: No. Park officials do not have authority to override the CWP statute that permits holders to carry concealable weapons, concealed or openly. (Remember though, not into buildings that have the proper signs).

3. Consistent with the recent Supreme Court holding in *New York State Rifle & Pistol Association v. Bruen*, and based on historical precedent, might South Carolina Parks be considered "sensitive places" for restricting the right to carry firearms?

   ANSWER: The Attorney General gave no opinion here. The Attorney General anticipates litigation here. My opinion is that parks are not sensitive areas like Courtrooms and police stations. If the parks officials try to push the issue that parks are sensitive areas, I would help fight that incorrect notion by all legal means.

For further explanation as to the legal reasoning, please refer to the Attorney General Opinion.

For hunting in state *forests*, review the chapter on hunting and keep abreast of all current hunting regulations. SCDPRT regulates all South Carolina state forests and state parks. Their website is: www.southcarolinaparks.com and their general information phone number is: (803) 734-0156. The visitor information phone numbers are: (803) 734-1700 or toll free (866) 224-9339.

Shooting Non-Game Birds and Ill Treatment of Animals

In general, be careful about pointing guns or shooting at animals when in natural or any other areas. Unless the animal is a state listed animal in season, and you have the right hunting license, do not shoot at it. If you are alleging self-defense, you better have some very compelling facts, arguments and preferably witnesses that explain the need to use deadly force against an animal. South Carolina law protects virtually every wild (non-game) bird that you will encounter anywhere in the state. Most birds from eagles, falcons, owls, and buzzards, to cardinals, bluebirds, sparrows, and finches are protected. The exceptions are the game birds that are subject to licensed hunting seasons like turkeys, doves, pheasants, and some ducks. However, make sure that you know how to identify these birds before shooting at them and make sure that you have a license and are in the right hunting season. As a final note, the English Sparrow, Pigeon, and Starling are considered feral and damaging. Those birds are not protected by South Carolina Law (Section 50-1-30(2)) and you can shoot them if otherwise safe and lawful to discharge a firearm under the circumstances. Again, be sure to properly identify the bird before shooting because birds aren't just flying targets.

Section 47-1-40 of the South Carolina Code of Laws prohibits the torture, tormenting, needless mutilation, cruel killing, or infliction of any unnecessary pain or suffering upon any animal. Shooting an animal can certainly meet this definition. Sections 16-11-510 and 16-11-520 provide for similar criminal liability.

State Farmers Markets

Section 5-190(D)(19) of the South Carolina Code of Regulations reads, "possession of firearms or fireworks is strictly prohibited on market properties, unless permitted in accordance with State law." Therefore, do not enter these properties with firearms unless you are carrying under a CWP. The language, *unless permitted in accordance with State law* also appears to mean those with exceptions like law enforcement or those with special permission from the presiding officer of the State Farmers Markets or the South Carolina Commissioner of Agriculture.

There are currently three State Farmers Markets in South Carolina. These are:

- Columbia State Farmers Market located at the: Southeastern Regional Market Terminal, 1001 Bluff Road in Columbia; the,
- Greenville State Farmers Market located at: 1354 Rutherford Road in Greenville; and the,
- Pee Dee State Farmers Market located at: 2513 West Lucas Street in Florence.

Pepper Spray

You may carry a spray can of pepper spray or other commercially available chemical irritant as described more fully in the *Tear Gas* section of this book. Tear gas type chemical irritants are specifically excepted from the criminal definition of poisonous gases in 16-8-10(13)(b) of the

South Carolina Code of Laws if the device used to carry the irritant on or about the person is designed to carry no more than 50cc of irritant. You do not need a concealed weapons permit to carry a chemical irritant like pepper spray either openly visible or concealed.

Review of Handgun Carry Exceptions

Again, the general rule is that it is illegal to carry a handgun, concealed or open. This rule is expressed in the first sentence of Section 16-23-20 of the South Carolina Code of Laws. A concealed weapons permit allows you to overcome this general prohibition in many situations if the handgun fits the definition of a concealable weapon. As mentioned earlier in this chapter, the South Carolina statutes create a laundry list of specific exceptions to the rule against carrying a handgun. We have already discussed some of the more pertinent exceptions but we will lay out the entire statutory list below. Some of the exceptions might seem redundant after reading the first part of this chapter but we thought it valuable to go through the entire list.

With or without a permit, you can carry a handgun under the following circumstances if you:

- are a regular salaried law enforcement officer, or a reserve police officer of a state agency, municipality, or county of the state or if you are an uncompensated Governor's constable, law enforcement officer of the federal government or other states when you are carrying out official duties while in the state (only federal government or out-of-state officers must be furthering official duties), South Carolina Code of Laws Section 16-23-20(1);

- are a deputy enforcement officer of the Natural Resources Enforcement Division of the Department of Natural Resources or a retired commissioned law enforcement officer employed as a private detective or private investigator, South Carolina Code of Laws Section 16-23-20(1);

- are a member of the Armed Forces of the United States, the National Guard, organized reserves, or the state militia ***when on duty***, South Carolina Code of Laws Section 16-23-20(2);

- are a coroner or deputy coroner, ***while engaged in official duties of his or her office***. A coroner or deputy coroner is considered engaged in official duties when going to, or returning from, the actual performance of his duties. However, coroners and deputy coroners must be certified and trained by the South Carolina Law Enforcement Division (SLED) in the proper use of handguns. (South Carolina Code of Laws Section 17-5-110)(See also S.C. Attorney General Opinion dated April 12, 2012 for more analysis and details);

- are a special investigator appointed by the solicitor of the 3rd judicial circuit, ***when on duty*** (South Carolina Code of Laws Section 1-7-533);

- are a member of, or are the invited guest of, an organization authorized by law to purchase or receive firearms from the United States or the State of South Carolina or are a member of, or an invited guest of, a club organized for the purpose of target shooting or collecting modern and antique firearms ***while you are at, or going to or from,*** the place of target shooting or shows or exhibits, South Carolina Code of Laws Section 16-23-20(3);

- are a licensed hunter or fisherman who is ***engaged in*** hunting or fishing or are **going <u>directly</u> to or from** your place of hunting or fishing in a vehicle or on foot. *Directly* does not include stopping for gas or coffee or any other diversion, South Carolina Code of Laws Section 16-23-20(4);

- are a person regularly engaged in the business of manufacturing, repairing, repossessing, or dealing firearms, or if you are the agent of such a person. This is applicable as long as you are ***carrying out the regular course of your firearm business***, South Carolina Code of Laws Section 16-23-20(5);

- are a guard authorized by law to possess a handgun and are ***engaged in*** protecting the property of the United States or an agency of the United States, South Carolina Code of Laws Section 16-23-20(6);

- are a member of an authorized military or civil organization while ***parading or going to or from*** your meetings, South Carolina Code of Laws Section 16-23-20(7);

- are in your home or on your real property, or if you have the permission of the owner or person in legal control of the real property, or if you are on property which you are in legal possession of or over which you have legal control, South Carolina Code of Laws Section 16-23-20(8);
- are in your vehicle and the handgun is secured in a closed glove compartment, a closed console, or in the trunk. You may also transport the handgun if it is in a closed container secured by an integral fastener and if that container is in the luggage compartment. It is legal to open the glove compartment, console, or trunk in order to retrieve a driver's license, registration, or proof of insurance in the presence of a law enforcement officer, South Carolina Code of Laws Section 16-23-20(9)(a);

- are carrying the handgun unloaded in a secure wrapper ***from the place of purchase to your home or fixed place of business***. It is also allowed in the same manner if you are in the ***process of***

moving your residence or place of business, South Carolina Code of Laws Section 16-23-20(10);

- are a prison guard and you are ***engaged in your official duties***, South Carolina Code of Laws Section 16-23-20(11);

- have a permit to carry from the State Law Enforcement Division if you are doing so under the conditions specified to permits, (Concealed Weapons Permit included), South Carolina Code of Laws Section 16-23-20(12);

- are the owner, person in legal possession of, or person in legal control of a fixed place of business or if you are an employee of such a business. (This provision does not apply for employees if the business is a place that sells liquor, beer, or wine for on premises consumption. Again, see the Carry at Work Chart in the CWP chapter for a handy reference of the rules for carrying a handgun at work), South Carolina Code of Laws Section 16-23-20(13);

- are a person ***engaged in*** firearms related activities ***while on*** the premises of a fixed place of business, which conducts as a regular course of business, activities related to the sale, repair, pawn, or use of firearms, or firearms training, unless the premises is posted with a sign limiting the possession of firearms to holders of permits, South Carolina Code of Laws Section 16-23-20(14);

- are ***transferring*** a handgun directly to or from a vehicle to a location specified in this section as a place where you can legally possess the handgun, South Carolina Code of Laws Section 16-23-20(15);

- are ***on*** a motorcycle and you have the handgun secured in a closed saddlebag or other similar closed accessory container attached, whether permanently or temporarily, to the motorcycle, South Carolina Code of Laws Section 16-23-20(16).

Maybe you have noticed a theme regarding the words and phrases that are in bold italics. All these emphasized words and phrases describe attributes like "while on duty," or "while going to and from," or "transferring." You must ensure that you understand these distinctions. If you have a concealed weapons permit, the rules are much more in your favor. If you do not, though, and you want to possess or transport a handgun, you are well advised to understand this list of exceptions. Failing to understand these distinctions might put you in danger of committing a crime under this statute without even knowing what you did wrong.

Law Enforcement Officer as a Party to a Civil or Criminal Action

Police and all other law enforcement officers can generally carry a handgun into a courthouse and even courtrooms, concealed or not. There are two exceptions however. The first is the protocol that the judge is the king of the courtroom. A judge can make it a rule in his or her courtroom that officers cannot have handguns.

Second, law enforcement officers are prohibited from carrying concealed weapons into a courthouse when they are a party to a civil or criminal action. This generally arises when an officer is a party in a divorce or domestic action. Family Court proceedings can strain emotions and it appears this prohibition is designed to prevent tragically violent reactions to sensitive testimony or unfavorable court decisions.

Mailing Guns

You cannot send a handgun through the regular mail. If you need to send a handgun, you must use a commercial carrier such as the type that has overnight and next day services. If you need to send a handgun through one of these commercial carriers, you must declare that the package contains a handgun and you must make sure it is unloaded and securely encased.

You can send rifles by U.S. Mail. However, you must declare it as a gun and make sure it is unloaded and securely encased. Unless you are a federally licensed firearms dealer, it is a violation of federal law to send a firearm by U.S. Mail or by any other carrier out of state unless you are sending it for repair or are returning it to a federal licensee.

Post Offices without CWP

For a full description of carrying guns at post offices, see the chapter on the *Concealed Weapons Permit*.

Minimum Age for Possession of Guns

You must be at least 18 years of age to purchase, own or possess a handgun in South Carolina. If you are 18 years of age or older, state law allows you to purchase a handgun from a private seller (including private individuals selling at gun shows). However, federal law still requires that a person must be at least 21 year of age to purchase handguns or handgun ammunition from retailers or anyone else selling pursuant to a Federal Firearms License (including FFL licensees selling pursuant to their license at gun shows). Remember again that you must be at least 21 years of age to obtain a South Carolina CWP.

Section 16-23-30(3) of the South Carolina Code allows youths under the age of 18 to temporarily possess handguns for instruction under the immediate supervision of a parent or adult instructor. It is clear that the intent of this section is that the parent or adult instructor is right there with the youth as the parent or adult supervisor instructs the youth on handling or operating the handgun. The parent or instructor should not loan the handgun to a youth unless the parent or adult instructor is certain that the youth will have immediate supervision the entire time that the handgun is in possession of the youth. It should also be noted that this section allows for those under 18 years of age in the Armed Forces of the United States, active or reserve, National Guard, State Militia, or R. O. T. C., to possess handguns when on duty or training.

Youths under the age of eighteen (18) years of age are also subject to restrictions under Federal Law. 18 U.S.C 922(X) provides that it shall be unlawful for anyone under 18 years of age to possess a handgun or handgun ammunition. Be aware that the law also makes it unlawful for someone to sell, loan, give, or otherwise provide a handgun or handgun ammunition to a person that is under eighteen (18) years of age. There are important exceptions to this general rule however. The first exception allows the ***temporary transfer*** of possession to someone under 18 years of age if the handgun and ammunition are possessed and used by the juvenile:

> (i) in the course of employment, in the course of ranching or farming related to activities at the residence of the juvenile (or on property used for ranching or farming at which the juvenile, with the permission of the property owner or lessee, is performing activities related to the operation of the farm or ranch), target practice, hunting, or a course of instruction in the safe and lawful use of a handgun;
>
> (ii) with the prior written consent of the juvenile's parent or guardian who is not prohibited by Federal, State, or local law from possessing a firearm, except–

(I) during transportation by the juvenile of an unloaded handgun in a locked container directly from the place of transfer to a place at which an activity described in clause (i) is to take place and transportation by the juvenile of that handgun, unloaded and in a locked container, directly from the place at which such an activity took place to the transferor; or

(II) with respect to ranching or farming activities as described in clause (i) above, a juvenile may possess and use a handgun or ammunition with the prior written approval of the juvenile's parent or legal guardian and at the direction of an adult who is not prohibited by federal, state or local law from possessing a firearm;

(iii) the juvenile has the prior written consent in the juvenile's possession all times when a handgun is in the possession of the juvenile; and

(iv) in accordance with State and local law;

The three other important exceptions allow for:

- a juvenile who is a member of the Armed Forces of the United States or the National Guard who possesses or is armed with a handgun in the line of duty;

- a transfer by inheritance of title (but not possession) of a handgun or ammunition to a juvenile; or

- the possession of a handgun or ammunition by a juvenile taken in defense of the juvenile or other persons against an intruder into the residence of the juvenile or a residence in which the juvenile is an invited guest.

There is no minimum age for possession of rifles and shotguns. (Remember that FFL dealers can only sell rifles and shotguns to purchasers 18 years or older). When it comes to possessing rifles and shotguns, SC law makes no requirement for supervision of minors by adults. However, be mindful of South Carolina hunting laws regulating hunting by persons under 18 years old.

Teach Children About Guns

What is your philosophy regarding children and your guns? You should research methods of training children about guns and employ a training program for children who might possibly come in contact with your guns. The chapter on gun crimes and liability discusses this topic further.

BB Guns, Pellet Guns, and Air Guns

There is no South Carolina law that specifically addresses BB, pellet, or air guns. However, Section 16-23-405(A), S.C. Code of Laws, defines a "weapon" as, *inter alia* (among other things), any other type of device, or object which may be used to inflict bodily injury or death. This broad definition covers all places and situations where you can commit a criminal offense simply by possessing a weapon. So, the best way to get a grip of this is by thinking of all the places where you need to be very careful about firearm possession. For instance, schools, government buildings, etc. In those places, consider a BB gun, pellet gun, or air gun the same as a firearm. Especially if the BB, pellet, or air gun is the size of a handgun.

Since there is no South Carolina code that specifically deals with BB, pellet, or air guns, local governments are free to enact laws that specifically deal with them. Therefore, a county, municipality or special governmental district can enact ordinances that put greater restrictions upon the use or possession of BB, pellet, and/or air guns.

Knives in General

South Carolina does not have a general prohibition from carrying of knives, concealed or not concealed. However, there are important statutory provisions that affect knife carry.

One deals with possessing knives in the commission of crimes. However, since this book is written to help law abiding citizens who do not engage in violent crime, we will not pay much attention to those criminal sections of the South Carolina code. If you would like to research further, see South Carolina Code of Laws Sections: 16-23-460(C), 16-23-490, 16-11-311, and 16-11-312. Basically, the prosecutor can tack on additional crime if the "base" violent crime is committed while the perpetrator has, or appears to have a knife in possession.

The major no-no is knives with a blade over two (2") long on school grounds. South Carolina Code of Laws Section 16-23-430(A) provides:

> *A) It shall be unlawful for any person, except state, county, or municipal law enforcement officers or personnel authorized by school officials, to carry on his person, while on any elementary or secondary school property,* ***a knife, with a blade over two inches long****, a blackjack, a metal pipe or pole, firearms, or any other type of weapon, device, or object which may be used to inflict bodily injury or death.*

So, the general rule is no possessing knives, with blades over two inches long, on school facilities (and functions). The penalty for being convicted with a knife that long is a felony record with the possibility of a fine of not more than one thousand dollars, or imprisonment not more than five years, or both. Further, the knife will be confiscated by the law enforcement agency making the arrest.

There is, however, a major exception for Concealed Weapons Permit holders on school grounds. South Carolina Code of Law Section 16-23-430(B) provides:

> *this section does not apply to a person who is authorized to carry a concealed weapon pursuant to Article 4, Chapter 31, Title 23 when the weapon remains inside an attended or locked motor vehicle and is secured in a closed glove compartment, closed console, closed trunk, or in a closed container secured by an integral fastener and transported in the luggage compartment of the vehicle.*

So, a CWP holder can possess a knife with a blade over two inches on school grounds, so long as the CWP holder puts the knife in one of the areas designated in the statute. These areas are inside an attended or locked motor vehicle and is secured in a closed glove compartment, closed console, closed trunk, or in a closed container secured by an integral fastener and transported in the luggage compartment of the vehicle. Those are the identical areas that a CWP holder can use for a concealable weapon, concealed (i.e., a handgun) while on school premises. See the "Rules for Schools" section of the Concealed Weapons Permit chapter for a complete discussion.

So, other than on school premises or during the commission of crimes or delinquency, there appear no statutory prohibitions against carry knives of any length. However, because the State has made no statutory preemption regarding knives, local governments are free to make local ordinances. Further, any facility that makes you go through a metal detector probably prohibits knives of almost any size.

Since this is a gun law book, we go through enough midnight oil and headaches trying to give you precise explanation of gun law. This section on knives is a bonus because so many have asked about it. We have done our best to find all existing law on knives and to analyze that law precisely. However, you are encouraged to do your own research and determine any prohibition of knives in your location and situation. For further research consider: South Carolina Code of Law sections 16-23-430, 16-23-490, 16-11-311, 16-11-312, 16-1-90(F), and 59-63-370(4).

Switchblade Knives

There are no South Carolina laws specific to switchblades. Therefore, for purposes of carry, treat a switchblade as you would any other knife. Federal law makes it illegal to sell or buy a switchblade knife unless it is made in the state of sale. Federal law pertaining to switchblades is codified in 15 U.S.C. §§ 1241–1245.

Chapter 6
Weapon Crimes and Lawsuits

Gun owners possess an incredibly powerful but also dangerous instrumentality. You hold a tool to protect your family, your country and yourself but it comes with a huge responsibility. The law punishes people who harm others with dangerous instrumentalities like guns. This chapter is designed to help you not become a criminal and not get sued as a result of your gun.

Criminal Law vs. Civil Liability

Guns can get you into trouble in both the criminal and civil realms of the law. Criminal liability generally comes when an individual intends to harm another. It can also come when someone does something so reckless or negligent that there is a reasonable expectation someone will get harmed.

A criminal case is usually the State versus the person accused of the harm. The state of South Carolina prosecutes criminal cases through its state attorneys. To find an accused guilty of a crime the State has the heavy burden of proving guilt beyond any reasonable doubt. Wrongdoers are held accountable through forfeiture of guns, jail time, fines, probationary sentences, and restitution. In general, a felony is a high-level crime with a possible sentence of more than one year in jail. Similarly, a misdemeanor is a lower level crime with a possible sentence of less than one (1) year in jail. However, this is not always the case. For instance, a violation of Section 16-23-465 of the South Carolina Code of Laws is a misdemeanor with a three (3) year jail time and a lifetime federal firearms disability. Be aware also that some crimes are state misdemeanors with the potential penalty of greater than two (2) years in jail that subject convicts to a federal firearms disability.

Civil law deals with non-criminal wrongs (although some criminal statutes provide for civil penalties). Generally, this is where an individual harms others through negligence. Negligence is acting in a manner that falls below the standard of care that a reasonable person would have used under the same circumstances. Civil law also has other theories of liability in addition to negligence.

While a civil court of equity has a broad array of tools to remedy wrongs, the main tool of the civil courts is money judgments. Private parties and their attorneys generally handle both sides of a civil dispute. Civil cases are proven by the lesser standard of *preponderance of the evidence* which simply means that the winner is the side that is more believable.

Crimes are a violation of written statutes that carry a penalty of gun confiscation, jail time, a fine, probation and payment of restitution to the victim. Civil wrongs are wrongs by people against other people that are not classified as crimes. The penalties for civil wrongs are money damages or an equitable remedy like an order to stop doing something or to specifically do something.

Let's take a closer look at how guns can get you into trouble both criminally and civilly. We'll start with the crimes and then discuss civil liability. For the sake of brevity, we will assume that you know crimes like murder and armed robbery. Usually, these crimes take a considerable amount of evil aforethought. Instead, we will identify some less obvious crimes that, none-the-less, carry serious criminal liability.

Reminder about the Lifetime Federal Firearms Disability

Before we get started though, a quick reminder about the lifetime federal firearms disability. As you go over the following crimes, pay attention to the potential penalty for a conviction or adjudication. Many of the crimes carry a sufficient potential penalty to saddle you with a lifetime federal firearms disability. This disability is explained more fully in the chapter on *Legal Disability and Executive Clemency*. With that important note out of the way, let's get back to the crimes that you must avoid.

Pointing a Gun at Someone

Never point a gun at someone unless in legitimate self-defense. Pointing a loaded, or even unloaded, gun at someone is a crime. Did you read that? It is a crime to point even an *unloaded* gun at another person. Under South Carolina Section 16-23-410, pointing a gun at someone is a felony that is punishable by a fine at the discretion of the court and up to five (5) years in jail. With that potential penalty, this offense also carries the penalty of a lifetime federal firearms disability. This section does not apply to theatrical or like performances.

If you must point a gun in legitimate self-defense, the criminal and civil courts will allow you a legal defense. We devote an entire chapter of this book to legal self-defense with a firearm so please refer to that chapter for a more thorough discussion. To keep it simple for now, it is a crime to point a loaded or unloaded gun at someone except for in legitimate self-defense.

Brandishing or Presenting a Firearm

The South Carolina Supreme Court was asked to determine a fine line definition of the rather nebulous term *present* or "brandish" a firearm as prohibited in Section 16-23-410. The Court found it necessary to define *present* because the legislature might have intended to prohibit not only directly pointing a firearm at someone, but also merely displaying a firearm as to threaten or cause fear.

The Court defined the term in In the Interest of Spencer R., S.C. Court of Appeals Opinion No.: 4668. In that case, the prosecutor charged a juvenile named Spencer with pointing or presenting a firearm. The arrest happened after police received a 911 call reporting he was in front of his residence with a gun threatening people at a school bus stop.

The incident allegedly arose out of ongoing turmoil between Spencer and some young ladies at his school. The young lady's mother testified that she was about to leave for work when she received a text message on her cell phone from her fifteen-year-old daughter, Angela, stating Spencer wanted to shoot and kill Angela. After receiving the text message, the mother drove to Angela's school and discovered the school suspended Spencer for three days after an altercation occurred between Spencer and one of Angela's friends. After the school day concluded, the mother drove to the bus stop to pick up her children. She testified Spencer lived three houses away from the bus stop, and when she passed by, she saw Spencer walk onto his driveway carrying a gun. She went on to say that he was holding the gun at a ten o'clock and four o'clock angle, with the bottom of the gun about level with his chest and the barrel in the air. She testified he sat down in a chair on the driveway that was visible from the bus stop, but he did not see her or turn in her direction. Additionally, he did not wave or point the weapon at her. After seeing Spencer, the mom called her husband because she felt threatened. Her husband arrived shortly thereafter, and they waited until the school bus arrived. When Angela and her friend, Brett, exited the school bus, the mom told them to hurry and get in her car because Spencer was "over there with some type of weapon." As she drove past Spencer's house, the mother stated she told the children to "stay low, don't look, duck down," but she did not look at the children to see if they followed her instructions. After she arrived at her residence, she called the police.

Brett testified when he walked up to the bus stop with Angela that morning, he observed one of Angela's friends slap Spencer. Brett explained that Spencer returned to the bus stop with his parents after the altercation and said he wanted to shoot Angela. Brett then said that when he and Angela got off the school bus later that afternoon, he saw Spencer standing in the driveway with a gun. He explained that Spencer was not waving or aiming the gun at them, but was holding it up. Brett then said that as he looked out of the window of the mom's car as he ducked down, he saw Spencer holding the gun and "staring us down like he wanted to shoot us."

Rodney, another student, testified that he also saw Spencer with the rifle that same afternoon. After he left the school bus, he walked by Spencer's house and saw Spencer sitting in a lawn chair in the driveway of his house with a gun between his legs and his hands on the barrel of the gun. Rodney asked Spencer what he was doing, and Spencer replied he (referring to Angela) "was going to shoot the bitch."

The Court found Spencer guilty of presenting a firearm. The Court defined presenting as "to offer for observation, show or display." An appeal followed. The question for the Court was did the facts in Spencer arise to presenting or pointing a firearm at another as prohibited in Section 16-23-410, S.C. Code of Laws.

After analyzing previous cases and definitions found in other State's statutes, the South Carolina Supreme Court defined the phrase "to present" a firearm in section 16-23-410 as: *to offer to view in a threatening manner, or to show in a threatening manner*. The Court also established the elements of the offense. The elements of presenting a firearm are: (1) presenting, (2) a loaded or unloaded firearm, (3) at another. Under this analysis, the order of delinquency against Spencer was upheld. The Court went on to say that,

> *Taken as a whole, Spencer's actions as to Angela were not that of an ordinary citizen engaged in the lawful use of a firearm on his property. Instead, the evidence demonstrates Spencer deliberately intended to show his rifle at Angela in a threatening manner. Even though Spencer did not wave or point the assault rifle directly at Angela, his decision to sit in view of the school bus stop for an extended period of time while displaying his assault rifle, combined with the events occurring that day and Rodney's and Brett's testimony that Spencer R. said he wanted to shoot Angela, constitute sufficient evidence to uphold Spencer's conviction.*

There are a couple of important takeaways here. First, as all other South Carolina gun laws that I can think of, the firearm offense applies *regardless of whether the firearm is loaded or not*. The point is that you can create a firearms offense whether the firearm is loaded or not. Second, whether a person gets convicted or not of *presenting* is determined by not only what happens when the firearm is present but also circumstances leading up to the time when the firearm become visible. Finally, the Court will look at the intention to show the firearm in a threatening manner (again, based on all of the circumstances).

So, merely sitting on a chair in your front yard cleaning a rifle, oblivious to what's going on around you, would probably never get you arrested or convicted of presenting. Likewise, marching back and forth in your front yard with a firearm, by itself, would probably not rise to presenting. It is only when the display of the firearm is combined with circumstances perceived as threatening that make the display illegal presenting.

Entering the Residence of Others while Armed

As mentioned in the *Concealed Weapon Permit* chapter, permit holders may not carry a concealable weapon, concealed, into the residence or dwelling of another person without the express consent of the owner or tenant. This is true for those without a permit under the general handgun prohibition of 16-23-20. This crime is a misdemeanor and can be punished by a fine of not less than $1,000 or up to one (1) year in jail or both under 16-23-50(A)(2). Further, the handgun will be confiscated under 12-23-50(B). If you have a permit, it will be revoked for five (5) years (see the *Concealed Weapons Permit* chapter). With respect to entering the residence of another with a long gun, the S.C. Code of Laws is silent.

Criminal Negligence

Section 16-3-60 of the South Carolina Code of Laws defines criminal negligence as the reckless disregard of the safety of others. Recklessness involves a very high degree of negligence where a person's actions show callous indifference toward others. Under this section, the definition is only used in conjunction with involuntary manslaughter which means the killing of another without malice. In the context of guns, examples might include shooting in an unsafe direction. For instance, some geniuses think that a 4th a July celebration is not complete without firing guns into the sky. If a bullet returns down and kills someone (which has happened), the shooter has committed involuntary manslaughter. Involuntary manslaughter is a felony with the penalty of not more than five (5) years in prison. It also brings a lifetime federal firearms disability.

Discharging a Gun into a Dwelling, Building or Vehicle

Under Section 16-23-440 of the South Carolina Code of Laws, it is unlawful to discharge a firearm at or into a dwelling, other building, structure, or enclosure, which is regularly occupied by people. It is also unlawful to discharge a firearm at or into a vehicle, aircraft, watercraft, or other conveyance, device, or equipment while it is occupied. This crime is very similar to reckless endangerment and you can be simultaneously charged for both. The penalty is up to a $1,000 fine or up to ten (10) years imprisonment or both and a lifetime federal firearms disability.

Taking a Law Enforcement Officer's Weapon

Under Section 16-23-415 of the South Carolina Code of Laws, it is unlawful to take a firearm, stun gun, or Taser® device from the person of a law enforcement officer or a corrections officer. Violation of this section is a felony with a penalty of not more than five (5) years of jail time or a fine of not more than $5,000, or both and a lifetime federal firearms disability. Additionally, taking it will almost certainly require you to engage in battery on a law enforcement officer which is a separate crime.

While you might think that you would never take a weapon from a law enforcement officer, it is possible that you could find yourself in a situation where you might get mixed-up with a law enforcement officer. This can happen either by mistake or because the officer is out of control and unlawfully posing an imminent risk of death or serious bodily injury to you or someone else.

First, let's look at some circumstances where you might get mixed up with a police officer. For simplicity sake, try to categorize law enforcement officers as either: uniformed and on-duty, plain clothed and on-duty, or plain clothed and off-duty.

The simplest scenario is if the officer is uniformed and on-duty. Attempting to take a firearm, stun gun, or Taser® away from a uniformed law enforcement officer is a felony. If you actually are able to take it away, you have likewise committed a felony.

If the officer is on-duty but is not in uniform, it gets a little tricky. Under these circumstances, you must know, or have a reason to think, that the person is a police officer and that he is on-duty. The court will judge your thought process by the "reasonable man" standard. This means that a court will try to objectively determine what a reasonable person would think under the same circumstances. In simple terms, would the average guy have thought that the person in plain clothes was a police officer and that he was on-duty at the time that you tried to take his weapon?

Here are two examples that demonstrate the two opposite ends of the knowledge spectrum:

> Not Guilty - You are walking on the street and you turn the corner and see a guy with a gun stuck into a woman's back. She has her hands up. You sneak up on the guy and are able to snatch his gun away from him. He is a plain clothes on-duty policeman.
>
> You took his weapon but a court might find that a reasonable person under the same circumstances would not have thought that the man was a law enforcement officer. One possibility is that you thought that the man was robbing the woman.
>
> Maybe Not Guilty – Same scenario except that you notice that the man is pulling handcuffs from his back pocket. Police usually carry handcuffs so there is some reason for you to believe that he is a police officer.

Probably Guilty - Same scenario except that you notice that the man has a badge clipped to his belt and is pulling handcuffs from his back pocket. Now you have two reasons to think that the man is a police officer. He is getting handcuffs and a reasonable person would think that the badge signifies a police officer.

Guilty – Same scenario except that you notice that the man also has a uniformed policeman standing right next to him. A reasonable person would not think that a uniformed police officer would stand idly by while a criminal sticks a gun in the woman's back.

South Carolina law does not prohibit off-duty law enforcement officers from carrying either open or concealed weapons. Officers don't even have to have a concealed weapons permit to carry concealed while in their street clothes. However, officers are under the policy of their individual department. In other words, each law enforcement office can institute its own policy about officers carrying guns while not on duty. It is not a criminal offense for the officer to not follow his or her office's policy but it might be cause for employment action like a suspension or termination. It seems very unlikely that any law enforcement administrator would restrict his or her officers from carrying a weapon under most circumstances. Therefore, it is a reasonable assumption that law enforcement officers are always carrying a weapon.

In any of the above circumstances, if the law enforcement officer gives you consent to take his or her weapon, there is no crime. It is probably very rare to have a law enforcement officer give you consent to take his or her weapon. However, situations might arise where consent is conceivable. For instance, an officer could be wrestling with a suspect and yell for you to take his or her Taser to subdue the suspect. Probably does not happen much but it is possible.

Secondly, while highly unlikely, it is conceivable that you encounter an out of control law enforcement officer who unlawfully attacks you or someone around you with an imminent threat of death or serious bodily injury. If you determine that you are or someone around you is under an imminent threat of death or serious bodily injury from an out of control officer, you have the right to use deadly force to defend yourself or others. Your actions will be judged on the reasonable man standard discussed in the self-defense chapter.

Guns at School

(For a more thorough discussion about guns on school grounds, make sure that you have read the *Rules for Schools* section in the *Possessing and Transporting Guns without a Permit* and the *Concealed Weapons Permit* chapters.)

The general rule is that you cannot bring firearms on to school property or functions. However, there are important exceptions that allow you to possess firearms under certain conditions. Barring possession under an exception though, possessing a firearm at any school is a felony punishable by a fine of up to $5,000 or imprisonment for up to five (5) years or both under Section 16-23-420. Section 16-23-430 provides for an additional or separate felony for bringing a deadly weapon unto elementary or secondary school grounds. The penalty under Section 16-23-430 is a fine of up to $1,000, a jail term not to exceed five (5) years, or both and you may also have your weapon confiscated if convicted or adjudicated. In addition to firearms, you can be charged for possession of knives with a blade over two inches long, blackjacks, metal pipes, metal poles, or any other type of object that can be legitimately deemed a weapon at an elementary or secondary (middle and high) school under Section 16-23-430. Both sections subject the convicted or adjudicated to a lifetime federal firearms disability.

Public Buildings

With or without a Concealed Weapons Permit, it is unlawful under 16-23-420 of the South Carolina Code of Laws to possess a firearm in any publicly owned building. This Statute has been discussed above in the *Guns at School* section so refer to that section for information on penalties. For non-school properties, this is generally interpreted to mean inside a building and not simply on the premises. For example, you can legally possess a firearm in the glove box of your vehicle in the parking lot of a public building but you cannot bring the same firearm into the building. An important exception exists, however, for interstate highway rest areas. Concealed Weapons Permit licensees are authorized to carry concealable weapons, concealed into interstate highway rest areas and possess them inside the rest areas.

No Firearms on the Capitol Grounds

Again, with or without a permit, Section 10-11-320 of the South Carolina Code of Laws makes it unlawful to discharge, carry, or otherwise have a firearm readily accessible while on the capitol grounds or within the capitol building. For a more detailed including the partial exception for CWP holders, see the *Can I Carry on the Capitol Grounds* section in the *Possessing and Transporting Guns without a Permit* chapter.

Trap or Trick Guns

Under Section 16-23-450 of the South Carolina Code of Laws it is unlawful to construct, set or place a loaded trap gun, spring gun, or any other similar device. A trap gun is a device, which might or might not include an actual gun, which is designed to be triggered by movement such as someone opening a door. As an example, people might consider constructing a trap gun mechanism to shoot or scare home invaders.

Merely constructing a trap gun is a misdemeanor punishable by up to a $500 fine and between 30 and 365 days in jail or both. If the trap goes off and someone is killed, you will probably be charged with murder. Even if the trap gun just goes off on someone, but does not kill that person, you might still be facing attempted murder.

You will discover later that the law never permits you to protect property with deadly force. The idea behind a trap gun is to protect property from an invader when the property owner is not around. Therefore, it is never a good idea to construct a trap gun. Find other ways to secure your property and leave the trap guns to Wile E. Coyote and the Roadrunner.

Forfeiture of Weapon if Crime Involves Concealed Weapons

Under Section 16-23-460 of the South Carolina Code of Laws, carrying a concealed weapon of the type usually used for the infliction of personal injury is a misdemeanor and the potential penalty is from $200 to $500 with a potential jail term of between 30 and 90 days. This section also provides that the weapon must be ***forfeited*** to the county or municipality. If you are convicted under this section, you will lose that weapon forever. So, you should assume that all concealable weapons (defined in the *Concealed Weapons Permit* chapter) and handguns are included in this definition of concealed weapon.

You must realize that this statute works alone or can be tacked-on to many other crimes if a concealed weapon was being carried during the commission of the crime. Violation of this section can be tacked-on to both violent and non-violent criminal offenses. This section does not prohibit you from carrying a concealed weapon pursuant to a CWP or any statutory exception that allows concealed carry. This also does not apply to rifles, shotguns, dirks, slingshots, metal knuckles, or razors; unless they are used with intent to commit a crime.

What must Law Enforcement do with Forfeited Firearms?

This issue is dealt with in a South Carolina Attorney General Opinion dated June 3, 2013. South Carolina Code of Laws Sections 16-23-50(2)(B) and 16-23-460 deal with forfeiture of a firearm to the government for violation of the statutes. However, the government (usually law enforcement) must follow procedures before depriving a person of the firearm. The person must have basic due process before deprivation.

First, there must be a conviction to permanently deprive you of the firearm. The firearm may be held for a reasonable time pending disposition of the criminal charge. This means that the firearm can be withheld during the pendency of all legal process including appeals. If the firearm is owned by a third party who is not implicated in the crime, the third party must be allowed an opportunity for hearing to determine if the third party is the rightful owner. If the third party is found to be the owner or otherwise rightful possessor, the law enforcement agency shall release the firearm to the non-implicated owner.

If implicated under 16-23-460 (concealable weapon), the Code requires that the firearm by forfeited to the municipality. Again, all due process explained above is required of the municipality. Once forfeited to the municipality, nothing prevents the municipality from giving possession to its police department.

What about a Pre-Trial Intervention (PTI) or "diversion program?" Pre-Trial Intervention is a process to cut short the prosecution of a criminal case, provided the accused voluntarily meets certain conditions set-out by the solicitor. Generally, the solicitor will agree to put a break in the prosecution process (moving towards trial and trial) provided the accused perform certain things within the PTI time-period like pay a cost, do community service, complete targeted training and/or education. Provided the accused completes the agreement within the time-period, the solicitor files a *nolle prosequi* meaning the case is dropped and there is no conviction. If you complete the PTI and the agreement is otherwise silent on your forfeited firearm, the Attorney General Opinion suggests that your firearm should be returned. However, be aware that the solicitor might include a forfeiture of the firearm as a condition of the PTI. If that is the case, you have agreed to the forfeiture as a condition of your case being dropped and you will not get the firearm back. Therefore, it is important to carefully read the agreement before signing and to negotiate the best agreement for you based upon your circumstance.

Police departments and municipalities are under the return of property statutes found in the South Carolina Code of Laws Section 27-21-20. This Section provides process such as notice and a period of time as well as diligent search for the rightful owner of property. The Attorney General Opinion explains how and why that Section is applicable to forfeited firearms.

Additional Penalty for Firearms in Business that Sell Alcohol

As mentioned previously in this book, under Section 16-23-465 there is an increased penalty for illegally carrying a firearm into a business which sells liquor, beer, or wine for consumption on the premises. This crime is a misdemeanor with the penalty of a fine of up to $2,000 or jail for up to two (2) years or both. See the *Concealed Weapons Permit* chapter for a full discussion of carrying a firearm into a business that sells alcoholic beverages for onsite consumption.

Drinking and Shooting

Under South Carolina Code of Laws Chapter 23-31-400(B), it is unlawful to use a firearm if you are under the influence of alcohol or a controlled substance. Violations are a misdemeanor and may be punished with a fine of up to $2,000 or imprisonment for up to two (2) years or both. There is an exception if you are required to use the firearm lawfully in self-defense.

If you are shooting and someone thinks you are drunk, the observers can call the police. If the investigating officer arrives and has a reasonable suspicion that you have been using drugs or drinking too much, you will be given a blood test or urine test or both to determine if you are in fact under the influence. If you refuse to submit to the test, that fact can and will be used against you in the criminal proceeding. However, while the results of any blood or urine test will be used in a criminal prosecution for using the firearms under the influence, the results cannot be used in a criminal prosecution for possession of the controlled substance.

If you are arrested for using a firearm while under the influence but the arresting officer does not request a blood or urine test, you can request such testing. If you know you have not consumed alcohol or used drugs, it is a good idea to get tested right there. If you do request the testing and the officer refuses to give you the tests, you cannot be prosecuted.

If used at trial, the results of the blood or urine test used at trial create certain legal presumptions. If the test reveals that you have .05% or less alcohol in your blood, it is presumed that you were not under the influence of alcohol at the time of the test. If the test reveals that there is greater than .05% but less than .08% alcohol in your blood, no inference is created either way (under or not under the influence). Finally, if the test reveals that you had .08% or greater alcohol in your blood, a presumption is created that you were under the influence at the time of the test.

These presumptions are only a starting point. It is still possible to show by other evidence that you were under the influence even though you had .05% or less blood alcohol level. The jury can consider other evidence like slurred speech or stumbling. There are also field sobriety tests which might indicate intoxication. It is also possible to have .08% or greater blood alcohol level and not be found under the influence. A jury decides if you were under the influence or not but you should never put yourself in that position.

This statute should not cause you to hesitate before using a gun in self-defense just because you had been consuming alcohol or were required to use prescription drugs. It is basically designed to prevent the purposeful use of firearms under the influence of alcohol or drugs for reasons other than self-defense. There are certainly circumstances that could arise where a person is drinking alcohol or under the influence of controlled substances and is confronted with a deadly threat that requires the defensive use of deadly force.

Possessing a Firearm While Unlawfully Dealing in Alcohol

It is unlawful under Section 61-6-4180 to possess a firearm or weapon while unlawfully dealing in alcohol. Under this section, if a person unlawfully manufactures, transports, or sells alcoholic liquors or aids or assists in any manner in one or more of these acts and at the time of the unlawful manufacturing, transporting, selling, aiding, or assisting has on or about his person or has on or in a vehicle which he uses to aid him in any such purpose or in his actual or constructive possession a firearm or weapon of like kind, he is guilty of a misdemeanor and, upon conviction, must be imprisoned not less than one (1) year nor more than three (3) years, or be fined not less than $500 nor more than $1,500. The three-year potential sentience of this state misdemeanor means that a conviction also brings a lifetime federal firearms disability. If the firearm is concealed while this statute is violated, the additional possible penalty is a $200 to $500 fine, jail time between thirty (30) and ninety (90) days, and forfeiture of the firearm.

Discharging a Firearm within 50 yards of a Public Road While Drunk

South Carolina Code of Laws Section 16-17-530(c) provides that any person who shall, while under the influence, or feigning [faking] to be under the influence, of intoxicating liquor, without just cause or excuse, discharge any gun, pistol, or other firearm while upon or within fifty yards of any public road or highway, except upon his own premises, shall be deemed guilty of a misdemeanor. Upon conviction, the penalty is a fine of not more than $100 or jail time of not more than thirty (30) days.

This statute seems like it would appear in a wacky laws book. While it is dealing with the serious topic of firearms, it is so odd that it deserves a second look. In plain English, the law basically says, "Unless you have a very good reason to do so, or you are on your own premises, it is against the law to shoot a gun within fifty (50) yards of a public road if you have been drinking or if you are faking that you were drinking." It is already illegal to shoot a gun while under the influence of alcohol except for in lawful self-defense, so why this additional charge? Also, is a bullet any less dangerous from 51 yards as opposed to 50 yards? Also, why would someone pretend to be drink while shooting a gun? Or why would anybody be pretending to be drunk anytime. For the legislature to deem this law necessary, it can only mean that somewhere; somehow; sometime in the past . . . somebody got hurt and some nut tried to use the excuse that he was only pretending to be drunk when he shot his gun within 50 years of a public road.

Allowing Mental Patients and Mental Prisoners Access to Firearms

It is a felony to provide a firearm to mental patients or mental prisoners. Section 44-23-1080 of the South Carolina Code of Laws provides that it is unlawful for anyone to willfully, or even negligently, provide mental patients or prisoners access to firearms. The fine is not less than $1,000 and not more than $10,000 and the jail time is not less than one year and not more than ten years. If the judge wants to, he or she can give you both the fine and the time. Also, because this is a felony, conviction or adjudication brings a lifetime federal firearms disability. Further, on top of these stiff criminal penalties, you might also get hit with a civil lawsuit. So, never provide a mental patient or prisoner even a chance to access your firearms. It's also a felony under federal law 18 U.S.C. 922(d).

Providing Prisoners with Firearms

Section 24-3-950 of the South Carolina Code of Laws makes it a felony criminal offense to furnish or attempt to furnish a prisoner under the jurisdiction of the Department of Corrections with contraband. *Any and all firearms* are defined as contraband in South Carolina Code of Regulations Chapter 33-1. It is likewise a felony for the prisoner to possess a firearm under this statute. The penalty is a fine of not less than $1,000 nor more than $10,000 or imprisonment for not less than one year or more than ten years, or both. Of course, you become subject to the lifetime federal firearms disability also.

Similarly, Section 24-7-155 makes it a felony for any person to furnish or attempt to furnish any prisoner in any county or municipal jail, prison, work camp or overnight lockup facility with contraband [a firearm] as defined in South Carolina Code of Regulations Chapter 33-1. The penalty is a fine of not less than $1,000 nor more than $10,000 or imprisonment for not less than one year nor more than ten years, or both. You can also add on the lifetime federal firearms disability.

If you are currently an inmate, Section 24-13-440 of the South Carolina Code of Laws makes it unlawful for an inmate of a state correctional facility, city or county jail, or public works of a county to carry on his person a dirk, slingshot, metal knuckles, razor, firearm, or any other deadly weapon, homemade or otherwise, which usually is used for the infliction of personal injury upon another person, or to willfully conceal any weapon within any Department of Corrections facility or other place of confinement. An inmate violating this section is guilty of a felony and, upon conviction, must be imprisoned not more than ten (10) years. A sentence imposed under this section must be served consecutively to any other sentence the inmate is serving.

Don't forget about South Carolina Section 16-23-460. Again, that section tacks on an additional misdemeanor for carrying a deadly weapon usually used for the infliction of personal injury concealed about his person. The charge is a misdemeanor with a fine of not less than $200 nor more than $500 or imprisonment not less than thirty (30) days or more than ninety (90) days. But the kicker is that the firearm must be forfeited also.

Criminally Negligent Use of a Firearm Before, During or After Hunting

Under Section 50-1-85(3) of the South Carolina Code of Laws, it is unlawful for any person to use a firearm or archery tackle in a criminally negligent manner while in preparation for, engaged in the act of, or returning from hunting. Criminal negligence is defined as the reckless disregard for the safety of others. A conviction under this section is a misdemeanor with four possible penalties depending upon the nature of the criminal negligence. Upon conviction:

(1) in a case where no personal injury or property damage occurs, a fine of not more than $200 or jail for not more than thirty (30) days;

(2) in the case of property damage only, a fine of not more than $1,000 nor less than $500 or jail for not more than six (6) months, and the court must order restitution to the owner of the property;

(3) in the case of bodily injury to another, a fine not less than $500 nor more than $2,500 or imprisoned for not more than two (2) years; if the bodily injury results in disfigurement, total or partial permanent disability, be imprisoned for not less than sixty (60) days nor more than two (2) years;

(4) in the case of death, be imprisoned for not less than three (3) months nor more than three (3) years. Violation of this subsection also brings a lifetime federal firearms disability because the potential sentence for this state misdemeanor is greater than two (2) years.

These are mandatory sentences so no part of the minimum fines and penalties provided in this section may be suspended by any Court in South Carolina.

In addition to the criminal penalties under this section, the South Carolina Department of Parks, Recreation and Tourism (SCDPRT) must immediately seize any hunting license of a person charged under this section and, upon conviction, the hunting privileges of the person convicted under Item (1) or (2) will be suspended for one (1) year. A person convicted under Item (3) will lose his privilege to hunt for three (3) years, and a person convicted under Item (4) will lose the privilege of hunting for five (5) years.

If the person is convicted under this section and then decides to hunt while his license is suspended under the provisions of this section, he must be fined not less than $500 nor more than $2,500 or imprisoned for not more than two (2) years and shall have his hunting privileges suspended for an additional five (5) years. The person may not obtain another hunting license until he has satisfactorily completed a hunter's safety program conducted by the SCDPRT.

Discharging a Firearm at a Boat Ramp or Landing

For some reason, boat ramps can really bring out the worst in people. Maybe the confrontation starts because someone's kid on a personal water crafts put a big rubber streak against someone's hot new graphics. Maybe it starts because some family decides to wash their boat on the ramp while there is a line of boats waiting to put into the water. Or, maybe it starts because some yahoo didn't take a picture of the bass before he threw it back into the water. For whatever reason, boat ramps breed confrontation. Just an opinion, but fresh water ramps usually have more testosteroned-up hotheads than do salt water ramps. Either way, under South Carolina Code of Laws Section 50-21-146, it is unlawful to discharge a firearm at a boat landing or ramp. A person who discharges a firearm at a public boat landing or ramp is guilty of a misdemeanor and, upon conviction, must be fined between $25 and $200 or imprisoned for between ten (10) days and thirty (30) days. This is in addition to other crimes that may apply. Some have suggested that this discussion about boat ramps might be better placed under the *Drinking and Shooting* section! If alcohol is involved there might be additional crimes tacked-on.

Teaching, Demonstrating, or Making a Firearm for Civil Disorder

Under Section 16-8-20 of the South Carolina Code of Laws, it is a felony to:

- teach or demonstrate to another person the use, application, or making of a firearm or destructive device which is capable of causing injury or death if the person knows, has reason to know, or intends that what is taught or demonstrated, will be employed unlawfully for use in, or in furtherance of, a civil disorder; or
- assemble with one or more persons for the purpose of training, practicing, or instructing in the use of a firearm or destructive device which is capable of causing injury or death to persons if the training, practice, or instruction is used in furtherance of an unlawful purpose or a civil disorder.

Upon conviction for a first offense, the convict must be fined not more than $5,000 or imprisoned for not more than five (5) years, or both. Upon conviction for a second or subsequent offense, the convict must be fined not more than $10,000 or imprisoned for not more than ten (10) years, or both. Because these are felonies, a conviction or adjudication under this section will also bring a lifetime federal firearms disability.

This section has some exceptions. Nothing in the section prohibits:

- an act of a law enforcement officer performed within his official capacity;
- training for law enforcement officers conducted by or for an agency or a political subdivision of a state or an agency of the United States;
- activities of the National Guard or of the armed forces of the United States; or
- classes intended to teach the safe handling of legal firearms for hunting, recreation, competition, or self-defense.

Increased Penalty for Using Concealed Weapon in Violent Crimes

If you are convicted of assault, assault and battery, assault or assault and battery with intent to kill or manslaughter and it appears at your trial that the assault, assault and battery, assault or assault and battery with intent to kill or manslaughter was committed with a concealed firearm, South Carolina Code of Laws Section 16-3-610 provide for an increased penalty. The section requires the presiding judge to, in addition to the punishment for the underlying crimes, add the increased penalty of additional incarceration time of not less than 3 months and not more than twelve (12) months, with or without hard labor, or a fine of not less than $200. The judge has the discretion to give either the jail time or the fine or both. Because either the underlying crime is a felony, or the increased penalty causes the combined potential jail time to exceed two (2) years for the underlying state misdemeanor, conviction under this section also subjects the convict to a lifetime federal firearms disability.

Additionally, Section 16-23-490 provides for an increased penalty for possession of a firearm during commission of, or attempt to commit, a violent crime. If a person is in possession of a firearm, or visibly displays what appears to be a firearm, during the commission of a violent crime and is convicted of committing or attempting to commit a violent crime as defined in Section 16-1-60 of the South Carolina Code of Laws, the penalty is a mandatory five (5) years in jail without parole or "good-time" in addition to the punishment provided for the principal crime. Again, because either the underlying crime is a felony, or the increased penalty causes the combined potential jail time to exceed two (2) years for the underlying state misdemeanor, conviction under this section also subjects the convict to a lifetime federal firearms disability.

Tear Gas and Chemical Irritant Weapons

Except for authorized law enforcement officers, Section 16-23-470 of the South Carolina Code of Laws makes it is unlawful to possess, use, transport, buy, or sell a tear-gas machine or a tear-gas gun if the projectile can or does contain greater than 50 cubic centimeters of tear gas. It is also unlawful to possess, use, transport, buy, or sell any parts, ammunition, shells, or equipment that may be used in a tear-gas machine or a tear-gas gun with a cartridge of over 50 cubic centimeters. A violation of the section is a misdemeanor and is punishable by up to a $5,000 fine and up to three (3) years in jail. Uh-oh: a potential sentence of up to three years in jail? Here is another example of a state misdemeanor with a potential jail sentence of more than two (2) years so the possibility of a lifetime federal firearms disability is, pardon the pun, triggered.

The statute does a poor job of defining tear gas because traditional *tear gas*, Mace, and pepper spray are distinct chemicals from one another. None of these compounds are gasses. However, they are all probably coved under this prohibition. What is commonly called *tear gas* is either orthochlorobenzalmalononitrile or chloroacetophenone, known respectively as CS and CN. These are the most common compounds used by law enforcement for riot control and other applications. Civilians can get their hands on CS and CN also. Dibenz(b,f)-1,4-oxazepin, abbreviated to CR, is another compound commonly called *tear gas* and used by law enforcement. At normal temperatures and standard atmospheric pressure, these compounds are not gasses but rather white crystals. To disperse the compound, the crystals must be put into a solvent and aerosolized. Mace is a trade name for another CN crystalline compound that must be put into a liquid and aerosolized. Pepper spray is oleoresin capsicum (OC) is extracted from chili peppers. OC is a dark orange, oily liquid, which must be put into a liquid and aerosolized. Without any better definition of tear gas from the statute, the best practice is to assume that any of the above compounds are defined as tear gas for the purpose of the prohibition.

Section 16-23-470 allows possession or use a tear-gas machine or tear-gas gun if is used only for self-defense and not capable of firing a shell with a capacity of more than 50 cubic centimeters of tear-gas. Some new items on the market maybe fit this exception. Manufacturers have created paint ball sized pepper spray (OC) balls for use with paintball guns and shotgun shells that fire pepper spray (OC) projectiles. So long as the projectile contains less than 50 cubic centimeters of pepper spray, these projectiles appear legal under the self-defense exception. Remember, however, that the gun and tear gas must only be possessed or used for self-defense.

Objects Designed to Cause Damage by Fire or Detonation

Section 16-23-480 makes it unlawful to manufacture or possess any object which is designed to cause damage by fire, ignition, or detonation. Here is another statute section that uses very broad and vague language such as: *any object which is designed to cause damage by fire,* so it is open for unintended interpretations. A torch can be used by a roofer to melt the tar on roof laps for better sealing, or a torch can be used by an arsonist to burn down buildings. So, should a person be prosecuted for possession of a torch as the existing overly-broad statute would allow, or should a person only be prosecuted for the misuse of the torch? You can probably think of items that are designed to cause damage by fire, ignition or detonation. In any case, manufacturing or possessing such an object is a felony punishable by a fine and up to five (5) years in jail. This felony also subjects the convicted or adjudicated to a lifetime federal firearms disability. Although typical retail fireworks use fire, they are designed for entertainment and not to cause damage by the fire or ignition. Therefore, it is unlikely that anyone would be prosecuted for using retail fireworks under this statute. You never know though.

Transfer of Handguns to Convicts, Minors & Mentally Incompetents

South Carolina Code of Laws Section 16-23-30(A)(1) makes it unlawful to sell, offer to sell, deliver, lease, rent, barter, exchange, or transport for sale any handgun to any person who has been convicted of a crime of violence in any court in the United States, the several states, commonwealths, territories, possessions, or the District of Columbia. It is also unlawful to sell, deliver, lease, barter, exchange or transport for sale any handgun to any person who is a member of any subversive organization, is a fugitive from justice, is a habitual drunkard, is a drug addict, or who has been adjudicated mentally incompetent under Section 16-23-30(A)(2). Similarly, it is against the law to sell, deliver, lease, rent, barter, exchange, or transport for sale any handgun to any person who is under the age of eighteen (18) years old under Section 16-23-30(A)(3). This does not apply to the issue of handguns going to members of the armed services, the National Guard, the state militia, or the ROTC when on duty or training or temporarily for instruction and under the supervision of the instructor.

Also, under Section 16-23-30(A)(4) it is unlawful to sell, offer to sell, deliver, lease, rent, barter, exchange, or transport for sale any handgun to any person who has been adjudicated unfit to carry or possess a firearm by a circuit court judge. Such adjudication will have been made after a law enforcement officer, prosecuting officer, or the court itself initiated an action on the fitness of an individual. A person can only be determined unfit after the opportunity for notice and hearing.

All of the crimes under 16-23-30 are felonies. A person, including a dealer, who violates these statutory sections, upon conviction, must be fined not more than $2,000 or imprisoned not more than 5 years, or both under Section 16-23-50(A)(1). Additionally, the handgun involved must be forfeited under Section 16-23-50(B). Because it is a felony, a convicted or adjudicated person is subject to a lifetime federal firearms disability.

What if I Find a Gun?

South Carolina Code of Laws Section 16-23-55 sets forth a procedure for returning a found handgun in the *Offenses Involving Handguns* Chapter (23) of the South Carolina Code of Laws. This section does not require turning over a found handgun to law enforcement nor does it create any penalties for not doing so. Presumably, the procedure is included in the *Offenses Involving Handguns* Chapter to help law enforcement and prosecutors recover discarded or lost handguns that were involved in crimes. The incentive is that the finder can own the gun "free and clear" from any claims of ownership in a little more than 90 days after turning it over to law enforcement. Law enforcement must make a diligent inquiry to determine the true owner of the handgun and determine whether the handgun was stolen or involved in a crime. Law enforcement must also advertise in the area newspaper that the gun has been found. If the handgun is not claimed within 90 days of the first publication in the newspaper, the finder can apply for the handgun but must also pay all advertising and other costs incidental to returning the handgun.

The applicant must be a resident of South Carolina, however, residency is not required of a person who is on active duty in the United States military and who is in possession of a current United States military identification card. The application is the same as if purchasing a handgun from a dealer. In other words, the applicant must complete the same purchase forms and go through the National Instant Criminal Background Check System (NICS) as if the applicant is buying a handgun from a local gun shop or any other federal firearms licensee. Incidentally, the NICS is mandated by the Brady Handgun Violence Prevention Act (Brady Act) of 1993, Public Law 103-159. The Act has done nothing to curb handgun violence by criminals and has only made it more difficult and expensive for law abiding citizens to exercise their right to keep and bear arms.

Machine Guns, Military and Sawed-Off Weapons

In common terms, it is unlawful for you to have anything to do with a machine gun or firearm commonly known as a machine gun, military firearm, sawed off shotgun, or sawed off rifle. Under South Carolina Code of Laws Section 16-23-220, 230 and 240 you are prohibited from possessing, buying, selling storing, transporting, renting, giving away, or just about anything that pertains to these weapons. If convicted, you could be fined up to $10,000 and jailed for up to ten (10) years or both. Conviction or adjudication also brings a lifetime federal firearms disability.

There are exceptions that allow you to legally possess these types of weapons. However, a detailed discussion of the exceptions is beyond the scope of this book. If you are interested in legally possessing these weapons, machine gun dealers are generally knowledgeable of the requirements.

One exception is for military personnel, law enforcement personnel and private citizens who have complied with the strict provisions of the National Firearms Act (NFA). The NFA has registration and tax provisions that are relatively straightforward but require detail beyond the scope of this book. Therefore, consult an attorney and the next chapter before possessing these types of weapons. Another exception is for weapons that are rendered harmless and not usable and are kept only for display as relics. Further, antique firearms are also exempted. Finally, there is a way that you can legally acquire these types of weapons through inheritance.

Possession of a Firearm by Those Convicted of Certain Crimes

Under Section 16-23-30(B) of the South Carolina Code of Laws, it is a felony for any person convicted of certain crimes of violence to own or possess a handgun. This is true even if the conviction originated in another state.

Crimes of violence are defined in South Carolina Code of Laws Section 16-23-10 as: murder, manslaughter (except negligent manslaughter arising out of traffic accidents), rape, mayhem, kidnapping, burglary, robbery, housebreaking, assault with intent to kill, commit rape, or rob, assault with a dangerous weapon, or assault with intent to commit any offense punishable by imprisonment for more than one year. Note that conviction is defined not only a as jury verdict of guilty but also *adjudication of guilt* through pleas of guilty, pleas of nolo contendere, and forfeiture of bail. A person, including a dealer, who violates Section 16-23-30(B), upon conviction, must be fined not more than $2,000 or imprisoned not more than 5 years, or both under Section 16-23-50(A)(1). Additionally, the handgun involved must be forfeited under Section 16-23-50(B).

One or more of the crimes of violence described above might not be designated as a felony but are state misdemeanors punishable by more than two (2) years in jail. So, even if the actual sentence or punishment was less, the fact that the state misdemeanor has the ***potential*** punishment of more than two (2) years in jail renders the convict ineligible to possess a firearm. Please see *Appendix I* for more information on federal firearms disability that results from a conviction of most federal and state felonies, federal misdemeanors with a potential jail term of more than one (1) year, or state misdemeanors with a potential jail term of more than two (2) years.

Armor Piercing Bullets

It is illegal to manufacture, sell, or deliver armor piercing ammunition to anyone other than law enforcement personnel. Armor piercing ammunition has a truncated cone and a core made of steel or another material of equal hardness. In 1994, the federal law added any ammunition with a full metal jacket if that jacket is more than 25% of the total weight of the bullet. If you buy ammunition from a reputable gun shop, you will never run into armor piercing ammunition. As to owning or possessing armor piercing ammunition, it is not technically illegal to own or possess armor piercing bullets unless you load them into a handgun or if you have the intent to commit a crime with the rounds.

It is also unlawful to use, transport, manufacture, possess, purchase, or sell any ammunition or shells which are coated with polytetraflouroethylene (Teflon). Ammunition coated with Teflon is considered armor piercing. A violation here is a felony punishable by a fine of up to $5,000 and jail for up to five (5) years. A violation will also subject the convicted to a lifetime federal firearms disability.

Illegal to Provide Guns to Illegal Aliens

In addition to any federal law, South Carolina Code of Laws Section 16-23-530 makes it illegal to knowingly sell, offer to sell, deliver, lease, rent, barter, exchange, or transport for sale into South Carolina a firearm to a person knowing that such person is not lawfully present in the United States. A violation of this section is a misdemeanor with a penalty of up to $2,000 fine, three (3) years in jail or both. Because this is a state misdemeanor with a potential jail term of more than two (2) years, a violation also subjects you to a lifetime federal firearms disability.

Just to make things fair, it is also illegal for the illegal alien to possess, purchase, offer to purchase, sell, lease, rent, barter, exchange, or transport into South Carolina a firearm. So, in addition to any other law the illegal alien is violating for being in the United States, this section provides for felony liability with a fine of not more than $10,000, imprisonment for not more than ten (10) years, or both. Because it is a felony, the violator is also subject to a lifetime federal firearms disability. But, if the person is an illegal alien, he or she probably doesn't give a hill of beans about any of these laws anyway so the prospect of a lifetime federal firearms disability is not much of a deterrent.

Possessing Stolen Handguns

Under South Carolina Code of Laws Section 16-23-30(C), it is a felony to knowingly buy, sell, transport, pawn, receive, or possess any stolen handgun. Under Section 16-23-50(A)(1), the penalty for a violation is a $2,000 fine, up to five (5) years in jail, or both. Additionally, the handgun must be confiscated under 16-23-50(B). Don't forget to also add a lifetime federal firearms disability because this crime is a felony.

Possessing Handguns with Altered Serial Numbers

Under South Carolina Code of Laws Section 16-23-30(C), it is also a felony to knowingly buy, sell, transport, pawn, receive, or possess any handgun from which the original serial number has been removed or obliterated. Again, under Section 16-23-50(A)(1), the penalty for a violation is a $2,000 fine, up to five (5) years in jail, or both. Additionally, the handgun must be confiscated under 16-23-50(B). Like previously, you can also add on a lifetime federal firearms disability because this crime is a felony.

Shooting at Trains

South Carolina statute 58-17-4100 prohibits the willful shooting of firearms at a train. The prohibition applied to all portions of a train, not just cars typically occupied by people, and it does not matter if the train is moving or not. It seems that this law was required because some people think it is either fun or challenging to hit trains with bullets. The penalty is not more than $500 fine or five (5) years in jail. This is a felony crime that will leave the convicted person with all of the troubles of a felony record and lifetime federal firearms disability. The person who shoots at a train might also be charged with other crimes if applicable. If the cars are occupied or someone is hurt or killed, even more charges will pile on. Do not point your muzzle at trains or anything else that you do not intend to kill or destroy.

Legal Defense to a Crime

You never want to get in the position of breaking the law and getting arrested or charged. However, there are legal defenses if you are arrested or charged. Say, for instance, that you are legally carrying your gun and forget it's there when you try to enter the gate area of an airport, or a courthouse or some other prohibited place. The fact that you actually forgot about the gun is a legal defense. Lack of knowledge is a legal defense.

Another legal defense is using your weapon for lawful self-defense. The lawful use of self-defense is a worthy of an entire chapter so the *Self-Defense* chapter will more fully discuss your right to defend yourself.

Civil Lawsuit Liability

Civil liability arises when someone is wronged in a manner that does not violate a criminal law or is in conjunction with a criminal wrong. A civil wrong can subject you to a money judgment. Some established bases for a civil lawsuit include: negligence, negligent entrustment of a dangerous instrumentality, assault, trespass, trespass to chattels, infliction of emotional distress, and nuisance. This list is not exhaustive. A court can use its inherent power to hear almost any dispute. But, for the purpose of this book, we will look at the abovementioned causes of action.

Negligence is conduct that falls below the conduct of a reasonable person under the same circumstances. It is important to understand that the standard is not subjective. This means that you are not judged on whether you think that your actions are reasonable. Instead, your actions are judged against what others think a reasonable person would do under the same circumstances. Therefore, it is wise to add a measure of caution regarding the handling and storing of your firearm because others might not think that your actions are reasonable.

Negligent entrustment of a dangerous instrumentality arises if you entrust your weapon to someone that you know, *or should know*, has a propensity to do purposeful or negligent wrongful acts. The person you entrust (lend) the weapon to can be an adult or a minor, competent or incompetent. So, be very selective about who you entrust your firearms with, if anyone.

Assault is placing another in imminent fear of an immediate harm. The idea is that the first person makes a second person fear that the second person will immediately be harmed by the first person. Again, the reasonable person standard is applied.

In the context of guns, assault can occur if a person simply brandishes a firearm. Under some circumstances, a person might reasonably fear harm from a firearm even when the person with the firearm had no intention to cause the fear. Facing civil liability for assault, you should never brandish or expose a firearm unless you are sure that no one around you will be placed in immediate fear as a result.

Trespass is an unauthorized entry upon the property of another. Be aware that sending an object like a bullet upon the property of another is also trespass. You do not have to intend to commit a trespass to be liable. Instead, you must only intend to go upon the property of another. Therefore, you can still be liable if you did not intend to trespass but you intentionally went on another's property. You are permitted to trespass in the event of an emergency or for self-defense.

Civil liability for trespass can accompany the criminal liability mentioned earlier in this chapter. For instance, you can be held criminally liable for entering a business with a concealed weapon when that business has posted a "No Concealable Weapons Allowed" sign. You can also be sued for money damages by the same business owner for the trespass.

Trespass to chattels is damaging or destroying the property of another. With respect to guns, liability arises when an errant shot destroys the property of another. Animals are considered property under the law. Therefore, if you accidentally damage another's building, vehicle, or pet, you can be sued for money damages.

You can be held civilly liable for intentional or even negligent infliction of emotional distress upon another. You must be aware that, under the right circumstances, a jury could find that your firearm caused another emotional distress. Your conduct must be extreme and outrageous, but, none-the-less, you can be held civilly liable for inflicting serious emotional pain upon someone.

Nuisance involves denying another the quiet enjoyment of their property. You can create civil liability for nuisance by creating noise or smoke with your gun. Also note that, while a nuisance cannot also be a trespass, a trespass can be a nuisance. Nuisance claims are barred against bona-fide gun ranges by the South Carolina Gun Range Protection Act discussed in the *Miscellaneous Gun Laws* chapter.

It should be noted that the family of Trayvon Martin filed a claim against the insurer of the homeowners association for the neighborhood where George Zimmerman and Martin's mother resided. There was a settlement in that case that is believed to exceed $1 million but there is no way to be sure. The theory of liability is that Zimmerman, while acting independently at the time, was a member of the neighborhood watch that was sanctioned by the homeowners association. As with all neighborhood association liability matters, periodic review of procedures, liability waivers, and insurance by an attorney or the insurer.

Keeping Guns Away from Children

The courts recognize that children are not simply "little adults" but rather immature people who are not as mentally developed as most reasonable adults. Children are not able to assess risk like adults can. Similarly, children cannot foresee the consequences of actions as most adults can.

You might have seen television programs where parents are shown hidden camera video of their children finding a gun. To the parents' horror, some of the children handled the planted guns and even pointed them at other children in the room.

In some circumstances, parents and custodians can be held liable for the actions of children when the parent or custodian knows the child has a propensity to act purposely or recklessly. Further, the doctrine of *Dangerous Instrumentalities* place liability on those who furnish dangerous things to tort-feasors. Also, adults directly supervising children can be held liable for the consequences that result from that adult's negligence.

For these reasons, adults must have a strategy for safely keeping guns around children. Maybe your strategy can be to combine a gun safe with an educational program like the NRA's *Eddie Eagle: Stop! Don't Touch, Leave the Area and Tell an Adult* program. Maybe you have one loaded pistol with a small finger pad gun safe next to your dresser and the rest of your guns unloaded in a safe. The authors are not making recommendations here but emphasizing the point that you must have some reasonable strategy for balancing the defensive safety of a firearm against the potential that a child can cause unintended harm.

Fortunately, there are many good products that prevent unauthorized or accidental access to guns. The most effective mechanism is called, not surprisingly, a gun safe. A finger pad gun safe can be placed in a nightstand and uses an electronic fingerboard that opens immediately with pin number. Also, there are trigger locks and bolt locks for guns that would not be needed for a threat. Finally, guns can be kept in places where children do not go like relative's homes or gun club lockers.

Handgun Locks may Provide Civil Lawsuit Protection

As discussed earlier in the purchasing chapter, federal law can provide limited immunity from a *qualified civil liability action*. Under 18 USC 922(z)(3), a qualified civil liability action is defined as a civil action for damages resulting from the criminal or unlawful misuse of a handgun by a third party if: 1) the handgun was accessed by another person who did not have the authorization of the lawful possessor; and 2) at the time the handgun was accessed it had been made inoperable by the use of a secure gun storage or safety device. For more discussion on this section of federal law, see the chapter on purchasing firearms.

Will My Insurance Cover Me if I get Sued or Arrested?

Homeowner's insurance and business liability insurance policies generally have a personal liability provision. Many people also have "umbrella" liability policies that supplement and increase liability coverage. In general, these policies provide liability indemnification for occurrences at the home or business, in or about a vehicle, or even anywhere else in public. These policies insure against the *negligent* acts of the insured but not the intentional acts of the insured. So, as you read through this civil liability section, keep in mind that you will not be covered if the act is considered intentional.

If you are sued for negligence, and the negligence is a covered occurrence in your policy, the insurance company will provide you with an attorney and defend the lawsuit. The policy will also pay if it is determined that another was injured as a result of your negligence. If you are arrested for a crime, liability policies will not cover you so the insurance company will not provide you with a defense attorney. There are, however, legal service insurance plans that provide you with an attorney if you are arrested or need other routine legal services. Those policies generally only cover the legal fees of defense but will not indemnify you against claims or judgments. See the *Self-Defense* Chapter for more discussion of insurance liability policies.

Chapter 7
National Firearms Act (NFA)

Robert K. Merting, Esq., Contributor.

What is the NFA?

The National Firearms Act (hereafter, "NFA") is a federal law enacted in 1934. The law used the Federal Government's taxation powers to require registration of and levy a transfer tax upon certain items defined as *firearms* in the Act. While the NFA did not make any firearms or items illegal *per se,* its original intent was to make ownership of said items too expensive and cumbersome for the average person. This was accomplished by making it illegal to make, possess, transfer, or move specified firearms or other items across state lines without proper registration, taxation, and notification. The transfer tax for most transfers was set at $200 in 1934 and has remained the same.

What is a NFA Firearm?

An NFA firearm is any item defined as a *firearm* in the National Firearms Act, 26 U.S.C. 5845. "Firearms" under the act fall into one of eight categories:

1. Shotgun with barrel(s) less than 18 inches;
2. Weapon made from a shotgun;
3. Rifle with barrel(s) less than 16 inches;
4. Weapon made from a rifle;
5. Any Other Weapon (capable of being concealed on the person);
6. Machinegun;
7. Silencer; or a,
8. Destructive device.

Besides these eight broad definitions or categories, the law goes on to further refine its own definition of *firearm*. The federal regulations that implement and regulate the NFA provide further detailed descriptions of what qualifies as a firearm under the statute. As with most statutes, appeals court decisions interpret and clarify the definitions.

It is important to note that the NFA defines firearm differently from the other major federal gun law: the Gun Control Act (hereafter, GCA). The GCA's definition of firearm includes all common pistols, revolvers, rifles, and shotguns as well as most NFA firearms.

Firearms under the NFA include items that are not what we typically consider firearms. For example, everyone knows a shotgun or machinegun is a firearm. However, virtually nobody would guess that a silencer or Claymore mine (a destructive device) is a firearm. But the NFA defines silencers and destructive devices as firearms. Therefore, to reduce confusion, we may refer to NFA firearms as NFA *items* in this book. While not statutorily accurate, we think calling them "NFA items" reduces confusion.

Most common (i.e. GCA) firearms are not NFA items. The NFA was a reaction to crimes by Prohibition era gangsters. The gangsters committed some of their more shocking crimes using machine guns, sawed-off shotguns, homemade bombs, surplus military firearms, and noise-reduction devices. While they also used "common" firearms in the crimes, the push to include common firearms, such as handguns, in the NFA failed. Therefore, "common" pistols, revolvers, shotguns and rifles are not regulated by the NFA. If you come across an item and are unsure if it is an NFA item or not, you should consult an attorney because the potential penalty for mere unlawful possession is up to a $250,000 fine and up to ten years in federal prison, per violation (26 U.S.C. 5871).

A Note on Machine Guns

While the original NFA did not prohibit any firearms, changes to the regulations in the GCA and the Firearm Owners Protection Act (hereafter "FOPA") did create outright prohibitions. The GCA prohibited civilian ownership of imported firearms with certain features. These same firearms could be owned if manufactured within the United States. This narrow prohibition would be lost in importance if not for the FOPA.

In 1986 the FOPA prohibited civilian possession of all machine guns not already registered and legally possessed prior to the enactment of the law. This created three classes of machine guns. The most valuable, fully transferable machine guns, were registered with the ATF prior to 1986 and were not subject to the GCA prohibition on importing. Machine guns that were subject to the prohibition on importing, but that had been imported and registered to dealers for demonstration to government buyers before 1986 became known as "Pre-May Dealer Samples." Machine guns registered after the enactment of the FOPA are known as "Post-May Dealer Samples.

Fully transferable machine guns can be owned by anyone legally able to own firearms and willing to go through the NFA item transfer process. The number of these guns is limited and demand for the items have pushed the prices many multiples higher than their semi-automatic counterparts.

Pre-May Dealer Samples can only be transferred to government entities or currently licensed Federal Firearm Licensees (i.e. FFLs). However, a FFL does not need to justify why it wants the firearm, and the FFL can keep a Pre-May Dealer Sample after it surrenders its license. The limited number of buyers, i.e. FFLs, reduces the demand for these guns. However, the allure to keep the firearm, and the ability to acquire such a firearm without any justification counteracts to increase the price.

Many times these firearms are worth nearly as much as a comparable fully transferable firearm.

Post-May Dealer Samples can only be transferred to government entities or to a currently licensed FFL with a law enforcement demonstration request. (i.e. a specific letter requesting the FFL acquire a particular machine gun for demonstration to the law enforcement department as part of a decision to purchase machine guns.) Due to the need to have a demonstration request, and the difficulty to acquire the same, these firearms have minimal value. In some instances, the parts of the gun may be more valuable than the firearm itself.

Unfortunately, for the average collector, the only machine guns available are the expensive fully transferable machine guns. When looking to buy such a firearm, we highly encourage you to use an experienced gun dealer and / or attorney to ensure you are not part of a scam.

What does it Mean to *Possess* an NFA Firearm?

The NFA does not define *possession* of an NFA item. Rather, it imposes restrictions upon the making, importing, or *transfer of possession* of the items. The distinction between *possession* and *transfer of possession* is more semantic than form. Only owners can possess registered NFA items and registered firearms can only be transferred upon the approval of ATF and the payment of a tax. Federal law defines transfer as the:

> *selling, assigning, pledging, leasing, loaning, giving away, or otherwise disposing of [an NFA firearm],26 U.S.C. Chapter 53, Section 5845(j).*

This broad definition should be of concern to anyone transferring or possessing NFA items. Keep in mind that transfer of possession presents criminal liability to both the transferor and the transferee. Therefore we highly encourage owners of NFA items to keep the firearms locked and away from anyone not authorized to have possession of the firearms. If you have any questions about letting someone other than you possess, shoot, borrow, keep, or buy your NFA firearm, please contact a gun law attorney for a consultation.

NFA Firearms Trusts

A common way to allow multiple persons to use a NFA item is by registering the NFA item in a NFA firearms trust. This purpose-specific trust can solve several legal problems associated with NFA items.

What is a Trust?

It's easy to think of a trust as a document. However, a trust is a legal relationship between people. The relationship is spelled out in the text of a written agreement. The main parties in this relationship are the settlor, the trustee(s), and the beneficiary(s). The settlor has property and transfers it to the trustee for the benefit of the beneficiary. For the rest of this handbook, we will use the term *trust* to refer to the paperwork and *trust relationship* to describe the more important relationship that the paperwork creates.

To explain, let's first go to a basic concept of law: legal "persons." You are a human person and a legal person. The law calls your human existence a "natural person." The law calls your legal existence a "legal person." As a legal person, you can own property, possess property, and sell property. With respect to NFA firearms, you can own, possess, and buy or sell them.

Likewise, a trustee is a legal person who can own and sell property. However, in a trust relationship, the trustee is constrained by the terms of the trust.

A trust relationship can be seen as a bucket. In fact, we have a visual prop that we use. It's a paper fast food chicken bucket with sheets from a legal trust glued on the outside. The entire prop is made of paper and ink. The point is that you can create a bucket, capable of legally holding and controlling property, by simply combining some paper, the right legal words, the right people, and the requisite intent to create a trust. Even though trusts do not have to be written, we only create trusts in writing because ATF does not recognize a trust unless it is in writing.

Trusts are created and authorized by law, specifically, your state's law. Your state's trust law can be in its statutes, case law, or a combination of both. Further, trusts are recognized and defined in the Federal IRS code (remember that the NFA was established as a firearms tax statute aimed at registration and curbing transfers). If it weren't for your state's trust law, the federal Codes and relevant cases from the Courts, trusts would not exist in the eyes of the law and we would not be able to rely on them. ATF requires that NFA firearm trusts comply with the state law of the applicant for transfer.

How Does a Trust Own Property?

A trust relationship only makes sense in the context of property. A trust relationship is created to own property, determine its use, and determine its ultimate distribution. To understand how to get property into a trust relationship, we should first take a step back and look at the concepts of *property* and *title*. Every law student's first year includes a semester-long course called Property. For the purpose of this handbook though, there's no need for that depth of understanding. Suffice it to say that property is something that a legal person can own and that ownership is recognized and (supposedly) protected by society.

When you think about the property that you own, you should think in terms of your titled property and non-titled property. Titled property generally describes items such as real estate, vehicles, and brokerage accounts. These types of property usually have some paper work indicating ownership and also require your signature on a piece of paper to transfer. When you sell a vehicle, you sign the back of the paper title. For real estate, you sign a deed. For a bank account, you write a check or sign a form closing the account. Titled property requires a "paper trail."

Non-titled property generally describes property that you own that does not have a paper proof of ownership and does not require a signature to transfer. Non-titled property includes items like figurines, musical instruments, furniture, and collections. To transfer non-titled property, you simply deliver the property over to the new owner (for money, or as a gift, etc.). Non-titled property does not necessarily require a "paper trail."

Now we get into the concept of *legal* versus *equitable* ownership. This distinction is at the core of trust law. To understand this concept, we have to go back to the origin of trusts in England at the time of the Crusades. Knights in the Crusades were landowners. When a knight went to distant lands, he would convey legal ownership to a caretaker with a deed. The knights would give the deed with a verbal understanding and agreement that the legal ownership would be conveyed back after the knight's return. To their dismay though, knights were returning to a caretaker who refused to transfer the property back. Shockingly, the courts of law saw the original transfer as an unfortunate, but legal, transfer of the property to the caretaker. Furious with that result, the knights begged the king for relief. The king referred the knights to another type of court - the court of chancery. In a court of chancery, the king's chancellor could decide a case according to his conscience as opposed to strict rules of law. The court of chancery thus created the legal principle of *equity*.

With respect to these property cases, it shocked the conscience of the chancellor that the caretaker could go back on his word and refuse to title the property back to the knight. The chancellor reliably found in favor of the knights. As the knights continued to prevail, it became known that the chancellor would continually rule that the returning knight is the rightful owner. Therefore, the law of trust relationships was created. From then on, even though the caretaker (trustee) was a *legal* owner for the time while the knight was away, the knight remained the *equitable* owner and beneficiary. The legal owner could hold the land (in trust) for the benefit of the equitable owner but would be compelled to convey it back to him when requested.

So, how does a trust own property? The trust never actually owns property but it can be seen as an ownership relationship. Remember, the trust paperwork creates a trust relationship. The settlor begins with both *legal* and *equitable* ownership of the property. The trustee, subject to the terms of the trust, takes *legal* ownership as trustee in trust for the beneficiary. The beneficiary, however, is the *equitable* owner of the property. In the strict legal sense, the trust never "owns" property. However, it is much easier conceptually to talk about the trust owning property. Most attorneys and people who deal with trusts regularly talk in terms of the trust owning property. So, from now on, for simplicity's sake, we will always talk in terms of the trust owning property and about transferring property to and from the trust.

The Roles in a Trust

In general, trusts have three required roles: settlor, trustee, and beneficiary. These roles are spelled-out in trust law and by the terms of the trust. A very important characteristic of trusts is that one person can take-on more than one role. However, trust law does not allow one person to be sole trustee and sole beneficiary. If that happens, legal title and equitable title *merge* and the trust is void. You don't want a void trust with NFA Items.

Going back to our knight and his land caretaker, we had all three roles performed by only two people. The knight played the role of settlor and beneficiary. The caretaker was the trustee.

In most NFA trusts, the settlor is also a trustee. He might be a sole trustee or co-trustee for reasons we'll discuss later. Also, in most NFA trusts, the beneficiary is someone other than the settlor. Most settlors also name successor trustees.

Settlor

The settlor is the person who has the trust drafted, signs as "Settlor," "Grantor," or "Trust-Maker" and funds the trust with property. In the case of NFA trusts, the initial funding is generally a recitation: "for $10 and other good and valuable consideration." The settlor is almost always a trustee. If the settlor is also trustee, he or she is entitled to possess NFA items owned by the trust.

Trustee

The trustee is the person who holds title to the property in trust for the beneficiary. The trustee is able to possess and transfer property like NFA items, cash, or any other legal property. In NFA trusts, the settlor is almost always a trustee because that person wants to be able to possess and transfer NFA items held in the trust.

Co-Trustee

A co-trustee is a person appointed by the settlor or trustee. Co-trustees can possess and transfer property in and out of the trust like NFA items and money. Most NFA trusts are drafted so that the settlor/trustee has the ability to remove a co-trustee or take any other action restricting or eliminating a co-trustee. Conversely, language in the trust generally provides that a co-trustee cannot remove the settlor/trustee or his successor. A co-trustee, other than the settlor/trustee, can also be a beneficiary.

Beneficiary(ies)

A beneficiary is one person (or more) who is ultimately entitled to the property of the trust. A beneficiary may be a minor. A beneficiary can be a current co-trustee and, therefore, be entitled to possession of an NFA item owned by the trust.

Dangers of Non-Attorney NFA Firearms Trust

The primary purpose of an NFA firearms trust is to purchase, hold, and use NFA firearms. This trust is not a "boilerplate" commercial trust found in retail software but has been carefully written by an attorney familiar with the NFA.

Without getting into details about each benefit, a properly attorney-drafted NFA firearms trust provides at least the following:

a. Current co-trustees are entitled to possession. For example, a settlor might go to Afghanistan for a period of time. His current co-trustees in South Carolina can continue to possess and use any NFA firearms owned by the trust.

b. Privacy. The trust is the owner and is generally named a generic name. Paperwork is done in the name of the trust as opposed to in someone's name. Trusts are private and not typically filed with a Court or government agency.

c. No local law enforcement permission is required.

d. The trust remains in effect through incapacity or death of the settlor and avoids probate.

e. Trusts do not require registration and formalities that corporations require.

f. A properly drafted NFA firearm trust includes restrictions on transferring firearms to prohibited persons and provides notice to trustees of these restrictions.

g. Properly drafted NFA firearm trusts are not the same as a boilerplate revocable living trust found in gun shop templates or in commercial trust software programs.

h. Once an item is transferred to a trust and tax paid, there is no need to pay for additional registration taxes each time a subsequent trustees is appointed.

Gun Dealers shouldn't Provide NFA Firearms Trusts

Gun dealers providing trust forms are in danger of engaging in the unlicensed practice of law, which is a felony under Section 40-5-310 of the South Carolina Code of Laws. The potential penalty is up to five years in prison and/or five a thousand dollar fine. Conviction of a felony strips the felon of his firearm rights and all firearms licenses. Is it worth risking your rights, business, and livelihood for a few hundred dollars?

NFA Firearms Inheritance

You can give or receive an NFA restricted firearm through inheritance. Remember though that NFA firearms not owned by a trust are subject to probate court. There is no other way to transfer the NFA firearm if it was owned by an individual. Even though the bequest might have been made in a Last Will and Testament – the Last Will and Testament requires probate and is not a probate-avoidance estate planning method. Some critical considerations for disposition through probate are:

a. Does the personal representative have a firearms prohibition?

b. Does the beneficiary have a firearms prohibition?
c. Does the destination state for the firearm have an NFA items prohibition? Is it for firearms only or suppressors too?
d. Which forms of shipment are legal?
e. Is the proper transfer paperwork filed with ATF before transferring or shipping?
f. Is the proper transfer paperwork filed with ATF in a timely manner and before the estate closed?
g. Is the item contraband?

Leaving an NFA item (NFA firearm) in the hands of an unwary personal representative leaves that person with tremendous potential criminal liability. That is why a trust, with supporting educational information, is far more preferable. Transfers upon death through inheritance require registration but are transfer tax free.

A Relative Brings Home a Machine Gun from War

Every now and again a family comes across a machine gun or other military item that a relative brought back as a war trophy. The typical scenario is a Thompson Automatic (Tommy Gun) from World War II. Alternatively, the family encounters a German or Japanese machine gun.

If the item was never registered on the National Firearms Registration and Firearms Record, it is considered illegal contraband by the ATF. ATF will accept the item and try to see if it was ever registered. If they can't determine it was registered, they will either destroy it or transfer it to a qualified law enforcement agency because there is currently no way to register machine guns to anyone except a government entity. Alternatively, the family can try to have a government owned museum accept the item and potentially receive a tax deduction for the contribution. This however can be risky without attorney-client privilege to shield the identity of the donor during negotiations.

If the firearm was registered, which is not uncommon with foreign machine guns captured as war trophies, the item could be worth many thousands of dollars if the registration can be located and straightened out.

The authors have experience helping beneficiaries with machine guns, both with and without registrations, and we advise cautious handling of such firearms. If you need assistance checking on a registration or disposing of such a gun, do not hesitate to contact a qualified attorney.

Transferring and Registering as an Individual

If you apply for registration as an individual, you must notify a chief law enforcement officer, provide two photographs, and provide two sets of fingerprints. The chief law enforcement officer can be the Chief of Police, the Sheriff, head of the State Police, a District Attorney or State Attorney, or any other person that is acceptable to the Director of ATF.

Applying for registration in the name of a corporation or a trust changes these requirements just a little. First you must provide documentation on the existence of the corporation or trust. Second you must identify the 'Responsible Persons' of the entity. 'Responsible Persons' are those persons who are able to possess and use the firearms owned by the Trust. Third, each 'Responsible Person' must complete an ATF Form identifying the person and providing a photograph and two sets of fingerprints.

Fortunately for the purchaser of NFA firearms, most dealers customarily handle the ATF paperwork on behalf of the purchaser and will guide you through the process.

Please be extra careful to know the law with respect to NFA items. If you have any questions, contact a firearms attorney.

Chapter 8
Self-Defense

Introduction

Especially when carrying a firearm, you should always avoid confrontation. The fact that you have a firearm on or near you during a confrontation takes things to the next level whether you intend it to or not. For instance, you can aggravate a simple argument into a criminal aggravated assault. You could have the gun taken from you and used against you. You could have an unknowing bystander think you are a perp and shoot you. You could have the police shoot you. My point here is not to discourage you from carrying, you should be carrying everywhere you can. The point is to go out of your way to avoid any type of confrontation. Consider your firearm only a shield and not a sword. It is your self-defense "fire extinguisher" for dire emergencies only.

No matter how hard you try to avoid bad people, though, a deadly situation can materialize at any time and in any place. This chapter will deal with lawful self-defense. Self-defense is an affirmative legal defense for actions that would otherwise be criminal. You have a right to inflict force upon others if you are legitimately defending yourself or others.

Under South Carolina law, if a person is charged with a crime, and subsequently claims self-defense, the burden is upon the prosecution to disprove beyond a reasonable doubt at least one of the elements of self-defense. If the prosecution cannot do so, then the claim of self-defense stands and the criminal charge is defeated.

Please read this chapter thoroughly because it is important that you know the law of self-defense. You should view this chapter as a whole and not as separate sections because some sections interact with other sections. If any chapter deserves to be read over and over, this is the chapter.

For a real-life case study of the law of self-defense in South Carolina, you should read the appeals opinions in State v. Jason Michael Dickey found at the SC Supreme Court website (SCCourts.org). Likewise, recent high profile shootings cases provide great lessons. For instance:

> *State of Wisconsin vs. Kyle Rittenhouse* (acquittal of Rodney King riots peacemaker) – (a good attorney is critical, use of force expert critical, don't be a self-appointed peacemaker, avoid situations where things can easily get argumentative and violent, avoid using open carry during unstable events like protests and riots, avoid situations where you feel like you have to bring a gun with you);
>
> *State of Florida vs. Curtis Reeves*, (acquittal of movie "popcorn" shooter - (avoid confrontations at all cost when you have a gun, you never know how a stranger will act, younger bully should not have confronted older man, a good attorney is critical, use of force expert is critical, a good jury is critical); and,

<u>*State of Florida vs. George Zimmerman*</u> (acquittal of HOA security patrol) – (not worth it to handle crime problems on your own, a good attorney is critical, use of force expert is critical, jury selection critical).

All three of these cases required the self defense shooter to go through years of severe stress, cost at least a million dollars in attorney as expert witness fees, and came down to a jury verdict that could have easily put the shooter in prison for the rest of his life.

You can get great self-defense mindset training by subscribing to a good YouTube channel. My favorite is: ***Active Self Protection***. They play videos of real encounters and then explain everything a good, sane, prudent, moral, and sober person should do in that real self-defense situation.

The Terrible Context of Self-Defense

It is unfortunate that our society has come to the point where honest and peaceful, law-abiding citizens have to carry guns during their normal daily activities. Guns are fascinating, "cool," and often beautifully built machines but one is primarily designed to cause serious damage to whatever its ammunition hits. Guns can be heavy, bulky, and can get clothes or purses greasy if not cleaned correctly. Also, guns cause stress because the carrier must be mindful of where the muzzle is pointed, keeping fingers off the trigger, the legality of possession and concealment, and preventing the gun from escaping into the hands of untrained children or unauthorized users. Carrying a gun consistently adds complexity to daily life. Even so, more and more people are carrying guns to defend against a deadly attack.

That being said, the criminals and crazy nuts generally have the advantage because they are not worried about the legality of using their weapon. In a survival situation, law-abiding citizens might hesitate because of uncertainty about the law of self-defense. Fear of criminal prosecution or a lawsuit can cause the *paralysis of analysis.*

One way to overcome the paralysis of analysis is to read this chapter over and over and to imagine self-defense scenarios in your mind as you go through your day. Think of scenarios that you often find yourself in. For instance, the next time that you are in a parking lot at night, think of how you would react if you encounter someone armed. Would you react differently if the threat is moving fast or slow or if any of the thugs have a knife as opposed to a gun? At what point would you consider the thugs' actions a deadly attack? At what point would pull-out your gun from its holster and shoot at the attackers? What could you do or would you do if other people are around? As another example, think of how you would react if you and your coworkers were held hostage by some armed robbers. If you have an opportunity to shoot the robbers while their backs are turned, is it legal to do so? Another example is to envision shopping in a crowded mall when some crazed gunman starts shooting with a rifle. Would it be legal to shoot back? Would it be more beneficial to find a good hiding place first or start firing back first? Think through the scenarios and then try to find the best answers in this book. I say "best answers" because sometimes there is not *the answer* but only the best answer given the circumstances and our legal system.

Another way is to have a few very simple rules. For instance, strangers should not know that you are carrying a gun, or see your gun, unless you are using it to defend against a deadly attack. At best, brandishing a weapon will get you into criminal liability or defeat your claim of self-defense. At worst, brandishing your gun will prevent you from effectively defeating the deadly threat. Owning the element of surprise is one way to overcome the built-in advantage that criminals have. Further, brandishing a weapon can be an ineffective deterrent to someone who is really out to victimize you. So, have simple rules like:

never pull your gun out unless you intend to use it to shoot at a legitimate deadly attack against you or someone you are protecting.

I expect that the people reading this book are law-abiding citizens who do not want to shoot somebody. Law abiding citizens carrying guns for self-defense are not a problem. It is the criminals and people with untreated mental conditions that are a problem. That being said, if you come into the predicament where you are required to use your gun, and you misjudge the situation, you might end up prosecuted, seriously injured or dead. None of these alternatives are welcome but they do happen.

On balance, the most important thing is that you have the ability to defend against a deadly attack. The justice system must be respected but you should not let it intimidate you from legally carrying your gun and using it if you have to. In the unfortunate context of defending your life with a gun, there are no great options. In the end, protecting your life, or the life of some other innocent person, is more important than anything else.

Distinction between Deadly and Non-Deadly Force

You must have a sound understanding of the difference between deadly force and non-deadly force. Deadly force is defined as force that is likely to cause death or great bodily harm. Clearly, any gun has the ability to cause death or great bodily harm. Similarly, a sharp knife and swinging a baseball bat have the ability to cause death or serious bodily harm. An automobile steered directly at another can cause death or serious bodily harm. Even the bare hands of a strong person can cause death or serious bodily harm to a weaker, more vulnerable or surprised person.

Alternatively, non-deadly force is force that is not likely to cause death or serious bodily harm. Spraying pepper spray is not likely to cause death or serious bodily harm. Similarly, the bare hands of a weak person are not likely to cause death or serious bodily harm.

If you are starting to realize that the differences between deadly and non-deadly force are not black and white, you are beginning to understand the concept. If the use of deadly force comes before a court of law, all facts relating to the incident will be carefully scrutinized.

The Four Elements of Self-Defense in South Carolina

Under common law in South Carolina, four elements must exist:

- You must be without fault in bringing-on the violent encounter between you and the other person(s);

- You must actually believe that you are in imminent danger of loss of life or serious bodily injury or you must actually be in such danger;

- You must use deadly force only if a reasonable or prudent man of ordinary firmness and courage would have believed himself to be in imminent danger of loss of life or serious bodily harm or, if you actually were in such danger, the circumstances were such to warrant a man of ordinary prudence, firmness and courage to use deadly force against the other person(s);

- Unless you are in a place that you are lawfully entitled to be, you had no other probable means of avoiding the danger of losing your own life or sustaining serious bodily injury than to act as you did in the particular instance.

The next sections look at these elements one-by-one.

Without Fault

In order to raise self-defense, you cannot be the aggressor or primogenitor of the violent encounter. While there are law cases that define the legal threshold of "without fault," simply put, you don't want to be perceived as one who started the whole episode that resulted in a violent encounter. Further, you are prohibited from doing anything to escalate an encounter. The law requires that you be *without fault*, not that you simply are less at fault than the other guy. Did you catch that? You must be without fault throughout the entire encounter with the other person.

Say that you are driving on I-26 and there is a jerk going slow in the left lane. Next to that guy is an SUV in the slow lane going the same speed as the jerk in front of you, thereby creating a rolling blockade. Your irritation builds with every passing mile. Irritation turns to anger and you start to tailgate the left lane loafer. After a few miles of tailgating, the loafer motions you to pull over for a closer encounter of the violent kind. You pull over and argue and then the loafer comes at you with some type of deadly attack. Under these facts, you are behind the eight-ball in gaining the legal defense of self-defense because you can be perceived by a jury as not being without fault in bringing about the violent encounter. There is a chance that you would be charged and that a jury could find that somewhere in those events you had some level of fault in either creating or escalating the episode.

Alternatively, say that you are on I-26 near Newberry at 1:00am and you get a flat tire. You pull over to repair the tire and you have your concealed weapon with you. Some opportunistic criminals see you in a vulnerable position and stop to "help." As they help you with the tire, one of the guys comes at you with a knife or gun. You pull out your weapon and shoot the attackers in self-defense. Under this simple fact pattern, you did not bring on the attack and you did nothing throughout the episode to escalate the attack. Therefore, you have much better facts to not get charged. Even if you do get charged you have not given the prosecutor and jury easy facts to nail you on the "without fault" element of legal self-defense like you did in the previous example.

Belief of Imminent Threat of Death or Serious Bodily Harm

You can only use deadly force in self-defense if the threat to you is imminent. Imminent means that you are under an immediate threat. In other words, someone is posing a bona fide threat of death or serious bodily harm to you right there at that location and at that time. Put another way, the threat must be right before both physically and in time.

As to the physical aspect of this element, the important factor is that the weapon presented against you must be capable of causing harm based upon the distance between you and the threat. A knife is a deadly weapon but it must be used in close range and by a person with the physical ability to use the knife. Pistols and shotguns are deadly weapons but they have deadly ranges that are generally less than rifles. A car can be a deadly weapon if it is traveling in the right direction and within a certain distance of a victim.

As to the timing aspect of this element, the important factor is that the attack occur immediately prior to, or contemporaneously with, your self-defense reaction. So, the time prong is not satisfied if someone calls you on the phone and says that he or she is going to come over and kill you. It is also not satisfied if someone creates a deadly attack towards you and you get away and then you go back and shoot the person. The threat must either directly proceed or happen contemporaneously with your self-defense actions.

The main point here is that, under a self-defense claim, juries will be asked to determine if the deadly object, if any, combined with the nature and circumstances of the attack, was right before you, right then and right there. We will next show a few simple examples that illustrate the self-defense element of *imminent threat.*

Assume that your spouse or romantic interest and you are out on a date and you get a phone call from your date's obsessively jealous or crazy ex. The ex begins to say that your date is bad for you and that, "if he can't have her, nobody can." The ex says that he is going to go to your house later that night and kill you. Hearing that news, you become scared because you know that the ex is a violent person, is bigger than you, and has been previously convicted of assault with a deadly weapon. To protect yourself, you drive over to the ex's house and shoot and kill the ex. Under these circumstances, it is very likely that you will be charged with murder and found guilty by a jury. The ex's threat was not imminent because the ex was talking with you over the phone and said that he would not kill you until later.

Now let's assume that the ex did not call you but rather surprised you by meeting both you and your date outside of the restaurant. From a short distance away, the ex begins to approach you in a very aggressive posture and pulls out a knife and says that he is going to kill you. You are honestly in fear for your date's life and your own. At that point, you pull out your concealed weapon and shoot him so that he is rendered immobile. Under these facts, you might get arrested but a jury has ample evidence to find that the threat was imminent. If you did get arrested, hopefully the prosecutor would see that you acted in legal self-defense and drop any charges against you. If the worst scenario occurs and you go before a jury, the jury would have good evidence for an acquittal.

Again assume that the ex surprises you both outside of the restaurant. Let's change the facts a little to say that the ex has no history of violent behavior that you are aware of, is much smaller than you, and never gives any indication that he has a deadly weapon. While "in your face," the ex tells you that he is going to get a gun out of the car and shoot you. You have no idea where the car is located but you know that it is not close because there are no cars directly around where you are standing. Believing that the ex is going to go to his car and get a gun to shoot you, you pull out your gun and shoot him right there. Even though the ex was saying that he was going to get a gun to kill you, and originally approached you in a somewhat threatening manner, you could be successfully charged with murder or manslaughter because there is weak evidence that the threat was imminent. In other words, the threat was not right before you, right then and right there.

The above scenario becomes more complicated if you do not shoot the ex then and there but, instead, stand your ground while the ex goes back to his or her car and returns with a gun. That type of scenario will be examined following the *Reasonable or Prudent Man Standard* element of self-defense. The next section will introduce you to the Protection of Persons and Property Act that provides a very important legal presumption that a threat is imminent under certain circumstances.

Imminent Threat Presumed in Home, Dwelling or Occupied Vehicle

To their great credit, the South Carolina General Assembly passed, and on June 9, 2006, Governor Sanford signed, the Protection of Persons and Property Act (the Act). The main purpose of that legislation is to create statutory legitimization of the "Castle Doctrine." The bill also gives statutory protection to "stand your ground" in most legitimate defensive situations. The Castle Doctrine is a very old doctrine of law that recognizes the adage that a person's home is his castle. It also extends that adage to include a person's business and occupied vehicle.

For the purpose of this section, the relevant portions of the Act (Section 16-11-440 (edited) of the South Carolina Code of Laws) provide:

> A person is *presumed* (emphasis added) to have a reasonable fear of **imminent** peril of death or great bodily injury to himself or another person when using deadly force that is intended or likely

to cause death or great bodily injury to another person if the person:

(A) against whom the deadly force is used is in the process of unlawfully and forcefully entering, or has unlawfully and forcibly entered a dwelling, residence, or occupied vehicle, or if he removes or is attempting to remove another person against his will from the dwelling, residence, or occupied vehicle; and

(B) who uses deadly force knows or has reason to believe that an unlawful and forcible entry or unlawful and forcible act is occurring or has occurred.

In plain English, this statutory section simply imputes you with a *legal presumption*. Legal presumptions are discussed later in this chapter. The legal presumption imputed to you is that the threat that you faced was imminent under the listed circumstances. Therefore, if you are required to use deadly force against another and those circumstances were in place, a jury trying you would be legally required to start with the presumption that the threat that you faced was imminent.

The statute is very specific as to the places where the presumption will arise. The threat must take place at a dwelling, residence or occupied vehicle. The statute defines *dwelling* as a building or conveyance of any kind, including an attached porch, whether the building or conveyance is temporary or permanent, mobile or immobile, which has a roof over it, including a tent, and is designed to be occupied by people lodging there at night. Conveyance here can mean anything from a million dollar rock star RV to a broken school bus attached to the side of a home. *Residence* is defined as a dwelling in which a person resides either temporarily or permanently or is visiting as an invited guest. Finally, *vehicle* means a conveyance of any kind, whether or not motorized, which is designed to transport people or property. This can be anything from an airplane to a car to a chartreuse microbus. There are also specifications regarding the nature of the attack such as the manner in which the intruder is entering the dwelling or vehicle.

In South Carolina vs. Gregory Duncan, the South Carolina Supreme Court opined on an important Protection of Persons and Property Act case that arose in Greenville County. In a nutshell, the opinion follows the plain language of the Act. The Act says that South Carolina "recognizes that a person's home is his castle." Further, "that it is proper for law-abiding citizens to protect themselves, their families, and others from intruders and attackers without fear of prosecution or civil action for acting in defense of themselves and others."

According to the opinion, four people were in the home of the person who shot in self-defense: the shooter (Duncan), his girlfriend (Templeton), and another couple who did not reside on the premises. They were all in the home together for whatever reason and the shooter's girlfriend Templeton displayed a picture of the shooter's daughter in a cheerleading outfit. The man from the non-resident couple (Spicer), made inappropriate comments about the cheerleader/daughter and Duncan asked Spicer to leave.

Spicer did leave but came back several minutes later. Spicer was opening the screened porch door when Duncan exited the front door of the house onto the porch with a gun. Spicer then began advancing across the porch and Templeton was between Spicer and Duncan and was trying to get Spicer off the steps and leave. Spicer continued to force his way onto the porch. Templeton claimed Duncan pointed the gun at Spicer and fired. Spicer died from the gunshot wound.

The solicitor filed criminal charges (presumably murder or manslaughter) against Duncan. Duncan's attorney immediately filed a motion to dismiss the charges based upon the Act. The trial Court granted the motion to dismiss (meaning the prosecutor could not further prosecute the charges against Duncan) and the prosecutor appealed. The Supreme Court ruled that it was proper for the trial Court to dismiss the case immediately without any further proceedings.

While this is a very good opinion and true to the intention of the Defense of Persons and Property Act, it should not be construed as a license to shoot people in your home absent a justifiable threat. The key facts here are that Templeton testified that Spicer continued to force his way onto the porch. Because Spicer continued to force his way onto the porch, Duncan was given the legal presumption of a "reasonable fear of imminent peril of death or great bodily injury to himself or another person." Remember that the Spicer was not a resident of the premises and was not a law enforcement officer acting in the performance of his official duties.

Persons and Property Act provides for Evidentiary Immunity Hearing

How does the Act work in the Courts? If you are involved in a self-defense shooting, and the prosecutor decides to prosecute you, you (and your attorney) have the ability to try to get immunity from the prosecution through the Act. Your attorney can immediately motion for an evidentiary hearing before the Court. The purpose of the hearing is to determine if you are eligible for immunity as a result of the facts of your case in light of the Act. If you show, by the preponderance of the evidence presented, that the facts in your case warrant immunity, the trial Court should immediately determine that you are immune from prosecution and dismiss the case. The State can then immediately appeal that decision.

If, however, the Court determines that you do not meet that preponderance of evidence standard, the prosecutor can continue the case towards trial. You cannot appeal that determination until after trial (with all of your other possible appeals). For a complete analysis by the South Carolina Supreme Court and Appeals Court, *See* *State v. John W. McCarty* (2022), *State v. Manning* (2014), *State v. Duncan* (2011), *State v. Curry* (2013), and *State v. Isaac* (2013).

The "Reasonable" or "Prudent Man" Standard

If you use deadly force to repel a deadly attack, you will be judged by the "reasonable man" standard. That is, if you are charged, the judge or jury will decide whether a reasonable person would have acted similarly under similar circumstances. Therefore, the facts surrounding the incident are very important. You are better served by facts that bolster the reasonableness of your use of force.

Consider this simplified example: you are approached by a person who points a gun at you and says that he or she is going to kill you. You have a concealed pistol. You draw your pistol and shoot the person. With these limited facts, your use of the pistol seems a reasonable use of deadly force. However, as we have already seen in the previous sections, additional facts can either bolster or diminish the *perceived* reasonableness of your response. If the encounter happened at night in a dark alley and the assailant demanded money and fired a shot towards you, those facts tend to bolster the perceived reasonableness of your response. Alternatively, the perceived reasonableness of your response is diminished if the encounter happened in daylight on a crowded street and an assailant wielded a bright orange toy pistol.

While your use of deadly force in any of the above scenarios might be perceived as reasonable, a jury could likewise perceive that they were not. The point here is that there is no clear line as to what facts make the use of deadly force reasonable. There are countless factual scenarios and judges and juries see things differently. Making things more difficult is the fact that a victim usually has only seconds to determine whether or not to respond with deadly force.

Reasonable Fear Presumed in Home, Dwelling or Occupied Vehicle

Similar to the statutory legal presumption of *imminent threat* discussed under the previous element of self-defense, the act provides for a presumption of reasonable fear of a deadly attack under certain circumstances. For the purpose of this section, the relevant portions of the act (Section 16-11-440 (edited) of the South Carolina Code of Laws) provide:

> A person is *presumed* (emphasis added) to have a **reasonable fear** of imminent peril of death or great bodily injury to himself or another person when using deadly force that is intended or likely to cause death or great bodily injury to another person if the person:
>
> (A) against whom the deadly force is used is in the process of unlawfully and forcefully entering, or has unlawfully and forcibly entered a dwelling, residence, or occupied vehicle, or if he removes or is attempting to remove another person against his will from the dwelling, residence, or occupied vehicle; and
>
> (B) who uses deadly force knows or has reason to believe that an unlawful and forcible entry or unlawful and forcible act is occurring or has occurred.

As before, this statutory section simply imputes you with a legal presumption. The legal presumption imputed to you is that you had a reasonable fear of an imminent threat of death or serious bodily harm. If the threat arose under the listed circumstances, a jury trying you would be legally required to start with the presumption that you had a reasonable fear of an imminent threat of death or serious bodily harm to you or someone else. As before, the statute is very specific as to the places where the presumption will arise. The threat must take place at a dwelling, residence or occupied vehicle. There are also specifications regarding the nature of the attack such as manner in which the intruder is entering the dwelling or vehicle.

Legal Presumptions

Now is a good time to discuss legal presumptions in general. The first thing you need to know about presumptions is that they are starting points in the law. This means that if certain conditions are met, the jury is charged with drawing certain conclusions based upon those facts. Be aware though that these presumptions can be overcome by evidence to the contrary. For example, you are presumed to be in reasonable fear of imminent death or great bodily harm if you use deadly force to stop an attacker or invader who is in the process of unlawfully and forcefully entering, or has unlawfully and forcefully entered a dwelling, residence, or occupied vehicle. However, this presumption can be overcome if evidence is presented that you clearly were never in fear of an imminent attack by the intruder.

Maybe you knew for a fact that your frail neighbor had plans to break into your house unarmed, while you were not at home, to steal some of your 1883 Carson City Silver Dollars. When you encounter the neighbor in your house, you see no weapons on the neighbor and the neighbor immediately runs away from you to get away. At no time are you in fear of a deadly attack. Not wanting the neighbor to get away, you shoot the neighbor in the back or side or maybe even in the chest. If charged with a crime and you raise the defense of self-defense under these facts, you will be imputed with the presumption that you were in reasonable fear of an imminent deadly attack. However, the jury has ample facts to overcome the presumption and find your use of deadly force unjustified under the circumstances.

No Other Probable Means of Avoiding the Danger

Under South Carolina common law, the fourth element of a successful claim of self-defense is that you had no other probable means of avoiding the dangerous threat other than to use deadly force upon the attacker. In other words, you have a duty to retreat if you had a reasonable opportunity to do so. However, the Protection of Persons and Property Act has done away with this common law duty under most of the circumstances that you are likely to face.

For the purpose of this section, the relevant portion of the Act (Section 16-11-440 (edited) of the South Carolina Code of Laws) provides:

> (C) A person who is not engaged in an unlawful activity and who is attacked in another place where he has a right to be, including, but not limited to, his place of business, has no duty to retreat and has the right to stand his ground and meet force with force, including deadly force, if he reasonably believes it is necessary to prevent death or great bodily injury to himself or another person or to prevent the commission of a violent crime as defined in Section 16-1-60.

In plain English, this section of the statute eliminates the common law duty to retreat and allows you to stand your ground and apply deadly force to a deadly threat. However, there are certain conditions that must be met to overcome the common law duty to retreat. These conditions are:

- You cannot be engaged in illegal activity at the time of the episode;

- You must be in a place where you have a legal right to be;

- You must reasonably believe that deadly force is needed to prevent death to you or someone else or to prevent a violent crime as defined in Section 16-1-60 of the South Carolina Code of Laws.

Assuming that you are not engaged in illegal activities and that you are in a place where you have a legal right to be, these conditions are pretty broad and allow you to stand your ground in most situation that you find yourself in. Remember also though that you must reasonably believe that deadly force is needed to prevent death or a violent crime. Again, if you are in your home, dwelling or occupied vehicle, under the conditions discussed in the *imminent threat* and *reasonable or prudent man standard* sections, this presumption is imputed to you.

Remember under the *imminent threat* element discussed earlier in this chapter, we created a scenario where an ex surprises you and your date outside of a theater. Again, we changed the original facts to say that the ex has no history of violent behavior that you are aware of, is much smaller than you, and never gives any indication that he or she has a deadly weapon. While, "in your face," the ex tells you that he or she is going to get a weapon out of the car and come back and kill you. You have no idea where the car is but you know that it is not close because there are no cars directly around where you are standing.

Instead of shooting the ex right then and there as in a previous scenario, you allow the ex to go to his or her car. From the other side of the parking lot, you see the ex retrieve what appears to be a gun or large knife from the car. A good distance away, the ex continues to yell that he or she is going to kill you and starts walking quickly towards you from way across the parking lot. Again, you have a concealed weapon on you. Even though you have a pistol on you, you clearly know that you are far enough away that you could start running back to the theater to get to safety. Assuming that you are not doing anything illegal and that you have not been told to keep off the theater property by the owners, you have no duty to retreat and you can use deadly force against the man if the threat evolves to the point where you have a reasonable belief that the ex poses an imminent threat of death or serious bodily harm to you or your date. Remember though, because you are not in a home, dwelling, or occupied vehicle, the imminent threat and reasonable belief elements will not be automatically imputed to you.

Under the same scenario, let's alternately assume that you were at the theater with your date prior to a drug deal. Your plan was to meet some drug buyers after the movie in the theater parking lot. You have the drugs ready for sale on you and your buyers are in the parking lot. In that case, you are engaged in illegal activity when the episode started. Looking back at the facts, it is clear that you have a probable means of avoiding the danger with your retreat. Therefore, there is a good likelihood that you would have a duty to retreat under those facts.

In any scenario, you should seriously consider the practicality of a retreat over standing your ground. The best practice is to always avoid any potentially deadly encounter by getting away. If you have a chance to safely walk or run away from a problem, certainly do so. A humiliating retreat beats getting shot, an arrest, holding cells, bail, jail, attorney's fees and the risk of jury misinterpretation any day.

These fact patterns are simple examples to help you conceptualize the law. For all self-defense scenarios, the more facts that you have to support your actions, the stronger your self-defense claim. As you might see, the best practice is to have the proper self-defense mindset when carrying a weapon for self-defense. If you can safely avoid the danger, take that option every time. But, if you reasonably believe that you or someone else is in imminent danger of death or serious bodily injury, you have the right to protect yourself or others with deadly force.

More on the Protection of Persons and Property Act

There are some important exceptions to the Act that you must be aware of. First, the presumptions do not apply in scenarios where the person being removed from a home, dwelling or occupied vehicle is a child, grandchild, is under the lawful custody of, or is under the lawful guardianship of, the person against whom the deadly force is used. So again, you should carefully think before taking actions related to domestic family situations.

Also, as mentioned earlier, the two presumptions discussed above do not apply if you are engaged in an unlawful activity or are using the dwelling, residence, or occupied vehicle to further an unlawful activity. So, if you are using your home, dwelling, or vehicle for illegal activity, do not expect the act to provide you with presumptions.

Finally, the presumptions discussed above do not apply if the person against whom you use deadly force is a law enforcement officer who enters or attempts to enter the dwelling, residence, or occupied vehicle to perform his or her official duties. This is true as long as the officer identifies himself in accordance with applicable law or if you knew or should have known that the person was a law enforcement officer. Because police are trained to assume that homeowners, residents, and vehicle occupants have weapons, police generally enter these places very openly and with conspicuous notice. Therefore, it is unlikely that you will be confronted with a law enforcement officer in a castle doctrine situation. However, it can happen so make every reasonable effort to identify any person before you consider using deadly force against them.

The above exception is only applicable in the usual scenario where a law enforcement officer enters a home, dwelling or occupied vehicle to perform his or her official duties and with conspicuous notice. However, if a law enforcement officer enters a home, dwelling or occupied vehicle not under those circumstances, the person who uses deadly force against the officer is imputed with the presumptions provided for in the act. Implicit in this exception is that the officer is not out of control, unlawfully out to kill or cause serious bodily harm to someone.

The act has two additional provisions that we have not yet discussed. The first is Subsection (D) that reads:

> (D) A person who unlawfully and by force enters or attempts to enter a person's dwelling, residence, or occupied vehicle is presumed to be doing so with the intent to commit an unlawful act involving force or a violent crime as defined in Section 16-1-60.

This section creates a presumption against the intruder. By the act of forcefully entering a dwelling, residence or occupied vehicle, the intruder is presumed to intend to commit one or more of a host of specified crimes. Technically, the Act imputes the intruder with the intent element necessary to convict that person for one or more of the following:

- Murder
- 1st & 2nd degree criminal sexual conduct (Rape)
- 1st & 2nd degree criminal sexual conduct with minors (Rape)

- 1st & 2nd degree assault with intent to commit criminal sexual conduct
- Assault and battery with intent to kill (Deadly threat or use of force)
- Kidnapping
- Voluntary manslaughter (Heat of Emotions Killing)
- Armed robbery
- Attempted armed robbery
- Carjacking
- Drug trafficking as defined in Sections 44-53-370(e), 44-53-375(C); or 44-53-375
- 1st & 2nd degree arson in the first degree
- 1st & 2nd degree burglary (breaking and entering a dwelling with the intent to commit a serious felony therein)
- Engaging a child for a sexual performance
- Homicide by child abuse, aiding and abetting homicide by child abuse, inflicting great bodily injury upon a child, or allowing great bodily injury to be inflicted upon a child
- Criminal domestic violence of a high and aggravated nature
- Abuse or neglect of a vulnerable adult resulting in death or great bodily injury

- Accessory before the fact to commit any of the above offenses

This is an added layer of legal protection for the victim of a crime that has to use deadly force in self-defense against an intruder.

Finally, the Act specifies that:

> (E) A person who by force enters or attempts to enter a dwelling, residence, or occupied vehicle in violation of an order of protection, restraining order, or condition of bond is presumed to be doing so with the intent to commit an unlawful act regardless of whether the person is a resident of the dwelling, residence, or occupied vehicle including, but not limited to, an owner, lessee, or titleholder.

Here is another example of the law going the extra mile to protect families against domestic violence. As we have repeated throughout this book, take special care to stay away from instances of domestic violence. This subsection imputes the intent to commit an unlawful act upon people that forcefully enter or attempt to enter dwellings, residences, and occupied vehicles in violation of a court order or bond condition. Generally this situation arises where one person in a relationship was able to go to a court and obtain an order preventing the other person from entering the dwelling or otherwise harassing the person protected by the order. A condition of bond might arise when someone is arrested for domestic violence and one of the conditions of getting out of jail on bond is that the person will not go around the alleged victim.

Under this subsection, the person breaking the conditions of an order or bond must not merely enter the dwelling, residence or occupied vehicle but must do so *forcefully* to be imputed with the presumption. It might be a criminal violation to break the order or condition but the imputation of intent to commit an unlawful act in the dwelling, residence or occupied vehicle only arises if the person enters or attempts to enter with force. In other words, if a sympathetic girlfriend lets her boyfriend with a restraining order into the house, and then the boyfriend becomes violent against the girlfriend, the boyfriend is not burdened with the presumption of intent to commit unlawful activity in the home. Therefore, if she is required to use deadly force against the boyfriend, she does not benefit from any presumption of intent to commit unlawful activity imputed upon the boyfriend.

In conclusion, the act codifies the castle doctrine and provides beneficial presumptions to those lawfully in their residence, dwelling or occupied vehicle. It also allows you to stand your ground and use deadly force against the deadly threat in most circumstances. In the end, the Act provides a strengthened legal basis for your claim of self-defense if you are not engaging in unlawful activity and in a place where you are legally entitled to be.

Police have No Duty to Protect You!

As mentioned at the beginning of this book, you are responsible to protect yourself from threats of death or serious bodily harm. The police are under no duty to protect you. Again, threats generally occur so quickly that it is impossible for police to respond in time. When seconds count, police are at best minutes away. This practical and legal reality is supported by longstanding Court decisions.

Warren v. District of Columbia is a leading case. In *Warren*, two women were upstairs in a townhouse when they heard their roommate, a third woman, being attacked downstairs by intruders. They phoned the police several times and were assured that officers were on the way. After about 30 minutes, when their roommate's screams had stopped, they assumed the police had finally arrived. The two women went downstairs and observed that the police never came. Further, the intruders were still there. For the next fourteen-hours the women were held captive, raped, robbed, beaten, forced to commit sexual acts upon each other, and made to submit to the sexual demands of their attackers.

All three women sued the District for failing to protect them, However, the D.C. high Court ruled in favor of the District and its police, ruling that it is a "fundamental principle of American law that a government and its agents are under no general duty to provide public services, such as police protection, to any individual citizen." Therefore, you cannot hold the police responsible for your protection – law enforcement is under no legal duty to protect you.

Defense of Habitation

In State v. Manning, a May, 2014 South Carolina Court of Appeals opinion that cited State v. Rye, a 2007 S.C. Supreme Court case, the Court reiterated the *defense of habitation* doctrine. Defense of habitation is another affirmative defense available to defendants charged with a shooting offense where the defendant alleges the shooting was in self-defense. The doctrine of *defense of habitation*, along with the common law *Castle Doctrine* and the common law doctrine of justified *self-defense* are common law doctrines that provide defendants with affirmative defenses to a charge of unlawful shooting.

The Manning Court described the defense of habitation as follows:

> Defense of habitation, which is separate from the common law Castle Doctrine, provides: [f]or the defense of habitation to apply, a defendant need only establish that a trespass has occurred and that his chosen means of ejectment were reasonable under the circumstances. Stated differently, unlike the defense of self-defense, the defense of habitation does not require that a defendant reasonably believe that he (or his property) was in imminent danger [of] sustaining serious injury or damage. Instead, the defense of habitation provides that

> [when] one attempts to force himself into another's dwelling, the law permits an owner to use reasonable force to expel the trespasser.

Unlike immunity under the Protection of Persons and Property Act (the "Act"), these defenses do not provide self-defense shooters with immunity from prosecution. In other words, the defendant can only employ these doctrines after the Act is found to not apply.

Self-Defense against Non-Deadly Attacks

As to non-deadly force, you have no duty to retreat if you are not engaged in an unlawful activity and you are attacked in any place where you have the right to be. Therefore, if you are legally anywhere and acting lawfully, you can stand your ground and punch a guy back if he starts punching you. Be careful though because non-deadly force can escalate into deadly force. So, if someone attacks you with non-deadly force and you fight back but the encounter escalates to the point where you respond with deadly force, you might not successfully raise a claim of self-defense if you are found to have escalated any portion of the encounter. It should be noted here that if there was mutual combat in the beginning, there might be ample facts with which a solicitor can make it difficult to sustain your assertion of without fault.

Be aware that attacks occur in seconds. Generally, you will be required to discern the level of threat instantly and respond. Again, the legal standard that will be applied to you is that of a reasonable man or woman under the same or similar circumstances. This is not a subjective standard. In other words, a jury will not be asked to determine what you thought was reasonable but what a reasonable man would think. Do you understand the subtle difference? Your actions will be judged by what the jury determines is reasonable under the circumstances. In all situations, keen situational awareness will make you more prepared to react correctly.

The "Alter-Ego" Rule

When it comes to defending others, South Carolina follows the "Alter-Ego" rule. This means that, if you intervene on behalf of another, you will not be allowed the legal defense of self-defense unless self-defense would have been available to the person you assisted. Put another way, a person who intervenes for another is said to "stand in the shoes" of the person on whose behalf he is intervening.

What does this mean? If you encounter a person who is under a threat of imminent deadly harm, and you step in to help, you legally "stand in the shoes" of that person. Therefore, if all four of the elements of legal self-defense are present for that person, you are also protected by that legal defense.

The Danger of Defending Others under the Alter-Ego Rule

There is a very dangerous aspect of the alter-ego rule. The person whom you attempt to assist must have the right to use self-defense under the situation. So, go back to the first element that must be present for legal defense: you must be without fault in bringing on the difficulty. When you "step into the shoes" of the person you are defending, you take the risk that the person you are defending has some fault in the episode.

Here is a factual scenario: say that you come around a corner and see a guy pointing a gun at a woman and he is saying that he will shoot her. You shoot the guy, and seriously injure him. The attack ends and the woman runs away. You then notice that she has a gun in the hand of the arm that was blocked from your view by her torso. Witnesses indicate that she was robbing the guy at gunpoint and that he responded by drawing his gun on her. Under these facts, you legally stepped into the woman's shoes but she did not have the legal defense of self-defense because the woman was not without fault in causing the man to draw his gun.

Preventing the Commission of a Violent Crime

You have no duty to retreat and you can use deadly force as long as you reasonably believe that your use of deadly force is necessary to prevent death, great bodily harm or to prevent the commission of a violent crime as defined by Section 16-1-60 of the South Carolina Code of Laws.

Protecting Yourself or Others versus Protecting Property

You can only use deadly force to prevent the use of deadly force upon you or someone else. You must have a reasonable fear that you or someone else is about to get killed or be seriously injured. You cannot use deadly force to stop non-deadly force. You cannot use deadly force to protect property. To protect property, you can only use non-deadly force. Therefore, if you reasonably believe that someone is threatening your property but not your person or someone else's person, you can only protect your property with non-deadly force.

This might sound like a contradiction to the Protection of Persons and Property Act because that act allows you to use deadly force to prevent certain attacks and invasions upon a dwelling. The confusion arises by the fact that real estate is often called "property" and dwellings are often referred to as "my property." When we say that you cannot use deadly force to protect property, we are referring to personal property and unoccupied real estate. When the act refers to property, it refers to occupied homes, dwellings, and private conveyances (cars, boats, motorcycles, private airplanes, etc.).

As an example of personal property or unoccupied real estate, look back to our earlier discussion of trap or spring guns. Spring guns are devices rigged-up to go off if someone opens a door or lifts a cover.

Historically, some people have installed trap guns to protect their property when the occupants are away. These devices are illegal because they are primarily designed to use deadly force to protect unoccupied property.

We live in a flawed world and the courts cannot monitor and fully understand every situation that happens. For this reason, the law creates certain principles. One principle is that life is always more important than things. Therefore, a court will never give you a pass for killing or causing serious bodily injury where only possessions are in danger.

Arson is a unique crime because it is a crime against property but there is a high likelihood of someone being burned in the flames. For instance, homes and businesses often have people in them around the clock. Therefore, even if the arsonist believes that someone is not in the building, there remains a very good chance that someone actually is in the building. Further, people who try to put the fire out can be seriously hurt or killed in the attempt. For these reasons, arson is generally not considered simply a property crime but also a crime of violence.

Can an altercation over possessions escalate from non-deadly force to deadly force? Yes it can. You can initially resist a property theft with non-deadly force. Thereafter, the thief's threat against you can become deadly. Maybe he or she later pulls a gun or knife or tries to run you over with a car. Maybe a thief places someone near you in a deadly choke hold. The iterations are endless. A non-deadly threat can escalate into a deadly threat.

Make sure that you understand this principle that the law puts life above things. You can never use deadly force to protect personal property or unoccupied real estate. Only non-deadly force can be used to protect these things. However, the act of protecting your property with non-deadly force can escalate into a deadly situation. If you are faced with a situation where the property threat has escalated into a deadly threat to you or others, you can use deadly force for legitimate self-defense. You might also be successful in raising the doctrine of defense of habitation as described earlier. However, keep in mind that you might have to go through a perilous prosecution and trial. Therefore, you should avoid using deadly force unless the four elements of legal self-defense are working in your favor anytime you use deadly force against another.

Criminal and Civil Liability

This book contains a more thorough presentation and analysis of common ways that a gun can get you into criminal and civil trouble in the Common Gun Crimes and Lawsuits chapter. However, for the purpose of this chapter, some criminal and civil liability concepts are briefly presented here.

Complete Defense to Criminal and Civil Action

If you shoot someone in legitimate self-defense, you have the possibility of an evidential immunity hearing to get the charge dismissed. You also have the common law affirmative defenses of self-defense, castle doctrine and defense of habitation in any subsequent criminal charge. Finally, you are protected from civil liability. In fact, the law provides that if you lawfully defend yourself, any person who sues you will end up having to pay your attorney's fees, court costs, all expenses associated with the lawsuit, plus any lost income as a result of the lawsuit. Unfortunately, if that person has little collectible money or property, you will probably never get a penny out of them.

Excusable Homicide

There are a few situations where you may kill someone (not in self-defense) but you are still not guilty of murder or manslaughter.

These cases are called excusable homicide. Let's say you are out downtown doing some shopping and someone pulls a gun on you and starts shooting. You fire back. You fire three shots. The first two hit and kill the assailant. The third goes slightly off target and kills a guy who is typing on his laptop in an overpriced coffee shop. Since you were justified in shooting at the first guy and since you did not intend to hit the second guy, the likely result is a finding of excusable homicide. Self-defense would apply to the first killing and excusable homicide would apply to the second killing. More common scenarios are accidental killings from gun cleaning and hunting accidents. The bottom-line is that accidental shootings are generally excusable homicide.

However, some accidental shootings will not be excused by the criminal courts. There is no excuse for acting grossly negligent. For example, someone shoots a gun in the air for a New Year's celebration. The bullet then comes down on the other side of town and kills someone. That type of behavior is so reckless and wanton that it rises to gross negligence and brings both criminal and civil liability. There are many other ways to be grossly negligent with a gun.

Criminal Manslaughter

Manslaughter is the killing of another but with some mitigating factor or factors. Say for instance that you think that you have a reason to shoot another person but you are wrong. As an example, a guy across the street has a tire iron in his hand and yells threats to kill you without making any attempt to cross the street towards you. He also says things that highly inflame you. As a response to his threats, you shoot and kill him. In this case, his threat of deadly force is not imminent enough.

However, the law has a means for cutting you somewhat of a break. That break is a manslaughter charge, as opposed to a murder charge. Manslaughter is killing another with some mitigating factor such as high emotions or heat of passion. Maybe a jury finds that his words and actions caused you to be highly enraged and it is reasonable that your emotions were inflamed. That determination might move you out of murder liability and into the lesser penalized manslaughter liability. In any case, whether you are tried with murder, manslaughter or nothing is a decision for the prosecutor and possibly the judge to make. Whether you are guilty or not is for the jury to decide.

Civil Negligence

A broad theory for recovery of damages in a civil lawsuit is negligence. Negligence is when a person's actions fall below the standard of care that should have been used in a particular situation. If you use a weapon for legitimate self-defense under the law, the Protection of Persons and Property Act aids you in defense of a civil claim like negligence. If you have acted in legitimate self-defense under the act, the civil lawsuit should be dismissed by the judge and you should be awarded the cost of your attorney's fees for defending yourself against the lawsuit.

Display of Weapons

You might be wondering when it is legal to pull a gun out and threaten someone. It is very simple, if it is not legal to shoot the person, it is also not legal to pull your gun and threaten to shoot the person. While threatening will not get you a murder charge, it will get you an aggravated assault charge. Aggravated assault is a felony and getting convicted will mean you can't own a gun. Remember, if the situation does not legally warrant shooting a person, it is a crime to threaten to shoot the person. Therefore, you should always be of the mindset that you will not pull out your weapon unless you, or someone else you are defending, are faced with the threat of death or serious bodily injury. See also the sections in this book about brandishing and pointing and presenting.

What if I Shoot Someone in Self-Defense?

If you have been forced to shoot someone in self-defense, you must consider competing concerns. First, there is the concern for the safety of you and others. Second, is the concern for the person who has been shot. Third, you must balance the need to give the police some very limited information against your right to remain silent.

For your own safety, or the safety of those you have defended, you should get to a safe place away from the person that you have shot. Once you determine that you are safe and the person is no longer a threat, make sure that someone calls the police. If anybody decides to give aid to anybody shot, the aid or assistance given must meet the level of care that any ordinary and reasonable person would be expected to give under the same or similar circumstances. In light of South Carolina's Good Samaritan Law found in Section 15-1-310 of the South Carolina Code of Laws, this means that the care cannot be reckless or wanton.

Why You Must Never Talk with the Police or Anyone Else

(Author's note: Contributor Sgt. G. Curtis Moore, Jr. does not join in this section.)

If you ever shoot someone, when the police come, tell them your name and give them your driver's license or other ID and your CWP if you have one. After that, demand to speak with a lawyer and do not say anything else. Period. **DEMAND TO SPEAK WITH A LAWYER AND DO NOT SAY ANYTHING ELSE**. When we say do not *say* anything, that also means do not write any letters or reports or sign anything. Further, do not make any apologies, agree to any "interviews," or talk with any reporters or bystanders. This includes not giving any statement to your family or friends.

I cannot stress strongly enough the importance of forcing yourself to not say anything and simply demanding an attorney. While there are several good reasons, the following are two of the strongest: first, our system of criminal justice is an imperfect system that has plenty of room for error and wrong results beyond your control. Law-abiding, innocent people can be found guilty as a result of the peculiarities and mechanics of the system. Forcing yourself not to say anything and demanding an attorney minimizes the chance of a wrong outcome. Second, people have a compelling urge to talk after a traumatic event occurs – especially if the person is involved in the event. Forcing yourself not to say anything and demanding an attorney overcomes this urge and minimizes the chance of a wrong outcome.

United States Supreme Court Justice Robert Jackson said in *Watts v. Indiana*, "under [our system] of criminal procedure, any lawyer worth his salt will tell the suspect in no uncertain terms to make no statement to the police under any circumstances." This is an expert in American Constitutional Law writing an opinion for a real case before the Supreme Court. He had an impressive history of litigating prominent national cases before being appointed to the Supreme Court. Even if indirectly, you must take his comment as a stark warning of the severe prejudice that will come from not remaining silent. Listen to his words again, "in no uncertain terms, make no statement to the police under any circumstances."

Here is a thought experiment to try. Find a quiet place, close your eyes and go through the next scenario several times in your head. Pretend that you are in a convenience store at night when three masked people suddenly come in to rob the place. One starts to point a gun at you and you fear for your life so you shoot and hit the robber. The other two robbers flee. You have just shot someone in lawful self-defense. The police arrive and approach you. You are scared and in shock but happy to see the police. You are a law-abiding person and you like the police and are eager to cooperate with the authorities.

How do you feel right now? Do you have an urge to tell the police something? Is there an urge to explain yourself? Do you want the police to think that you are cooperating? Do you want the police to like you? Do you feel uncomfortable just standing there not answering questions from the police? Do you think that if you don't say something to the police they will think that you are trying to hide something? Would you have an urge to respond if you hear the clerk tell wrong facts to the police? Do you feel like the police would not arrest you if you tell them what happened? Do you think it will all just go away and that an attorney will only make a bigger deal out of the situation? Do you worry that an attorney will be too expensive? All those thoughts are normal but they bitterly betray your best interest.

Most police and prosecutors are very dedicated professionals who do an excellent job of protecting us every day. They generally want to help law abiding citizens. But you must understand their role in our criminal justice system. Our society has placed the responsibility of prosecuting suspected crimes upon the prosecutor and the responsibility of gathering as much evidence as possible on the police. They would be derelict in their jobs if they did not gather as much evidence as possible and use the criminal justice system to its fullest legal effect against the accused. Being a creature of the state, they have tremendous resources and training and receive a high degree of respect and credulity from juries. Also, a trial might not occur until a year or more after the shooting. The police officer's interpretation of what you said can change over time or prosecuting attorneys can develop alternate arguments based upon the way you worded the story. Last, but certainly not least, as we will explain more fully below, the rules of evidence **can only work <u>against</u> you** and not for you if you open your mouth and speak with someone. The point is, the rules are against you right from the start and you are up against a behemoth. The most vulnerable time is the time between the shooting and the time that your attorney arrives by your side. In the next sections. we will discuss some of the things that can happen if you decide to talk with the police (or anybody else).

To help you see how the rules will work against you and not for you, consider the South Carolina rules of evidence. South Carolina follows the general rule that hearsay is not admissible as evidence in a trial. What is hearsay? Hearsay is *a statement, other than one made by the declarant while testifying at trial or hearing, offered in evidence to prove the truth of the matter asserted.* How does this rule apply to a statement that you make to the police? Let's say that you were involved in a self-defense shooting and you speak with the police and that the only thing that you tell them was that, "I was in fear for my life." Now say that you are at trial for shooting the attacker and that you have raised the defense of self-defense. An element of self-defense is that you were in reasonable fear of imminent death or serious bodily injury. The policeman that you spoke with is called to the witness stand. If your attorney asks the officer to repeat what you said, that officer cannot say that you said, "I was in fear for my life," because that testimony is inadmissible as hearsay. Why? Your statement was not made at trial and it is being offered as evidence to prove the matter asserted (that you were in fear for your life). So, your statement to the police that you were in fear for your life will not help you at trial. Notice how it is the ***rule*** working against you and not the police officer. The officer might believe that you are innocent and might hope that the jury acquits you. But, no matter how decent and nice the police office is, or how much the officer is "on your side," it is the rule working against you and not the officer.

While that news is bad enough, the bad-bad news is that there are important exceptions to the general hearsay rule. The one you need to know about here is that any disserving statements or admissions that you make **are admissible** as evidence. So, even if you are completely innocent, you might say things to the police that can later be presented to a jury as a disserving statement or an admission of guilt. You might say the most trivial things or convincingly explain your innocence with thorough detail, but the way you say something could be interpreted by a jury as an admission. You should never run that risk. Never! Keep quiet and let the facts speak for themselves.

The foregoing should be enough to convince you not to talk with the police under any circumstance. Again, this is not an indictment against the police but rather a simple fact of the mechanics of the rules of evidence and the justice system. The *Miranda* warning tells you that anything that you say, can and will be used against you in court. But, the warning fails to inform you that nothing that you say can or will be used to help you in court. In other words, the rules are rigged so that any statement that you make can only hurt you but never help you.

But, if the foregoing reason was not enough, let's go though some more reasons. Let's imagine again that you were forced to shoot somebody who presented you with an imminent threat of death or serious bodily harm. You then find safety and call the police. The person that presented you with the threat survives the shooting. When the police come, you say nothing until an attorney is by your side. If it ever comes to a trial, there should be facts to back you up. Maybe there were also witnesses there that will back you up. If only the attacker and you were on the scene, it is simply your version of the episode against the other guy's and you have made no statements that can be used against you.

Now let's change the facts and say that you said some things to the police. What if the officer misinterprets a word because of your accent or the manner with which you said something? What if the officer had an impression of you that is not correct? What if the officer mistakenly writes a statement down differently from what you said? What if an officer recalls your statement differently because a year has passed by before a trial begins? Once you say something to the police, it becomes your word against the other guy AND the police at trial. By talking with the police (or anybody else) without having an attorney by your side first, you have doubled the risk of a wrong outcome though witness error. If you talk with more people, including family and friends, before waiting until you have a lawyer by your side, you triple, or quadruple the risk. What do we mean by witness error? Witness error is communication malfunctions and people make mistakes in communication all of the time. People misinterpret information, forget things, see things through their own world view, import prejudices, can develop ulterior motives, and can simply lie at times.

Maybe you have played the communication game that starts with a classroom full of people sitting quiet. The teacher whispers a phase into one person's ear at one side of the room. That student leans over and whispers the phrase to the student next to him or her. The phase is passed from desk to desk, up and down each row, until the phrase reaches the last student at the far end of the room. The teacher then tells the last student to close his or her eyes while the teacher writes the phrase on the board. The last student is then told to shout out the phase. Invariably, a burst of laughter erupts because the shouted phase is nothing close to the original phrase. The message became corrupted and distorted though human communication. While this communication gets a lot of laughs in school, witness error through miscommunication is not funny when somebody is facing serious criminal charges.

Police are only allowed to convey the statements that they were given. If you say nothing to the police, you give the officer and jury no room to misinterpret your words. The officer will likely give a brief testimony of the facts on the scene and will offer up no statement that can be subjected to damaging examination by lawyers. Alternatively, if you talked to the officer, your words or statements are open to mistakes, misinterpretations, jury prejudices and damaging examination by attorneys. Moreover, the general public tends to hold the police in very high regard so juries tend to believe the testimony of a crisply dressed police officer more than others.

You will greatly simplify your defense if you are only required to contend with the guy that you were forced to shoot. In a practical sense, if it is your word against the other guy's, and your attorney can discredit the other guy, the prosecutor's case is all but lost. Similarly, if the other guy simply doesn't show up to court or refuses to testify, the prosecutor has no witnesses and the case has a good chance of getting dropped. So, why would you disadvantage yourself by talking with anyone?

Still another reason is that talking to the police will not keep you from getting arrested. For shootings, police make arrests based upon the evidence and the circumstances at the scene. The decision is almost never based upon what you say or do not say. If the police arrive and see one guy shot and you there possessing gun that shot him, they are very likely going to make an arrest and your words will not get you out of the arrest. If you are arrested, you will spend some time in a holding cell and be required to post a bond. Nobody likes the disgusting smell, obnoxious drunks. and baloney sandwiches in holding cells but that awful experience comes and goes relatively quickly and you can handle that. Arrests can even be expunged from your record. But, if you say anything to the police or anyone else, you can never get those words back and they can cause you much more grief than an arrest.

Yet another thing that can go wrong is that you might make inadvertent inaccuracies that are later used to attack your truthfulness and credibility. For instance, you tell the police that three guys barged into the convenience store, one started to point his gun at you and you feared for your life. As you try to describe the incident in more detail, you say that all three of the guys had guns. It turns out that only two of the guys had guns and the other had a thin aluminum can that he grabbed off the shelf. Even though it is an insignificant fact, a prosecutor can use your incorrect observation to attack your judgment and credibility.

Know also that the police are permitted to lie to you or deceive you to get you to make a confession. For example, the police can have a cassette recorder at your conversation and then stop the recorder to have some discussion "off the record." What they do not tell you is that you are being videotaped or that another recorder is running. Alternatively, you might have sympathy for the person that was injured or that person's family. Maybe you think that reaching out by saying you're sorry will make you feel better or somehow help the grieving family. The police might suggest that writing a sympathy letter or apology will make you feel better. You can be sure that your sympathy letter or apology will be turned into a confession. Just like you train to be better at your job, police go through extensive training to extract the maximum comments from you. You must protect yourself against saying anything.

As an additional indication of the built-in disadvantage of talking to the police, think of the dynamics of a post-shooting questioning. Again, you are upset, frightened, and probably surrounded by a growing crowd of onlookers. You want to get out of there and go home right away. Alternatively, the police are comfortably at work. They have all the time in the world. In-fact, as time goes on they start getting paid overtime. Since they are already uniformed and working, they might be happy to get a few more hours at time and a-half. Meanwhile, you are wishing you were home in your favorite chair. All of the pressure is on you to say something that you think will get you out of there. You must resist the urge to give your side of the story or to seem cooperative in the hope that the police will release you from the scene.

This might be a good place to talk about the length of time from a shooting until you have an attorney by your side. That time is dependent upon what type of relationship you have with an attorney. An organized crime kingpin probably has his criminal attorney's number listed as a favorite in his cell phone. When he calls his attorney, the attorney is at the scene within a matter of minutes. However, most people do not have a close relationship with a criminal attorney. So, realistically, the first thing that you have to do is decide upon a lawyer to call. That decision might take some time because of asking references or thumbing through advertisements. After you decide upon an attorney, more variables come into play. Is the attorney available when you call? Does that attorney have a conflict of interest? How far away from the scene is the attorney's office? Is it rush hour? Does the attorney make jail calls? All those variables affect when the attorney can first be by your side. So, the answer is that it can range from minutes to days. No matter if it is minutes or days, do not speak with the police without a lawyer by your side.

So, remain silent because silence might prevent you from saying something that will get you in trouble (even though you have done nothing wrong). Attorneys can work a lot more effectively with your silence than with comments that you have made. There is an old saying among lawyers that it is hard to hook the fish that never opens his mouth.

The best practice is to not give statements to ANYONE until your attorney arrives. Even if you do not give statements to the police, you can still give problematic statements to others on the scene. Anything that you say to anyone can and will be used against you in court. If your family or friends are with you, make an agreement that it is in everyone's best interest not to say anything until your attorney arrives. Even your family and friends can misinterpret things that you say. Imagine how terrible a friend or family member will feel if he or she must get up on the stand and repeat something really stupid that you said? Do not put that burden on them. Keep quiet and do not give any statements until you have your attorney at the scene. You will have plenty of time to speak with your family and friends once your attorney arrives and everything settles down.

Trust in the facts on the scene and the circumstances that led to your use of deadly force in self-defense. There will likely be physical evidence and witnesses to back you up so why not just sit quiet until you get a lawyer beside you? The fact that you sat quiet until you had the assistance of legal counsel can never be used against you in court. Resist the natural temptation to explain yourself because remaining silent will only help you and never hurt you. Best advice, do not be the guy who painfully joked in jail, "I had the right to remain silent, just not the intelligence to do so."

One last note, if you safely have opportunity to do so, call 911 as the life-threatening situation is developing. That way, a dispatcher might hear and record the situation as it unfolds. Also, calling 911 will show that you tried to get help from the police before the situation escalated to deadly force. Make it clear that you are in fear for your life. Keep 911 as a speed dial in your cell phone and use it if you can.

Remember that every defendant is entitled to an attorney. If you cannot afford a private attorney, a public defender attorney will be provided for you. So, whether you hire a private attorney or have a public defender appointed for you, there is no excuse not to have an attorney by your side.

Recapping this section, what do you do if you shot someone in legitimate self-defense?

1. Find safety right away.
2. Put your gun back into your holster or pocket.
3. Give the police your name, address, and driver's license or other ID and your CWP if you have one.
4. DO NOT TALK TO THE POLICE OR ANYONE until your lawyer is with you.

The bottom line is that you must follow Justice Jackson's admonition: **"in no uncertain terms, make no statement to the police under any circumstances."**

Homeowner's, Auto, and Umbrella Insurance Policies

Homeowner's insurance and business liability insurance policies generally have a personal liability provision. Many people also have "umbrella" liability policies that supplement and increase liability coverage. In general, these policies provide liability indemnification for occurrences at the home or business, in or about a vehicle or even elsewhere in public. Be aware that these policies insure against the *negligent* acts of the insured and not the intentional acts of the insured. The use of a weapon in self-defense is considered intentional and will not be covered by these insurance policies. So, if you are sued, you will not be provided an attorney by your insurance company and you will not be covered for any judgment against you. As mentioned earlier, the South Carolina Code of Laws give you complete relief from civil liability if you use deadly force in lawful self-defense. As far as your insurance carrier is concerned though, you might be stuck with hiring your own attorney.

4 Simple Rules for Making Sense of Self-Defense

You might feel like the law of self-defense is more complicated than you would like. It is. But it probably must be to balance the individual's need to protect him or herself against the public's need for a civilized community. Again, the best practice is to start organizing your thoughts now into a few simple rules for yourself. If you live by these simple rules, it is very difficult for you to face criminal or civil liability:

- Do not start or escalate trouble with other people. If you do make a mistake and start trouble, eat your pride and get away before it escalates any further and deadly force comes into use. Convince yourself that you are being the most courageous because you need to get away with the gun. Remember that you must be without fault throughout the entire episode to successfully raise the affirmative defense of self-defense if you use deadly force;

- Never draw your gun unless you legitimately feel like you or someone else is in immediate danger of death or serious bodily injury;

- If you step in to use your gun in defense of another, you better be sure that the person you are defending is without fault throughout the entire episode.

- If you shoot someone, demand an attorney right away and do not speak with anyone until he or she is at your side.

Conclusion

You have a right to defend yourself but you must understand when and how you can do so. Your attitude should always be that your weapon is for defense and that you will pull it out from concealment and use it only when the circumstances legitimately necessitate it. Your actions will not be judged by whether you think they are reasonable but rather by what a jury thinks a reasonable person would do under the same or similar circumstances. Knowledge of the law of self-defense should give you confidence to carry your weapon legally and intelligently. This knowledge should also make you not afraid of the law if you need to use your weapon against a legitimate immediate threat of death or serious bodily injury.

Chapter 9
Miscellaneous Gun Laws

Guns Exempt from Bankruptcy and Creditors

On May 19, 2017, Governor McMaster signed into law an exemption from creditors of three thousand dollars ($3,000) in value in any rifle, shotgun, pistol, or any combination not to exceed three firearms. See South Carolina Code of Laws Section 15-41-30(15). This means that if you have judgement creditors, or have filed bankruptcy, the creditors or bankruptcy trustee is prohibited from collecting from you up to 3 firearms or a total value of firearms of $3,000. Bankruptcy and creditor protection can be complicated and can require planning so see an attorney if you have any questions.

The Shooting Range Protection Act of 2000

Section 31-18-20 of the South Carolina Code of Laws defines a shooting range as an area of a property which is designed, utilized, and operated for the firing of firearms. Also, for an area to be a shooting range, the firing of firearms must be the usual, regular, and primary activity occurring in the area. Finally, the area must be remote enough so that a projectile could not reasonably be expected to escape the boundaries of the range. Alternatively, the range must have a sufficient barrier that would have the same effect. If the range meets these criteria, it is a shooting range for purposes of the act. The main thrust of the act is to limit noise nuisance lawsuits against shooting ranges by neighboring landowners.

In *Shaw v. Coleman*, the South Carolina Appeals Court determined that even a shooting area in a 1 acre residential property qualified as a shooting range under the act. This does not mean that any shooting area qualifies but it does show that the courts interpret the concept of a "shooting range" broadly as the statute intended it to.

There are several situations which must be considered when analyzing this act. First, consider the situation where the complaining party buys property near the range after the range is already operating. In those instances, the complainer is not allowed to bring a noise nuisance suit against the shooting range, the owners of the shooting range, the operators of the range, or the users of the range unless there is a substantial change in the use of the property. Even if there is such a substantial change in the use of the property, a noise nuisance lawsuit must be brought within three years from the beginning of the substantial change.

Next is when a neighbor complains that a range is established after the complainer already owned the nearby property. In this situation, any noise nuisance action must be brought within five years after the establishment of the range or within three years after a substantial change in the use of the range. If a range stops all shooting activity for a period of at least three years, any resumption of shooting activities is considered establishment of a new range for purposes of the act. The three-year period is tolled if all shooting activity ceases due to legal action against the range, its owners, its operators, or its users.

In addition to the limits that the act places on lawsuits, the legislation also limits control over shooting ranges by local governments. First, it forbids local and state government agencies from using a noise control ordinance, regulation, or rule to require a shooting range to limit or eliminate shooting activities if the range has been operating on a regular basis since January 1, 2000. It also forbids local and state government agencies from applying noise control ordinances, regulations, and rules to a shooting range if that shooting range complied with all noise control ordinances, regulations, and rules in effect when it was established. This protection endures so long as there has not been a substantial change in the use of the range. Finally, a local or state government agency may not apply any noise control ordinance, regulation, or rule to a shooting range if the range was in existence prior to the enactment of the regulation. Again, this is true so long as there has been no substantial change in the use of the range.

The act does not limit the ability of a local government to regulate the location and construction of a new shooting range. Further, the act requires county governments to prominently display a warning sign on all primary highways approaching a range. At a one mile radius from each shooting range, a sign must be erected that reads, "SHOOTING RANGE-NOISE AREA". The warning sign must also conform to the Manual of Uniform Traffic Control Devices and the policies of the Department of Transportation.

Restrictive Covenants & Homeowner's Associations

There might be other law in play when it comes to shooting ranges. For instance, a subdivision might have restrictive covenants that prohibit shooting ranges or discharge of firearms. Restrictive covenants are contractual in nature and not affected by the protections of the act. Restrictive covenants run with the land and are enforceable by the property owners in the development. If a property is encumbered by a restrictive covenant that prohibits shooting, shooting on the property would violate the covenant and subject the landowner to the penalty provided by the covenants or contract law.

State Rep. Phyllis Henderson asked the SC Attorney General for an opinion regarding the right of homeowners in an HOA/Covenant community to carry firearms in common areas *South Carolina Attorney General Opinion, June 29, 2018*. The issue is: while gun possessors have more carry options when at home and within his or her property lines, what if you live in a covenanted subdivision with lands owned communally by your homeowner's association? Can you carry a firearm on those common areas as if you were on your own property? While the Attorney General did not go as far as a yes or no answer, the opinion did set-out legal authority and theories and suggested that it might depend upon each subdivision's individual ownership structure and covenants. In general, it would seem that joint ownership of title (such as your name as a fractional owner on a deed) to the land in question will provide much better legal "cover" than would you simply being a member of the HOA that is on the deed as title owner.

Civil Lawsuit Protection for Gun and Ammunition Manufacturers

Section 15-73-40 of the South Carolina Code of Laws gives gun and ammunition manufacturers greater protection from civil lawsuits. This statute was enacted as a response to increased products liability lawsuits against gun and ammunition manufacturers. Plaintiffs began bringing defective product lawsuits against manufacturers not founded on a basis of individual guns being mechanically defective but rather on other grounds like the inherently dangerous nature of guns. This statute provides that any defective product case must be based upon a firearm being either defectively designed or constructed. Further, for a plaintiff to sustain a product liability lawsuit, the defective design or construction must be the proximate cause of the injury or death.

Local Governments Cannot Confiscate Guns During an Emergency

Section 23-31-520 has been amended to prevent counties, cities, and other political subdivisions like special districts from confiscating guns during an emergency. After the Hurricane Katrina damage in Louisiana, the City of New Orleans authorized law enforcement officers to go door-to-door confiscating firearms from private citizens. Guns were confiscated from individuals at their homes with no allegation of any wrongdoing. The goal was simply to disarm private citizens during a state of emergency. This action shocked the conscience of many who assumed that governments would not confiscate guns from law abiding citizens expecting the protection of a firearm during an emergency.

Over twenty-three states including South Carolina responded by either enacting new laws or amending existing laws to prevent local governments from confiscating firearms. South Carolina did not limit the confiscation prohibition to just emergencies. Instead, the local government preemption law discussed in Chapter 1 was amended to include the following language urged by Robert Butler, "[t]his article denies any county, municipality, or political subdivision the power to confiscate a firearm or ammunition unless incident to an arrest or a courtesy summons to appear." (A courtesy summons to appear is a notice to appear before the court for formal criminal charges without handcuffing and hauling the suspect to jail.)

The effect of this law is to prevent local governments from confiscating guns from a private party unless in coincidence with some type of criminal charges. No matter if an emergency is occurring or not, a local government in South Carolina cannot go around confiscating guns unless the persons who they are confiscating from violated some criminal laws and are being arrested for the violation.

Remember earlier that we said that a local government cannot make a gun law more restrictive or at odds with state law. Therefore, a local government cannot get around this confiscation provision by making up a gun law more restrictive than state law and then confiscating a gun during an arrest for that local government regulation. So, Legislative Consultant Robert D. Butler did a great job of recommending language for this law that prevents local governments from attempting to confiscate guns from law abiding citizens during an emergency.

Assault Weapons Ban

In 1994 Congress passed what is commonly called the assault weapons ban. As part of a larger crime bill, the legislation defined "assault rifle" and made the manufacture, importation, and possession of assault rifles (manufactured or imported after enactment) illegal. It is important to note that the weapons banned were not fully automatic machine guns like the Army and Marines take into battle. Instead, the highly political bill attempted to demonize semi-automatic guns that only looked like military assault rifles with the label "assault rifles." The bill also outlawed the sale of normal capacity magazines by allowing only reduced capacity magazines capable of holding no more than ten cartridges. The "assault weapons" ban ended on September 13, 2004 and is no longer the law of the land.

The "assault rifles" banned were generally semiautomatic weapons that are readily available today in gun shops. Expiration of the law does not mean that you can buy or possess machine guns and other military weapons. It does, however, allow you to purchase many military style rifles in semi-automatic-only configurations with the normal magazines designed for the rifles (i.e. 25-30 round capacity).

Modifying Semi-Automatic Assault Rifles

Modifying assault type weapons can be a tricky legal endeavor. You are well advised to not make modifications to an assault type weapon without thoroughly studying the applicable law. Even after considerable study, many attorneys are left scratching their heads. But you can be sure that federal prosecutors will be able to prosecute violations when they need to. Do not modify, or have someone else modify, assault weapons unless you are completely sure that your modifications are legal.

A thorough analysis of modifications is beyond the scope of this book. If you want to do further study, a good place to start is on the internet. There are several books written solely for explaining the law of modifying semi-automatic rifles. You can also go to the primary sources of the federal statutes and implementing regulations. Following are the cites: 18 USC 922(r), 18 USC 925(d)(3), Section 5845(a) of the Internal

Revenue Code, 27 CFR 478.39 and 479, and 58 Federal Register 40587 (July 29, 1993). Reading these sections is almost as fun as reading the tax code.

Law Enforcement Officers Safety Act (HR-218)

The U.S. Congress passed the Law Enforcement Officers Safety Act in 2004 (LEOSA). Under the act, a current or retired law enforcement officer can carry a concealed firearm in any U.S. state or territory. The authorization comes with some conditions.

Federal statute 18 USC 926(B) sets forth the parameters for currently employed officers. First, the officer must be a currently qualified law enforcement officer employed by a state, county, or municipality. When carrying a concealed weapon, the officer must carry his or her government issued photographic law enforcement identification. This allows carry anywhere in the United States and territories. The Act does not apply to machine guns, silencers, and destructive devices.

A qualified law enforcement officer is an employee of a governmental law enforcement agency who:

- is authorized by law to engage in or supervise the prevention, detection, investigation, or prosecution of, or the incarceration of any person for, any violation of law, and has statutory powers of arrest;

- is authorized by the agency to carry a firearm;

- is not the subject of any disciplinary action by the agency;

- meets the standards, if any, established by the agency which require the employee to regularly qualify in the use of a firearm;

- is not under the influence of alcohol or another intoxicating or hallucinatory drug or substance; and,

- is not prohibited by federal law from receiving a firearm.

Make sure that you are qualified under these rules if you want to carry.

The act does not usurp any state law that restricts possession of concealed weapons on private property or government property. Therefore, out of state officers in South Carolina who encounter businesses with properly installed "no concealed carry" signs should not carry in those stores. Likewise, out of state officers should abide by all other South Carolina laws regarding concealed carry on private property or government property. If the officer is on duty, the officer falls under the rules for officers on duty. The officer must follow all federal firearms restrictions. Remember that this rule allows for concealed carry by qualified officers. Officers carrying under this rule should not open carry as they would while on duty.

Retired officers are covered under 18 USC 926(C). Basically, the restrictions are the same for current officers. However, the retired officers must meet the following conditions:

- The officer must be retired in good standing from service with a public agency as a law enforcement officer;

- retirement from the public agency must not have been for reasons of mental instability;

- before retirement, the officer must have been authorized to engage in or supervise the prevention, detection, investigation, or prosecution of, or the incarceration of any person for, any violation of law, and had statutory powers of arrest;

- before retirement, the officer was regularly employed as a law enforcement officer for an aggregate of 15 years or more; or retired from service after completing any applicable probationary period of such service, due to a service-connected disability, as determined by such agency;

- the officer has a non-forfeitable right to benefits under the retirement plan of the agency;

- during the most recent 12-month period, the officer has met, at the expense of the individual, his or her state's standards for training and qualification for active law enforcement officers to carry firearms;

- is not under the influence of alcohol or another intoxicating or hallucinatory drug or substance; and,

- is not prohibited by federal law from receiving a firearm.

Further, the retired officer must have the following identification:

- a photographic identification issued by the agency from which the officer retired from service that indicates that the individual has, not less than one year before the date the officer is carrying the concealed firearm, been tested, or otherwise found by the agency to meet the standards established by the agency for training and qualification for active law enforcement officers to carry a firearm of the same type as the concealed firearm; **or**

- a photographic identification issued by the agency from which the officer retired from service as a law enforcement officer; **and,**

- a certification issued by the state in which the officer resides that indicates that the retired officer has, not less recently than one year before the date the officer is carrying the concealed firearm, been tested, or otherwise found by the state to meet the standards established by the state for training and qualification for active law enforcement officers to carry a firearm of the same type as the concealed firearm.

So, retired officers need both a certificate of firearms qualifying within a year and a government issued photo identification showing that you are a retired law enforcement officer meeting all the other requirements of this statute.

Section 23-31-600 of the South Carolina Code of Laws requires all South Carolina law enforcement agencies to issue qualified retired officers the applicable identification card and documentation of training. This section implements the federal law and creates a statutory mandate for South Carolina agencies. It also provides agencies with authorization to charge a reasonable fee for the cost of processing.

Under this act, current and retired officers need to be careful about carrying a concealed weapon outside of their own state. One thing to consider is that the officer must know the places where carry is prohibited under the laws of the other state. Another consideration is that many states provide which private individuals and businesses can prohibit concealed carry on private property. Remember too the federal rules about not carrying in the sterile area of airports and on commercial aircraft and public transportation.

Security Officers and Private Security Companies

Private security companies, security officers and private investigators are regulated and licensed under South Carolina law. The statutory provisions regarding these entities begin at Section 40-18-20.

SLED executes the provisions of Section 40-18-20 through regulations starting in Article 9, 73-400, South Carolina Code of Regulations. SLED issues two different licenses: Security Weapons Permit and the Security *Concealed* Weapons Permit. Please note that these permits are wholly separate from the concealed weapons permit issued under 23-31-205, South Carolina Code of Laws and discussed in Chapter 4 of this book. Do not confuse the two.

Security Weapons Permit

Under this statute (40-18-100), SLED may grant a Security Weapons Permit to carry a specified firearm to a person who is at least twenty-one years of age, is eligible to possess firearms, and is licensed or registered as a security officer. Application for the permit must be made on SLED form PD/PS-8, Revised 6/05, available at: sled.sc.gov. The fee for private security officer initial registration is $110.00.

Applicants must submit with the application one complete set of the applicant's fingerprints on SLED fingerprint cards. Just like for the Concealed Weapons Permit application, make sure that you use SLED fingerprint cards for the application. The permit is for one year and renewal applications are available on the SLED website or by calling SLED.

Applicants must also submit proof of training. The standard basic training course consists of four or more hours of training by a certified private security company training officer and must consist of the latest material provided to the trainer by the South Carolina Technical College Private Security Training School. The basic training must be completed, a written examination administered and scored, accurate results of the testing documented in the employer's files, and application for registration received by SLED before the security officer begins duties at a client site. The required written examination must be designed by the company certified training officer and must consist of questions taken from the lesson plan performance objectives used by the trainer. Applicants who successfully complete the basic training will, upon issuance of a registration card by SLED, be designated as a Registered Private Security Officer.

An alternative basic training course approved by SLED may be substituted for standard basic training. For consideration of approval by SLED, an alternative training course must be developed and conducted by an agency or educational institution accredited by a nationally recognized accreditation authority recognized by SLED. Any applicant who successfully completes alternative basic training will, upon employment by a licensed private security entity, qualify for registration by SLED as a Certified Private Security Officer.

Additionally, a security officer applicant must complete an additional minimum two hours of orientation and training by a certified company training officer. The training must be sufficient to ensure:

- the safe, accurate and proper use of equipment to be used by the security officer;

- knowledge adequate to properly and competently perform the duties and responsibilities specific to the assignment of the officer; and,

- additional topics specified by the employer.

If you want to be licensed to carry a firearm while on duty as a security officer, there is an added training requirement. In addition to the training discussed above, a private security officer who will be authorized to carry a firearm must, before being issued, authorized or permitted to carry a firearm on duty, successfully complete a course approved by SLED, consisting of a minimum of four hours of training by a private security company certified training officer or law enforcement firearms instructor currently certified by the South Carolina Criminal Justice Academy, in the safe and proper use of the specific type(s) of firearm(s) to be issued or carried. This firearm training must:

- adhere to the lesson plan(s) and course(s) of fire provided by the South Carolina Technical College Private Security Training School; and,

- include a demonstration of the safe and competent use of the firearm on a range supervised and documented by a private security company certified training officer or law enforcement firearms instructor currently certified by the South Carolina Criminal Justice Academy.

It is important that you keep records of all training for licensure. Accurate and complete documentation of all training of each private security officer must be retained by the employer and submitted to SLED as required. Complete and legible copies of each employee's training records must be furnished by the employer to the employee and must be retained by the employee as his permanent training record. Upon request by SLED, training documentation must be made available by the employing entity and the employee for inspection.

Upon change of employer, a registered private security officer must furnish to the new employer documentation of all training received. If such documentation is not available and cannot be secured from the immediate past employer, the new employer is required to conduct and document currently required minimum training. Mere possession of a registration card does not serve as documentation of required training.

Failure of an employer and registered security officer to retain required training records is a violation punishable by suspension or revocation of the company license and the security officer's registration. Private security officers must not be issued or use equipment or devices for which they have not successfully completed training adequate to ensure the proper, accurate and safe use of such equipment. Documentation of such training must be maintained by the licensee and be available for inspection by SLED.

The permit application and renewal must specifically reauthorize the type of firearm to be used by the applicant while acting as a security officer. This means that the security officer must choose the firearm to be used for security officer work. The applicant must thereafter prove proficiency with that specific firearm and only become licensed to use that specific firearm while on duty as a security officer. This firearm must also be approved or issued by the security officer's employer.

Once issued the license, a person issued a Security Weapons Permit may only carry a firearm in an open and fully-exposed manner while in uniform and performing security duties or while in a vehicle en route directly to or from a security post or place of assignment. If the security operation requires the security officer to carry a concealed weapon, each security officer must obtain a Security Concealed Weapons Permit.

Security ***Concealed*** Weapons Permit

In its discretion, SLED may issue a Security Concealed Weapons Permit to a registered security officer to carry, whether concealed or not, a firearm about his person, even though he is not in uniform or on duty if SLED determines that the additional permit would enable the security officer to better perform his assigned duties. The authority conveyed by the permit may be restricted by SLED. A violation of any rules associated with a Security Weapons Permit or a Security Concealed Weapons

Permit is a misdemeanor and can also bring civil penalties. Further, if you commit another crime while on duty like aggravated assault or manslaughter, you will face felony charges.

Remember that a Security Concealed Weapons Permit under Section 40-18-100 is completely different from a Concealed Weapons Permit under Section 23-31-205 et seq., South Carolina Code of Laws. While these licenses seem very similar, the Security Concealed Weapons Permit is less defined and leaves the holder more open to confusion than a Concealed Weapons Permit. SLED determines for each individual applicant and tailors the Security Concealed Weapons Permit to that applicant. Therefore, one permit holder may have a completely different set of rules than another permit holder.

Even though it seems that a Security Concealed Weapons Permit grants the holder the same authority as a Concealed Weapons Permit, it remains advisable for Security Concealed Weapons Permit holders to also get a Concealed Weapons Permit. Getting both is probably redundant but it prevents any gaps or ambiguities between the two permits.

Chapter 10
Conclusion

Your Brain is Your First Line of Defense

In South Carolina and the United States, you have gun rights that are the envy of much of the world. A firearm gives you a powerful weapon to repel criminals, drug-crazed maniacs, terrorists, a foreign government, and even possible tyranny from our own government.

Remember, however, that your brain is your first line of defense. Think about dangerous places and situations and avoid them. Think about ways to secure your person, vehicle, and home so that criminals pass you by for easier targets. Watch the Active Self Protection YouTube channel. Take firearms and self-defense training courses together with family and friends. Support politicians and organizations that have a proven record of supporting your right to keep and bear arms. If you do not have one already, get your concealed weapons permit and carry your gun with you in a good holster. Finally, read this book again and feel free to contact me with any questions that you have.

South Carolina and the United States need more people who are willing to own and legally carry firearms for legitimate self-defense. However, if you do choose to possess and carry firearms, strive to be an intelligent and responsible gun owner. Look first for ways to protect your family, you, and your property with your brains instead of bullets.

What You Should Have Learned from This Book

This book has given you a good look at South Carolina weapons law. You should now be more competent to possess, carry and assess the appropriateness of using a weapon. You should also have gotten the message to get a concealed weapons permit if you do not already have one.

The Bottom Line

Self-defense is a fundamental human right. But defending yourself can be dangerous if you don't have the tools. The tools that you need are your weapons and knowledge of the law. We hope that this book has helped you understand the law. If it has not, read it again. If it has, tell a friend to get a copy.

About the Author & Contributors

Dr. Stephen Fulton Shaw is a practicing attorney in both South Carolina and Florida. He holds a J.D. and a Ph.D. from the University of Florida and was the recipient of the book award in legal history. His masters and undergraduate work were at Florida State University. He served for several years on staff with former U.S. Representative Cliff Stearns who led the charge for a national right to carry law. He has handled federal and state criminal self-defense shooting cases, firearms dealing cases, gun range lawsuits, CWP denials and the successful GrassRoots Gun Rights S.C. appeal. He has also counseled firearms dealers and drafted many NFA gun trusts.

His interests include research, firearms, writing, and legal education. He chairs the annual S.C. Gun Law Continuing Education seminar for judges and attorneys.

He holds a defensive pistol certificate from the Defensive Training Group and a CWP in both South Carolina and Florida. His memberships include SC Carry and the NRA. He is married to his

South Carolina native wife Melanie Donna (Moore) Shaw from Laurens County.

Jim Kelley graduated from the University of Florida College of Law and has been a litigation attorney for over 15 years. With a lifelong interest in weapons, he has developed a deep knowledge of firearms law. He is a member of the International Defensive Pistol Association and the NRA and his training includes target and combat shooting as well as hand-to-hand defensive tactics. He chairs a popular gun law seminar for Ohio attorneys and has instructed gun law in Florida. Jim holds a Florida CWP.

Sgt. G. Curtis Moore, Jr. is lifelong South Carolina resident with over 25 years of law enforcement experience. His Military Police experience includes action in both Operation Just Cause in Panama and Operation Desert Storm in the Middle East. He holds a degree in Criminal Justice from Piedmont Technical College. He was a City of Greenwood police officer for seven years and retired as sergeant from the Lander University Police Department.

Henry R. Schlein is an attorney with the Cummings Law Firm, LLC, in Summerville, South Carolina, practicing primarily in Charleston, Berkeley, and Dorchester Counties. His law practice includes criminal and family law, as well as gun rights cases and pilot certificate actions. He was admitted to the South Carolina Bar in 1999. He served for 21 years on the Charleston Police Dept. and retired in

1996. He is a graduate of the FBI National Academy, 133rd Session. He served for 4 years in the U. S. Naval Submarine Service. He is an NRA certified law enforcement firearms instructor and a SLED certified CWP instructor. He is also a commercial pilot and flight instructor and was the chief pilot for the Charleston Police Department.

Robert K. Merting is a South Carolina firearms, estate planning, and corporate attorney experienced in the National Firearms Act (NFA), the International Trafficking in Arms Regulations (ITAR), and general South Carolina firearm laws. He brings his passion for firearms to his statewide practice and routinely helps clients acquire firearms regulated by the NFA and untangle firearms with missing or incomplete registration papers.

His experience prior to private practice includes work at Milliken & Company and several positions working at the defense contractor Jankel Tactical Systems. He is proficient in general corporate law including administrative law with regulatory agencies such as the ATF and DDTC.

Originally from the Low Country, Merting is a graduate of Wofford College where he dual majored with a B.S. in Computer Science and a B.A. in Business Economics. He received his Juris Doctorate from Washington and Lee University School of Law.

Major Mike Nunn, Esq. is originally from Columbia, SC and he earned his undergraduate and law degrees from the University of South Carolina. Mike was a senior litigator at Aiken Bridges in Florence, SC for 27 years whose primary focus was medical malpractice, products liability and governmental tort liability defense. Mike is a Fellow of the

American Board of Trial attorneys, the minimum requirement of which is to be lead counsel in at least 100 jury trials.

Mike became a reserve deputy with the Florence County Sheriff's Office in 2006 and in 2009 left private practice to accept the position of General Counsel and Public Information Officer with the Sheriff's Office where he continues to serve with the rank of Major. Mike is a graduate of the South Carolina Criminal Justice Academy as a Class One police officer who is involved in all aspects of the Sheriff's Office including Patrol, Criminal Enforcement, Investigations, Narcotics and SWAT.

Mike is a member of the National Criminal Enforcement Association and a featured writer for the association's nationally publicized magazine "Criminal Enforcement." A frequent speaker and lecturer on topics effecting law enforcement, Mike is also a NRA Certified Firearms Instructor and SLED Certified CWP Instructor.

About the Legislative Consultant

Dr. Robert D. Butler has an interesting blend of educational achievements. He started with a B.S. in Social Science Multi-disciplinary Studies (Political Science, Psychology, Sociology) from Michigan State University, and then he completed one half of the MBA program at Michigan State University before deciding to pursue a non-business career choice. Dr. Butler next obtained a Doctor of Chiropractic degree from Sherman College of Straight Chiropractic (where he was valedictorian of his class), and then opened a private practice in Lexington, SC. After a career ending injury, Dr. Butler obtained a J.D. from the University of South Carolina School of Law where he was inducted into the Whig and Robe Society. As a handicapped person unable to physically endure working eight hours a day, Dr. Butler has instead served as a home bound volunteer legislative consultant in the fight to protect our Second Amendment rights. His training in the social sciences allowing him to better understand people, combined with his attention to detail honed as a physician, and his specialized knowledge of the law make for one unique Second Amendment activist.

Authors' Final Notes

The author and contributors are deeply indebted to Dr. Robert Butler for his vital input and careful review of the statutes and case law discussed in this book. South Carolina gun owners also owe him a debt of gratitude for his tireless work defending the right to keep and bear arms.

Similarly, South Carolina Chief Deputy Attorney General Jeff Young is widely credited for courageously introducing and getting the CWP law in South Carolina passed. When he introduced the legislation in the General Assembly, it was widely regarded as "dead on arrival." But he doggedly drove the legislation through the House and Senate and made it law.

Last, but not least, NRA Master Trainer and Certified SLED CWP Instructor Mark Bilicki for his knowledge and support.

I also wish to thank Sharp Shooters Gun Range and City Range in Greenville as well as ATP Gun Shop and Range in Summerville. Likewise, Wofford College, Charleston School of Law, and Low Country Graduate Center who have been excellent in allowing me to host my academic Shaw's South Carolina Gun Law Seminars for attorneys and judges.

Finally, thank you to the purchasers who have established this book as the premier gun law resource in South Carolina.

Appendix I
Federal Firearms Disability and Removing a Legal Disability

Federal Firearms Disability in General

Under federal law, there are nine categories of persons prohibited from possessing firearms. It is a federal felony for you to possess a firearm if you are a:

- Person under indictment for, or convicted of, any crime punishable by imprisonment for a term exceeding one year (most violent felonies and some misdemeanors);

- Fugitive from justice;

- Person who is an unlawful user of, or addicted to, any controlled substance;

- Person who has been declared by a court as mental defectives or has been committed to a mental institution;

- Illegal alien, or alien who was admitted to the United States under a nonimmigrant visa;

- Person who has been dishonorably discharged from the Armed Forces;

- Person who has renounced his or her United States citizenship;

- Person subject to certain types of restraining orders; or

- Person who has been convicted of a misdemeanor crime of domestic violence.

People who are prevented from possessing firearms under federal law are commonly said to have a *lifetime federal firearms disability.*

How do you know if you have a legal disability?

First, those with a Federal or State felony conviction almost always have a legal disability. More specifically, according to 18 United States Code (U.S.C.) 922(g), you have a legal disability if one of the following applies to you:

- **Criminal** - you have been convicted in any court of a crime punishable by imprisonment for a term exceeding one year;

- **Fugitive** - you are a fugitive from justice;

- **Drugs** - you are an unlawful user of, or are addicted to any controlled substance (as defined in section 102 of the Controlled Substances Act (21 U.S.C. 802));

- **Insanity** - you have been adjudicated as a mental defective or you have been committed to a mental institution;

- **Aliens** - you are an alien and are illegally or unlawfully in the United States; or have been admitted to the United States under a nonimmigrant visa (as that term is defined in section 101(a)(26) of the Immigration and Nationality Act (8 U.S.C. 1101(a)(26))). This prohibition does not apply to aliens who are law enforcement officers of a friendly nation and are on law enforcement business, are designated by the State Department as a foreign official or a distinguished foreign visitor, are admitted to the USA for hunting or sporting purposes or have a lawful hunting license, or are an official representative of a foreign government under certain conditions as provided in 18 USC 922(y)(2);

- **Court Martial** - you have been discharged from the Armed Forces under dishonorable conditions;

- **Renunciation of Citizenship** - you have renounced your United States citizenship;

- **Violence Injunctions** - you are subject to a court order that was issued after a hearing of which you received actual notice, and at which you had an opportunity to participate; restrains you from harassing, stalking, or threatening your intimate partner or your child or the child of your intimate partner, or engaging in other conduct that would place your intimate partner in reasonable fear of bodily injury to such partner or child; and (C)(i) the order includes a finding that you represent a credible threat to the physical safety of your intimate partner or your child or the child of your intimate partner; or (ii) the order by its terms explicitly prohibits the use, attempted use, or threatened use of physical force against your intimate partner or child that would reasonably be expected to cause bodily injury; or

- **Domestic Violence Conviction** - you have been convicted in any court of a misdemeanor crime of domestic violence.

What is a crime punishable by a term of imprisonment exceeding one year?

Those who have been convicted of a crime with a potential jail term of more than 1 year are burdened with a federal firearms disability. This disability is based on the maximum potential penalty that you could have been given for the crime. It is not based on the sentence the convict actually receives. If the convict received a sentence of two years of probation, but could have gone to jail for up to 5 years, the legal disability applies because of the potential term of 5 years.

However, there are a couple of exceptions to the above general rule. 18 U.S.C. 921((a)20) specifically says that any Federal or State offense pertaining to antitrust violations, unfair trade practices, restraints of trade, or other similar offenses relating to the regulation of business practices is exempted from this definition. Therefore if you are convicted of a crime and could have gone to jail for more than 1 year but the crime involved an antitrust violation; you do not have a legal disability.

The same statute also provides an exception for ***state*** crimes which are misdemeanors in the state of conviction and which carry a maximum term of imprisonment of 2 years of less. This one is pretzel logic, we know. The general rule is that a legal disability arises when a person is convicted for crimes punishable by imprisonment of more than 1 year. Then the statute excludes state misdemeanors which are punishable by imprisonment for 2 years or less. This contradiction is prima facie evidence that the federal government's right hand does not know what its' left hand is doing. Anyway, this means that if you were convicted of a state misdemeanor that is punishable by up to two years in prison, you do not have a legal disability.

If I plead guilty to a felony, does that mean I was convicted?

Under 18 USC 921(a)(20), the definition of a conviction is based on the law of the jurisdiction where the proceedings were held. If the proceedings were in South Carolina, you will be out of luck. Section 16-23-10(6) of the South Carolina Code of Laws defines a conviction as all cases which end in pleas of guilty, pleas of nolo contendere, or forfeiture of bond. This statute directly defines the term for purposes of handgun crimes (South Carolina Code of Laws Section 16-23 et seq.).

The bottom line is that, if you plead guilty, nolo contendere, or had a forfeiture of a bond in a South Carolina court to a crime that is a felony that carries a potential penalty of greater than 1 year in jail (or misdemeanor that carries a potential penalty of more than 2 years in jail), you have a legal disability. If the proceedings were held in another jurisdiction and you plead to the charges, you may or may not have a legal disability depending upon that state's definition of conviction.

What if I was convicted of a felony but didn't have an attorney?

Sorry you are out of luck. Unfortunately, if you didn't get an attorney; the federal law does not relieve you of your legal disability. If you are charged with a crime, you should always seriously consider hiring an attorney. We're not trying to generate business here, it is just a simple fact that your chances of a favorable outcome increase dramatically if you are represented by competent counsel.

What if my Felony has been pardoned or expunged?

18 U.S.C. 921(a)(20) provides that any conviction which has been expunged, or set aside, or for which a person has been pardoned or has had civil rights restored shall ***not*** be considered a conviction for purposes of this chapter, ***unless*** such pardon, expungement, or restoration of civil rights expressly provides that the person may not ship, transport, possess, or receive firearms. This means that if you have a conviction for a crime which would normally make you ineligible, but you have been pardoned or achieved an expungement; you generally do not have a legal disability. It is important that any conditions or terms of the pardon or expungement do not provide specific language that prohibits you from shipping, transporting, possessing or receiving firearms. So, if you have already received a pardon or expungement, and the authorities placed a condition or term in your pardon or expungement that prohibits you from shipping, transporting, possessing, or receiving firearms; you still have a legal disability. If your pardon or expungement has no such specific prohibition, your legal disability has been removed. If you are seeking a pardon or expungement, it is wise to make every effort to ensure that your pardon or expungement will not

have any specific firearms terms or conditions. Without a specific firearm term or condition, the pardon or expungement will remove your legal disability.

What if I plead nolo contendere to a crime of domestic violence?

Again, 18 USC 921(a)(20) bases the definition of a conviction on the law of the jurisdiction where the proceedings were held. If the proceedings were in the State of South Carolina, you will be out of luck. The South Carolina Code of Laws define *conviction* as cases that end in pleas of guilty, pleas of nolo contendere, or forfeiture of bond (Section 16-23-10(6)). Therefore, if you plead nolo contendere in a South Carolina court to domestic violence, you have a legal disability. If the proceedings were held in another jurisdiction and you plead to the charges, you may not have a legal disability. In that case, you must determine that state's definition of *conviction*.

What if I was convicted of a crime of domestic violence but didn't have an attorney?

There may be good news for you, 18 USC 921(a)(33)(B)(i) provides that a person shall not be considered to have been convicted of a crime of domestic violence, unless the person was represented by counsel in the case, or knowingly and intelligently waived the right to counsel in the case; ***and*** in the case of a prosecution for such an offense for which the person was entitled to a jury trial in the jurisdiction in which the case was tried, the person must have either been tried by a jury, or the person must have knowingly and intelligently waived the right to have the case tried by a jury, by guilty plea or otherwise.

If you didn't have any attorney, you might not have too much room for excitement because, in most cases, you will probably be found to have knowingly and intelligently waived that right. If you did not waive that right, the court almost certainly appointed you an attorney.

The same is true of trial by jury. If you were entitled to one, the court almost always makes sure you either get one or knowingly and intelligently waive that right. If you knowingly and intelligently waived either of these rights, you still have the legal disability. So, even if you did not have an attorney or did not have a trial by jury, you probably still have the disability. However, if you have real doubts about whether you legitimately waived your right to an attorney and trial, you might want to speak with a lawyer and make the argument.

What if my crime of domestic violence has been pardoned or expunged?

If your federal firearms disability is the result of domestic violence (even if it was a state misdemeanor charge with a potential penalty of greater than 2 years in jail), Section 18 USC 921(a)(33)(B)(ii) provides for identical results as for felonies under 18 U.S.C. 921(a)(20). So, look at the section above that deals with expungement or pardons of felonies for guidance.

Removal of a Legal Disability

The South Carolina Constitution gives the executive branch the power to grant full or conditional pardons and to restore the civil rights of criminals convicted under state of South Carolina crimes. This power is also referred to as executive clemency. It is totally within the discretion of the executive branch. This means that if you are denied, you cannot file a lawsuit to have a court review the denial. It also means that writing to your state representative or state senator won't do you any good. The South Carolina Executive Branch has no authority to pardon federal crimes.

Removal of a legal disability for federal crimes was settled in the court case *Beecham v. United States*. In that case, the U.S. Supreme Court held that those convicted under most federal felonies (or misdemeanors with a potential jail term of over 1 year) remain subject to the federal firearms disability until their civil rights are restored through a federal, not a state, procedure. Therefore, those convicted of violating certain federal crimes (who have had their civil rights restored by a state law or procedure) are still, nonetheless, prohibited by federal law from possessing firearms.

Unfortunately for those convicted under a federal crime, there is no general federal statutory procedure for restoring civil rights to federal felons. While the Bureau of Alcohol, Tobacco and Firearms (BATF) is authorized under 18 U.S.C. 925(c) to restore federal firearms privileges to an individual convicted of a felony, it has not been permitted to expend funds for this purpose since fiscal year 1992 (although it may restore rights to corporations). So, at this time, an individual that has been burdened with a federal firearms disability may extinguish the disability only through a presidential pardon.

Eligibility

Eligibility for a pardon is based upon the type of sentence you initially received. If you:

- received probation, you must be discharged from supervision, pay all restitution, and pay all other fees associated with the criminal conviction;

- were sentenced to go to jail and were released on parole, you must pay all restitution and other fees. You must also either complete five years of parole or if your maximum parole period is less than five years, you must complete the maximum;

- were sentenced to jail and have served all of your time, you are eligible when you pay all restitution and all other fees associated with the criminal charge;

- are still in jail, you must have extraordinary circumstances which warrant the granting of the pardon. You must also pay all restitution and all other fees associated with the criminal charge; finally,

- are still in jail but have an illness, if the illness is terminal and you have a life expectancy of one year or less, you can apply as long as you have paid all restitution and all other fees.

How do I apply for Executive Clemency?

Your application for executive clemency begins by getting an application from the South Carolina Department of Probation. You then carefully fill-out the application and send the completed application, along with letters of reference and a fee of $100 to the Department of Probation.

Application

The application itself is a simple two page form. It asks for general information like your name, address, and social security number. It also asks more invasive questions like all prior arrests and convictions. You then have to dig through your memory or records for every address and place of employment for the past five (5) years. Finally, you must give the reason **why** you are seeking the pardon. The reason might be that you want to go out and get a gun or that you want a gun around the house. However, why would you do that when you can simply make the general statement that **you would, once again, like to enjoy the full rights and benefits of citizenship.**

Certified Copies of Documents

Once you have the application completely filled out, you will need to attach certified copies of all documents showing that all the restitution and other fees associated with the criminal charge have been paid in full. Certified copies are not simple photocopies. Certified copies are photocopies that are made by the Clerk of Court or other authorized official. The copies must be made directly from the original court file or the official records by the clerk. Further, a certified copy will include a certification, by the clerk, placed upon the photocopy. A certification is a stamp, crimp, seal or other mark placed upon the photocopy that includes language to the effect that the clerk certifies that the photocopy is a true and accurate reproduction of the official original.

Fees for Certified Documents

Almost always, the clerk charges a fee for the certified copies. Be prepared to pay the fee in cash or money order because many times the clerk will not accept a personal check or credit card. Word to the wise, any time you need certified copies, call the clerk for the exact amount of the fee and stop at the ATM to get the appropriate amount of cash before going to the courthouse. If you are using the mail, mail only money orders and not personal checks. If you don't send a money order or cashier's check, the clerk will invariably send you back your paperwork and you'll be back to square one.

Courthouse Security

One more word to the wise, if you go into the courthouse, you will usually have to go through a security check with metal detectors. You can make this check much easier by bringing minimal "stuff" with you into the courthouse. Leave your chrome motorcycle keychain, pocketknife, and historic pewter dip cans in the car. If you are going into a federal courthouse, leave your cell phone, pager, blackberry, and PDA in the car too because they will not let you bring them in.

Letters of Reference

You will need to include three letters of reference along with your application. As a practical matter, look for people who know you well and who are in a position to observe your current behavior and character.

The letters should include the name, address, home phone number, and work phone number of each person who is writing the letter of reference. The letters must be recently dated and must be signed by the person vouching for your character. Most importantly, the letter **must specifically state that the writer is in favor of your pardon**.

Application Fee

When you mail off your application, you must include the application fee. Currently, the fee is $100 and it must be paid by money order or cashier's check. It should be made out to: The South Carolina Department of Probation, Parole, and Pardon Services. Like your request for certified copies, if you fail to include the fee in the proper form, they will return the application to you unprocessed and you'll be back to square one.

The Role of the Department

Once you have sent off a complete and accurate application, your fate is in the hands of the Department of Probation, Parole, and Pardon Services. They will verify all the information contained in your application, including the references. The Department generally requires about seven to nine months from the time you file the application until the date of your pardon hearing.

A pardon hearing is where you will orally present your reasons why you should be pardoned to a single or multiple decision-makers.

You will be notified where and when the hearing is being held. The proceeding will have courtroom type decorum so you should conduct yourself as if you were about to go to court. You should be dressed in a suit and tie if you are male or business attire if you are female. Speak only after first standing up and use your best manners towards the decision makers and all others at the hearing. The hearing should last less than an hour.

It is preferable that you have a lawyer for this hearing but it is not required. If possible, you should elicit witnesses and testimony favorable to you and include evidence that will help you. If you do not have a lawyer, follow the instructions that the Board provides you with regarding allowable witnesses and evidence.

If you are denied a pardon, the decision of the Board is final for that application. Because this is not a judicial proceeding, there is no appeal and there is nothing you can do except reapply. There is nothing that prevents you from reapplying immediately. However, as a practical matter, you should probably give yourself a little time to further improve your circumstances. Alternatively, if the membership of the board changes you can reapply and hope for better results with the new board.

Does a Pardon Clear (Expunge) My Record?

No. When completing a job application, the conviction should be listed and then indicate that the conviction was pardoned. Only an expungement expunges your records with law enforcement offices.

Do I Need a Pardon to Register to Vote or Vote?

No. Once the sentence is fully satisfied, you automatically regain your right to vote.

How Long will the Pardon Process Take?

The application process is lengthy since all the references and information must be verified. On average, it takes about seven (7) to nine (9) months from the time the pardon application is received until a pardon hearing date is scheduled for in-state applicants. The process can take longer for the applicant who is an out-of-state resident. Cases are scheduled in the order in which they are received. If the person who is applying for a pardon has been laid off or faced with possible job termination pending the results of a pardon hearing, they must so indicate on the application under "Reason for Requesting Pardon," and attach statements concerning the circumstances.

Does a Pardon Clear Me from a Sex Offender Registry?

No, a pardon will not relieve you of the requirements of continuing to register as a sex offender.

How can I get Relief from a Federal Felony?

While state felonies can be addressed by a state's executive clemency process, at this time only a Presidential pardon can get rid of a federal felony. The process for requesting a Presidential Pardon begins by completing an application available from the U.S. Department of Justice website: http://www.justice.gov/pardon. It is highly recommend that you consult a firearms law attorney before applying.

In the future, one further avenue of relief may be available to those with a federal felony. Under 18 U.S.C. § 925(c), a person may make application to BATFE for relief. The basis for the application is that the applicant's record and reputation are such that the applicant will not be likely to act in a manner dangerous to public safety. If the Attorney General denies your application, you may then file a petition with the United States District Court for the district in which you reside for judicial review.

However, Congress has de-authorized funding to BATFE to process an application under this statute. An applicant was denied BATFE action on his application and took the matter to the District Court. His case was appealed to the Fifth District Court of Appeals. In US v. McGill, the Appeals Court concluded that district courts lack subject matter jurisdiction to consider section 925(c) applications filed by individuals because Congress, by withdrawing funds to the BATF to process such applications, intended to suspend the relief provided by that statute. The court went on to say,

> *There is no reason to spend the Government's time or taxpayer's money to restore a convicted felon's right to own a firearm. Thus, while section 925(c) remains on the books and has not been repealed, Congress has effectively suspended its operation. Until such time as Congress reauthorizes funding, BATF is legally prohibited from processing applications for relief under section 925(e), and the courts are accordingly precluded from judicial review of the denial of such applications.*

So, even though 18 U.S.C. § 925(c) remains on the books, an individual can expect no relief. That's because BATFE will not even process the application and the courts will not entertain a lawsuit to force them to.

Appendix II
Getting the Qualified Non-Resident Form R-168

If you are a qualified non-resident, your completed SLED Form R-168 must be signed by the county assessor in which your South Carolina property is located. It might be a good idea here to review dealing with government offices, certified copies and certification of documents. We discussed certified copies earlier in the chapter on executive clemency but you might not have had a need to read that chapter.

If you need an official document from a government official, you should always have a game plan before getting into your car and driving to the government office. If you don't, there is a great chance that you will waste a lot of time and get very frustrated. You might waste time driving through downtown streets looking for the office. You might waste time wandering around the building looking for your office. And worst of all, you might waste time standing in the wrong line.

The three best planning tools are this book, the internet and your phone. After reading this book, search the internet or your phone book for phone numbers and addresses. Make sure that you call the office first and find out who you need to see to get what you want. Find out which office they are in and verify the address. Sometimes the official will give you directions or landmarks. If they are not too busy, they often help with other valuable advice like where to park and when the office goes out for lunch. Mainly though, try to identify a specific person in the office who is familiar with issuing the type of document that you are looking for. A Plan, don't leave home without it.

As an example, we investigated getting a SLED Form R-168 from the Greenville County Assessor's Office. The first number that appeared on the County's website connected us to an automated phone router that started with the, "press one for this, press two for that" routine.

After pushing quite a few buttons and getting forwarded to several live employees, we were directed to the precise office that we needed. Then, within that office the staff had to ask around for the person in the office with experience with the SLED Form R-168. After a few more seconds on hold and more forwarding to different desks, we were finally speaking to the precise person who actually issues the Form R-168 certification.

This is not at all meant to be a criticism of the Greenville County office. The office was very courteous, concerned and helpful. It is probably just relatively rare that the staff gets a call from an out-of-state property owner looking for a SLED Form R-168. Once we found the right person, she knew exactly what to do. The point here is to spend the time in the comfort of your home reading the internet and calling the government offices instead of driving around downtown streets and wandering around buildings.

Another important point is that certified copies are not regular photocopies. You will not need a certified copy of the SLED Form R-168. Instead, the official will issue the original that you have brought to the official's desk. But, if SLED requires supplemental information from you beyond your original application, they might ask for certified copies of some documents.

Certified copies are photocopies that are made by the Clerk of Court or other authorized official. The copies must be made directly from the original court file or the official records by the clerk. Further, a certified copy will include a certification, by the clerk, placed upon the photocopy. A certification is a stamp, crimp, seal or other mark placed upon the photocopy that includes language to the effect that the clerk certifies that the photocopy is a true and accurate reproduction of the official original.

Almost always, the clerk charges a fee for certified copies. Be prepared to pay the fee in cash or money order because many times the clerk will not accept a personal check or credit card. Word to the wise, any time you need certified copies, call the clerk for the exact amount of the fee and stop at the ATM to get the appropriate amount of cash before going to the courthouse. If you are using the mail, send only money orders or cashier's checks and not send personal checks. If you don't send a money order or cashier's check, the clerk will invariably send you back your request for the certified copies and you are back at square one.

Courthouse Security

One more word to the wise, if you go into the courthouse, you will usually have to go through a security check with metal detectors. Many larger counties have public records offices separate from the courthouse but the smaller counties often have "all-in-one" buildings.

You can make this check much easier by bringing minimal "stuff" with you into the courthouse. Leave your chrome motorcycle key chains, pocketknives, and your prized historic pewter dip cans in the car. If you are going into a federal courthouse, leave your cell phone, pager, blackberry, or PDA in the car too because they won't let you bring one in. Federal marshals will not even let you store the electronic device with them or in or near the building. Instead, you will end up walking back to your car to store your device.

Appendix III
Fingerprints

This Appendix describes the process of obtaining fingerprints in greater detail than the body of the book. First, you should call a qualified law enforcement agency convenient to you and ask for the hours of public fingerprinting. (For brevity's sake, I will substitute "qualified law enforcement agency" or SLED approved fingerprint technician with simply "police station.") Sometimes, you can pop in to a police station and get an officer to provide fingerprints. However, this is the exception more than the rule. You are well advised to call the police department's non-emergency number and ask for a firm confirmation of their fingerprinting hours.

Remember that any police station can complete your fingerprint card. If you live closer to a North Carolina police station than a South Carolina one, feel free to get your prints at the North Carolina station (they might be able to charge you more though). If you are a student, go to your university police station. If you are a qualified non-resident and live in Washington, D.C., feel free to go the J. Edgar Hoover Building and get fingerprinted by the FBI there. The point is that you can get your prints done at any police station. Before wasting your time and gas, though, make sure that you are driving to a bona-fide police office that does fingerprints.

Once you have confirmed a time to arrive at the police station, bring the two cards provided by SLED, your driver's license or other qualified identification and the required fee in cash or money order. You will then enter the police station and usually find a reception window. Inform the reception officer that you are there to get fingerprints. The reception officer will generally have you sit in the reception area and wait for a police officer to come through some door to greet you. You can use the time to verify that you have the fingerprint cards, a valid ID and the cash with you.

After the officer greets you, you will be led down a hall to the fingerprint area. The office will have either an old fashioned wood and steel fingerprint board or a new-fangled digital imager. The main difference is that the old type requires that your fingers roll in a washable ink and the new type does not require ink. Both require that the officer take your hand and roll your fingers, thumbs and palms over the imaging surface.

Try to keep your hands and fingers very loose and allow the officer to do all of the work. There is a tendency to try to roll your fingers yourself but that might cause you to blur the image. If you are getting a digital image the officer can cancel the image before printing it on the card but if you are using the ink, a blur can require you to get a new card and come back another day. Try to relax and let the officer do all of the work.

Your fingerprint cards will have spaces for information. Be sure to fill out all of the information requested. Be very careful to have the officer place his or her information on the card also. Again, I say, be careful to get this information from the officer because even the most innocent person has a primeval urge to get out of a police station as fast as possible. If you do not get the information and signature of the officer, your application will be rejected.

Made in United States
North Haven, CT
04 November 2026

21763964R00186